T0305117

CE Marking, Product Standards and World Trade

For Laurel

CE Marking, Product Standards and World Trade

David Hanson, Ph.D, J.D.

Associate Professor of International Business,
Duquesne University

Edward Elgar
Cheltenham, UK • Northampton, MA, USA

Published by
Edward Elgar Publishing Limited
Glensanda House
Montpellier Parade
Cheltenham
Glos GL50 1UA
UK

Edward Elgar Publishing, Inc.
136 West Street
Suite 202
Northampton
Massachusetts 01060
USA

A catalogue record for this book
is available from the British Library

ISBN 1 84376 773 2

Printed and bound in Great Britain by MPG Books Ltd, Bodmin, Cornwall

Contents

v

Tables

Acknowledgements

The research for this book was funded in part by a three–year Market Development Cooperators Program grant from the International Trade Administration in the US Department of Commerce. Their help is gratefully acknowledged.

Our MDCP grant funded the development of CITRA, the Center for International Regulatory Assistance at Duquesne University. The mission of CITRA is, in part, to promote US exports by helping US companies meet CE Marking requirements. The MDCP grant gave us the opportunity to meet with hundreds of people in Europe and the US who are involved in some aspect of the CE marking process. These meetings were conducted in partnership with our ITA contact team.

A great deal of the information on which this book is based was gained through these meetings. However, it would not be fair to cite individual people on specific points. Many times, we met in groups and it would be difficult to determine who said what in the course of often vigorous discussions. At the time of these meetings, I had not decided to write a book on the basis of our findings. We therefore did not tell the people with whom we met that their comments might be cited in print.

Many thanks to Dr Mary McKinney, my partner in our CITRA adventure. I am also very grateful for the project support and personal friendship of Marge Donnelly and Indrek Grabbi, our MDCP grant administration team, Stanley Warshaw, consultant, bon vivant and standards expert and Sylvia Mohr, Standards attaché at the US Mission to the EU. Thanks guys, we couldn't have done it without you.

I would also like to express my deepest appreciation to the people listed below for their generosity in sharing their time and expertise on CE marking. Whatever I know about CE marking, I have largely learned from them. My errors, omissions and misunderstandings are, of course, mine alone.

Dan Bart	TIA, Washington, DC, USA
Ed Bert	Pine Instruments, Pittsburgh, Pa., USA
Thomas Beyer	Pennsylvania Department of Community and Economic Development, Germany
Valbert Biaggo	IMQ SA, Milan, Italy

Colin Brazier	Consul to the US, United Kingdom
Steve Buxton	Underwriters Laboratory, Netherlands
Malcolm Carlisle	Morgan Lewis, London, UK
Kevin Carr	National Institute of Science and Technology, Gaithersburg, Md, USA
Alain Cauwe	US Embassy, Brussels, Belgium
Chris Cerone	Advamed, Washington, DC, USA
Graham Chalmers	British Standards Institute, Hemel Hempstead, UK
Marco Chirullo	Weber Shandwick Adamson, Brussels, Belgium
Lalit Chorda	Thar Designs, Pittsburgh, Pa, USA
James Ciglar	NEMA, Alexandria, Va., USA
Dave Clifton	Technical Standards Information Service, Georgia Technical University, Atlanta, Ga, USA.
Roger Cranville	Pittsburgh Regional Authority, Pittsburgh, Pa., USA.
Dorota Dabrowska	American Chamber of Commerce, Warsaw, Poland
Brian Deane	Pulva, Pittsburgh, Pa, USA.
Els Dedobbeleer	Eucomed, Brussels, Belgium
Estelle Desmit	EOTC, Brussels, Brussels, Belgium
Gerald DiFrango	SMC, Pittsburgh, Pa., USA.
Joe Dhillon	National Institute of Science and Technology, Gaithersburg, Md., USA.
Mark Downs	Department of Trade and Industry, London, UK
Margaret Donnelly	International Trade Administration, Washington, DC, USA
David Eardley	Directorate General Enterprise, Brussels, Belgium
Allen Edgar	Queen's College, Belfast, Northern Ireland
Geert Eggermont	UNIZO, Milan, Italy
Christian Favre	International Standards Organization, Geneva, Switzerland
Janos Fejes	Testing Station for Explosion Proof Equipment, Budapest, Hungary

Acknowledgements

Robert Ferrigamo	European Environmental Bureau, Brussels, Belgium
Ian Frazier	Ministry of Labor, Paris, France
Gordon Gillerman	Underwriters Laboratory, Washington, DC, USA
L. Gourtsoyannis	NORMAPME, Brussels, Belgium
Indrek Grabbi	International Trade Administration, Washington, DC, USA
Manuel Guiterrez	American Society of Mechanical Engineers, New York, NY, USA
James Hanson	Consultant, Colombia, Maryland, USA
Kirsten Hentschel	US International Trade Administration, Brussels, Belgium
Ed Hynes	Royal and Sun Assurance Company, Manchester, UK
David Jefferys	Medical Device Administration, London, UK
Rene Kik	MIREC, Eindhoven, Netherlands
Andrew Kirby	Bureau Veritas, London, UK
David Knuti	US Commercial Service, Budapest, Hungary
Katharine Koch	Lille, France
Kathleen Kono	ASTM International, Conshocken, Pa.
Anthony Hampden-Smith	Morgan Lewis, London, UK
Anette Huizinga	ICT Milleu, Eindhoven, Netherlands
Holly Lawe	Technical Standards Information Service, Georgia Technical University, Georgia, USA
Dirk Langner	BundesFinanzMinisterium, Bonn, Germany
Jan C.M. van Leet	Department of Health, Hague, Netherlands
Miroslaw Lewinsk	Department of Industrial Policy, Warsaw, Poland
Peter Maas	NEN, Hague, Netherlands
Marcello Manca	Underwriters Laboratory, Milan, Italy
Thomas McClenaghan	Directorate General Enterprise, Brussels
Lois McElwee	Bush International, Pittsburgh, Pa., USA.
Jaques McMillan	Directorate General Enterprise, Brussels, Belgium

Bernhard Mertens	CENELEC, Brussels, Belgium
Artur V. D. Miedjen	EMA, Hague, Netherlands
Sylvia Mohr	US Embassy, Brussels, Belgium
Colin Moore	US Embassy, Brussels, Belgium
Dirk Mortiz	Bundesfinanzministerium, Bonn, Germany
Csaba Nagy	Institute for Medical and Hospital Engineering, Budapest, Hungary
Barbara Neiciak	Polish Embassy to the EU, Brussels, Belgium
Christine Nelson	US Food and Drug Administration, Gaithersburg, Md., USA.
Theo Nussfelder	CEpartner4U, Hague, Netherlands
Joanne Overman	National Center for Standards and Certification Information, Gaithersburg, Md., USA.
Sanford Owens	US Commercial Services Bratislava, Slokavia
Volker Pilz	Bayer, Leverkusen, Germany
Guiseppi Pirillo	Consortio Technoimprese, Milan, Italy
Michal Pirozynskio	Office of Registration for Medical Products and Medical Devices, Warsaw, Poland
Anne Rasanen	Sun Microsystems, Brussels, Belgium
Christaan Reyners	TUV-Rheinland, St. Augustine, Germany
Rosa Ring	Hungarian Accreditation Board, Budapest, Hungary
Andrzej Rostkowski	Polish Center for Testng and Certification, Warsaw, Poland
Stewart Sanson	CEN, Brussels, Belgium
Suzanne Sene	US Embassy, Brussels, Belgium
Irene Skolnick	Dymax, Pittsburgh, Pa., USA.
Paulina Skowronska	POLFARMED, Warsaw, Poland
J. Barbara Sloan	EU Office, Washington, DC, USA
Jake Slegers	American Chamber of Commerce, Bratislava, Slovakia
J. Leen de Smet	European Information Centre, Brussels, Belgium

Acknowledgements

Jan Erik Sorensen	World Trade Organization, Geneva, Switzerland.
Kvetoslava Steinlova	Slovak Office of Standards, Metrology and Testing, Bratislava, Slovakia
Janusz Szymanski	Polish Standards Committee, Warsaw, Poland
Cyril Theys	CETECOM, Brussels, Belgium
Agustà Thorsbersdottir	EFTA, Brussels, Belgium
Dr. Timm	HVBG, Bonn, Germany
Christina Timo	Comitato Elettrotecnico Italiano, Milan, Italy
Peter Valentovic	IBM Slovakia, Bratislava, Slovakia
Herve Vialle	EOTC, Brussels, Belgium
Andras Vincze	Hungarian Institute for Testing and Certificiation, Budapest, Hungary
Maurice Wagner	Eucomed, Brussels, Belgium
Fred Willian	Manchester Chamber of Commerce and Industry, Manchester, UK
Ken Zillmer	Advanced Testing Services, Beaver Falls, Pa. USA

1. Introduction

1. THE CE MARK

Turn over your keyboard. Look on the frames of your glasses. Examine the back of your VCR. Look at the equipment used in your doctor's office or in industrial machine shops. You are likely to see a stylized 'CE' somewhere on the manufacturer's nameplate. If you are French, the letters 'CE' may stand for 'conformité Européen'. If you are not, you might assume they don't stand for anything. Either way, this symbol is the CE mark. By placing the CE mark on the product, the manufacturer has pledged that the product meets a series of safety standards that have been established by the European Union.

The European Union introduced the CE marking system in 1985 (European Council, 1985). The system was developed by the European Union to promote free trade within the Community. Before the development of CE marking, trade was being limited by a relatively new type of non–tariff trade barrier, the growing differences among the EU member states in nationally mandated product requirements. By 1986, analysts at the World Bank estimated that over 21 per cent of all imports into the Netherlands were subject to hard core non–tariff trade barriers. For the EU as a whole the figure was 15.8 per cent. Between 1981 and 1986, the number of non–tariff trade barriers increased in Germany by 36 per cent, in France by 30 per cent and by 24 per cent in the EU as a whole. (Laird and Yeats, n.d.). Most of these barriers were created by inconsistent national product requirements

The development of the CE marking system has largely ended the tendency for inconsistent national product requirements to block trade within the European Union. At the heart of the CE marking system are a set of product safety standards and a series of conformity assessment procedures that are used to prove that these standards have been properly implemented. These EU requirements override national requirements. Participating countries are not allowed to impose any additional product standards or certification requirements on products covered by the CE marking system that could interfere with the free flow of goods within the Union.

The European Union is encouraging the broader adoption of the CE marking system outside Europe through technical support development programs, free trade arrangements and mutual recognition agreements. Australia, for example, has adopted the CE marking system for regulating medical devices. The EU has signed free trade agreements with Mexico and Brazil. The EU is also providing incentives for foreign governments to adopt the CE marking system.

Both Japan and China seem to be moving away from more protectionist product safety standards and conformity assessment requirements towards programs that resemble the CE marking system. Japanese practices have been far more contentious than anything the Europeans or Americans have invented. Most Japanese industrial standards are developed by the Japanese Industrial Standards Committee (JISC), an arm of the Ministry of International Trade and Industry. The ministries of Posts, Health and Welfare, Transportation and Construction have responsibilities for the development of specialized standards in their sectors. Japanese corporations are highly involved in the standards development processes. These standards are often used as a shield to defend domestic markets and as a sword to enter foreign markets (Stern, 1997). There is nothing in the New Approach that is as overtly protectionist as the Japanese system.

However, the Japanese system may be changing. Two smaller manufacturers of high technology products in the Pittsburgh region have separately reported that Japanese customs authorities had admitted their products, although they lacked the Japanese conformity mark, because they had been CE marked.

Until July 2003, China had two systems for product standards and conformity assessment. Many goods exported to China had to be approved to the CCIB Safety Mark system of product standards or the CCEE 'Great Wall' requirements. Products traded within the Chinese domestic market also had to meet the CCIA system requirements. As a result, imported goods had to comply with two sets of standards and conformity assessment requirements while domestic products only had to comply with one. Worse, the two systems did not have the same requirements. In some instances, the requirements were inconsistent ('China's CCC Mark', 2003).

This policy of treating imported goods differently from domestic goods for regulatory purposes is clearly inconsistent with GATT and obligations under the WTO. China has therefore gone to a unified system of CB standards and the CCC system for ensuring the conformity of higher risk products. Both programs are remarkably similar to the CE marking system ('China's CCC Mark', 2003).

2. CE MARKING AND US–EU TRADE

The European Union is the largest foreign market for American business. It is in a virtual tie with Canada as the leading market for US exports. In 2001, US exporters sold $177 billion in merchandise goods to the European Union. In comparison, US exports to Canada in 2001 were valued at $163 billion. US exports to Mexico in 2001 were valued at $101 billion. Japan as a market for US exports came in a distant fourth with a value of $57 billion in 2001 (US Census Bureau, 2001)

CE marking has also liberalized trade within the EU. This has provided major benefits to American exporters as well as to their European counterparts. In the past, US exporters would often have to redesign and re–document their products to meet fifteen different, and often conflicting, requirements. By complying with the CE marking requirements, US exporters can now sell the same product throughout an extended European market. This is a major advantage.

However, many American manufacturers are encountering difficulties in complying with the CE mark requirements. CE marking is fast becoming a major trade issue in US–EU relations, both as a specific issue and as an example of the more general problem of trade restrictions emerging from inconsistent national patterns of domestic regulation.

US exporters may find that the CE marking system has introduced new costs for product development and certification. Manufacturers can experience an expensive learning curve while adopting to a new system such as the CE mark. The flexibility and decentralized nature of the system can create interpretative ambiguities and lead to costly mistakes. American exporters may also have a harder time than their European peers in developing useful working relations with the CE mark administrators.

The problems associated with CE marking emerge at several levels. At the most basic level, many American manufacturers who want to export to the EU are having difficulties complying with the CE mark requirements. The United States Trade Representative, in the *Annual Report on Foreign Trade Barriers* (2001a), singled the CE mark system for particular attention:

[T]he advent of the EUs 'new approach', which streamlines technical harmonization and the development of standards . . . based on 'essential' health and safety requirements, generally points toward the harmonization of laws, regulations, standards, testing quality and certification procedures within the EU. . As demonstrated by the extensive list of standards–related issues below, differences in this area represent a significant portion of US–EU trade concerns. (p. 110)

This is not a new complaint. The same basic issue was raised in the report on trade barriers for 1995, 1996, 1999 and 2001 (USTR, 1995, pp. 16–18; USTR, 1996, pp. 1–2; USTR, 1999, pp. 93–94; USTR, 1999, pp. 110–111).

The Transatlantic Business Dialog is a group of international business leaders who have been charged by the governments of both the EU and the US with examining the state of US–EU commercial relations. According to the *Annual Report* (Transatlantic Business Dialog, 2000);

> The US–EU trade relationship is one of the largest and most important bilateral trade relationships for the United States. But the existence of heterogeneous standards and duplicative regulatory requirements on both sides of the Atlantic adds greatly to the cost of exporting . . . Such redundant testing and certification increase the base cost of exports by up to 15 per cent . . . A typical US machine manufacturer may spend $50 000 to $100 000 annually complying with foreign regulatory requirements – an overwhelming burden to small– to medium–sized exporters. (p. 5)

In 1997, the Semi–Conductor Equipment and Materials Association (SEMI) surveyed semi–conductor fabrication equipment manufacturers on the impact of CE marking. They estimated that the annual world–wide cost of compliance is between $300 and $500 million. US equipment manufacturers are expected to spend between $95 and $135 million on CE marking. The average cost for certifying one type of machine was $92 000. The estimates for CE mark maintenance costs were lower, around $47 000 per product line. (Harpstead, 1998; 'SEMI Study . . .,' 1997: 'SEMI expects . . .', 1997).

The impact of CE marking for smaller businesses can be significant. Hanson and McKinney (n.d.) surveyed over 1800 smaller Pennsylvania manufacturers in order to assess the impact of CE marking on their exports to the EU. The respondents reported that they had lost, on average, over $380 000 per year in European sales, or 15 per cent of the expected export revenues. Based on these numbers, the estimated total loss in state export revenues would be over $240 000 000. These results are roughly consistent with an observed decline of $184 000 000 in Pennsylvania exports to the EU at a time when Pennsylvania exports were increasing overall. A senior trade official attributed the decline in shipments to Europe to problems Pennsylvania manufacturers were encountering when trying to comply with the requirements of the CE marking system (Cranville, 1999).

The Organization for Economic Cooperation and Development asked a number of trade associations to estimate the time and cost requirements for complying with product certification requirements. Estimates for businesses selling to the EU ranged from $200 to $50 000 and time delays ranged from one week to six months. One third of the respondents said that foreign regulatory requirements prevented them from entering foreign markets, even though their products met widely accepted safety standards (Organization for Economic Cooperation and Development, 1996).

Why should CE marking pose a problem? What can be done about it? To find some answers, we should look more deeply into the nature of standards and their potential impact on international trade.

3. STANDARDS AND CONFORMITY ASSESSMENTS

The definition of a standard is simple. According to the International Standards Organization:

> Standards are documented agreements containing technical specifications or other precise criteria to be used consistently as rules, guidelines or definitions of characteristics to ensure that materials, products, processes and services are fit for their purpose. (International Standards Organization, 2003)

Industrial standards are an important, if generally unrecognized, feature of the modern industrial landscape. The development of widely accepted product compatibility standards is essential in a decentralized industrial world. We can play video tapes in our VCRs because the manufacturers have followed the specifications in the VHS tape standards. The electric alarm clocks in our bedrooms wake us up on time because they were designed and built in accordance with the US standard of 110 volt, 60 cycle household current.

Safety standards provide assurances that we are not likely to be injured or killed when we use a product. Hair driers in the US and the wiring in American houses likely to carry the UL logo to symbolize that they conform to the safety standards developed by Underwriters Laboratory. The seatbelts in our cars will have been developed in accordance with automotive standards in order to make sure we have a better chance of walking away from an accident.

Standards can be classified by origin and enforcement. Product requirements that are mandated by government agencies to meet regulatory goals are called 'technical requirements'. However, the pattern in both the EU and US is for public agencies to use private standards to achieve regulatory goals. This is blurring the distinction between a 'standard' and a 'technical requirement'. We will therefore use the term 'standard' to refer to the relevant safety and environmental specifications in the EU and US, even where their use is mandated by government agencies.

Another way of classifying standards is by content rather than by purpose. Standards are conventionally classified as being 'design based' or 'performance based'. A design standard will describe how a product should be, logically enough, designed to achieve a specified goal. A performance standard simply describes what the product has to be able to do and not how it should be designed to achieve that goal.

The standards we will be discussing have generally been developed by non–profit 'standards development organizations'; that commonly follow a prescribed procedure of industry consultation for standards development. Standards can also be developed by individual companies. The specifications for the Microsoft and Apple computer operating systems are two examples. 'Open' standards are released for unrestrained use by other groups. This was the Microsoft strategy. With 'proprietary' standards, the issuing company retains legal control over the use of the standard by others. This was the Apple strategy.

'Conformity assessment' requirements constitute the other part of the standards system. A conformity assessment procedure is simply the way in which a manufacturer proves that s/he has accurately implemented the standard into his or her product. Conformity assessment requirements may range from nothing, to self–declaration by the manufacturer, to a requirement that a third party must review the design, certify the manufacturing processes or test the finished products.

The rigor of the conformity assessment will often depend on the availability of information on product performance from other sources prior to use and the consequences of product failure. Compatibility standards rarely have any associated conformity assessment requirements. Any failure to properly apply a compatibility standard is likely to become apparent during the installation of the product or initial operation of the system.

Safety standards are more likely to involve some sort of conformity assessment procedures. Watching a crib go up in flames could be a very painful way to discover that the manufacturer's claim that a baby blanket is fireproof is, in fact, inaccurate. In order to protect the public welfare, manufacturers of safety–critical products are often required to provide assurances that their products really meet the required safety standards. These conformity assessment requirements may also be associated with product quality assurance systems.

Manufacturers of products that pass a given set of conformity assessment requirements are typically allowed to use a particular 'certification mark'. The UL logo is an example of a certification mark. Manufacturers hire Underwriters Laboratory to review their products and manufacturing processes. If the products and processes meet UL standards, then

Underwriters Laboratory gives them permission to place the UL logo on the product.

The CE is also a certification mark. However, there are two major differences from the UL example. By law, products covered by the New Approach directives must be CE marked before they are sold or placed into service in the European Economic Area. Under the CE marking system, the manufacturer is ultimately responsible for making sure that her products have legitimately passed the conformity assessment requirements. The manufacturer does not have to register the use of the CE mark logo or to get permission from any regulatory agency before using it.

In contrast, Underwriters Laboratory is a private organization that does not have the authority to require manufacturers to use the UL logo. However, the UL logo is trademarked. No one can use the logo without permission from Underwriters Laboratory.

4. STANDARDS AND INTERNATIONAL TRADE

We have seen that national differences in product safety standards and conformity assessment requirements can pose significant barriers to international trade. For insiders, the development and enforcement of national standards that are based on the unique properties of their products can serve to protect national markets. For outsiders, the use of unique national standards in export markets can limit market access. As a result, the international struggles to differentiate or harmonize national standards in different countries are often key elements in the on–going competition for international markets.

Consider some of the ways in which national differences in mandatory product safety standards can raise a manufacturer's costs. Ideally, most manufacturers would like to be able to ship from any production line to any market, world–wide. Product development costs would then be minimized and the supply chain could be optimized for fast, flexible and low cost distribution.

As a result, many exporters would generally prefer to have a single set of standards and conformity assessment requirements that can be applied in all major markets. The ideal is expressed as one standard, one test – accepted everywhere. (European Telecommunications Standards Institute, 2002). This would make it easier for a business to sell products from any production line to any market in the world. However, this is an unlikely outcome. The extent reality falls short of this ideal will make a difference to business.

The impact of national differences on exporters' costs will depend on the nature of the differences among standards used in different markets. The second best scenario might be to have the same standards used in both markets with the only differences in who carries out any required conformity assessment procedures. However, conformity assessment procedures may involve third party reviews of company quality assurance systems, such as ISO 9000. They can also involve product inspection and testing. The costs of any mandatory conformity assessments are generally borne by the manufacturer. There are fifteen national certification marks on the back of the power supply for the author's laptop. Even if they all involved testing to the same set of standards, managing fifteen different conformity assessment requirements and agencies would be both expensive and administratively difficult.

Manufacturers frequently find that they are facing different, but congruent, sets of standards and conformity assessment requirements in different markets. They are then able to design and build one product that meets both sets of requirements. However, this will generally involve the introduction of additional product features, manufacturing steps or conformity assessment requirements that would otherwise not be required.

For example, the ASME (American Society for Mechanical Engineering) Boiler Code ensures pressure vessel safety through the use of thicker walls and lower stress welds. The harmonized standards implementing the European Pressure Equipment Directive are based on thinner walls and radiographic assays of the welds. Manufacturers can meet both sets of requirements by using thicker walls, thicker welds, and radiographic testing. Manufacturing costs, however, will be higher.

Other combinations of congruent standards are common. One set of requirements might apply to production and production certification requirements. This strategy is heavily emphasized in the CE marking program. A majority of the conformity assessment modules are based on the widely accepted ISO 9000 series of production quality certification requirements. Other sets of standards could focus on product performance. The associated conformity assessment procedures would probably involve product testing. This is also an option for high risk products covered by the CE marking system.

The worst situation for a business would be to confront inconsistent product requirements in different markets. If a product were in compliance with the requirements of one country, it would then be out of compliance with the requirements of another country. As a result, it would be impossible for a company to sell the products manufactured in one production line to both countries.

For example, European national standards often specify the types of metals that can be used for the fabrication of pressure vessels. It is not uncommon for these specifications to only cover alloys produced by national industries. Pressure vessels made in accordance with one set of national, standards are likely to be inconsistent with the materials requirements developed in neighboring countries. The CE marking system was supposed to eliminate these types of inconsistencies. We will revisit this issue in our discussion of the Pressure Equipment Directive in Chapter 7.

The potential combination of, for example, national differences in worker certification requirements, design, production line and service review, the mandated use of certified components and required product testing could raise costs substantially. This is especially true if each jurisdiction were to require separate conformity assessment procedures to assure compliance with national requirements.

The costs imposed by inconsistent standards and conformity assessment requirements will also depend in part on the circumstances of the manufacturer. For multinationals, inconsistent standards are likely to raise costs and reduce flexibility, but not keep them out of any major markets. When faced with the unique requirements of a particular market, multinationals are more likely to have the option of designing and building a product that will meet these specific regulatory requirements.

However, this is not a costless option. Clearly, additional product development and certification costs will be incurred and some supply chain flexibility will be sacrificed. In addition, the manufacturer is likely to have some incentives for manufacturing the product in the market where it will be sold in order to take advantage of local regulatory expertise. This could contribute to the erosion of the manufacturing base in the home country. Over half of all the products sold by 3M in the EEA are manufactured in Europe. In part, this is done in order to make it easier to meet local regulatory requirements.

The nature of a standard and the associated conformity assessment requirements can have an impact on the cost of manufacturing the product. A company manufacturing a product with well–established technologies may want to use design standards. Good design standards often summarize a wide range of good engineering practices. On the other hand, a manufacturer that is introducing a new design or technology may prefer the flexibility provided by a more general performance standard.

Smaller corporations are more likely to have one assembly line for all products. Complying with international differences in standards can be very expensive. They would probably prefer to have international differences in required standards to apply only to components that could be changed for different markets. Multinational corporations are more likely to dedicate specific assembly lines to different markets. Complying with international differences would be less expensive. Systems covering designs and manufacturing processes would not be a major barrier to market entry.

These considerations lead to one conclusion. Different types of standards are likely to have different impacts on manufacturers in different circumstances. The dream of one standard, one test; accepted everywhere may not be the most effective way to develop an international system for standards. The interests of manufacturers and the public may be better served if multiple ways of achieving equivalent levels of product safety are available.

In general, the costs of regulatory compliance are more burdensome for smaller companies than larger ones (Judd, Greenwood and Becker, 1988). Many small companies sell products that have been designed to US standards and built on a single assembly line to serve all markets. Under these circumstances, free trade would require identical product standards and not just congruent standards. Managers in smaller companies are also less likely to have access to the services of standards experts to help with CE mark compliance.

Gaining access to international markets is often as important to smaller companies as to the major multi–nationals. Fast growing small companies are likely to manufacture highly sophisticated products or components that meet very specialized niche demands. If so, they may find that a relatively low volume of production could exhaust the requirements of the US market. To grow, they would have to export.

These considerations have an impact on the participation of smaller businesses in international markets. In 1992, 37 655 small businesses (with fewer than 500 employees) were responsible for $30.5 billion in exports, or 12.7 per cent of the US total. The average value of exports per company was $808 443. In 1999, 50 547 smaller businesses accounted for a total value of $42.1 billion in exports. On paper, the average value of exports is $832 868 per firm. In constant 1992 dollars though, this is $785 657, a decrease of 6 per cent from the 1992 level (International Trade Administration, 1999). In other words, small business participation in international trade has been declining.

As Solomon (1986) pointed out, the US economy is substantially dependent on the success of smaller businesses for prosperity. Businesses with fewer than 500 employees accounted for 80 per cent of all US private sector employment in 1999 and they contributed over 20 million new jobs between 1974 and 1984. During this period, the total employment provided by the Fortune 500 companies declined by 1.5 million jobs (US Census Bureau, 2001). A lot of this growth in small business employment is fueled by product innovation. Although small businesses account for only 5 per cent of total private sector research and development expenditures, they account for 40 per cent of new product innovations. On average, smaller companies bring new products to market in 2.22 years. For the Fortune 500 companies, the time to market was 3.05 years. A delay of one year in the introduction of a new high technology product can slash product life cycle earnings by 50 per cent (Solomon, 1986).

There are several reasons why CE marking can be a difficult barrier for smaller companies interested in exporting to Europe. Modifying a product to meet CE marking requirements is, to a large extent, an up–front fixed cost. A substantial portion of these costs are tied up in learning about the new requirements, analyzing the product to determine what changes have to be made, sourcing components and going through the necessary tests and conformity assessment requirements. These costs must be incurred whether the company sells one product or a hundred in the EEA. However, these fixed costs may be impossible to justify unless volume sales are almost guaranteed. A small company with an initial order from the EU for one widget at $35 000 may well wonder if it is worthwhile spending $20 000 and six months of effort to get the CE mark. However, if a company is not willing to invest in CE marking for the initial sale, then there will not be any future sales to Europe. Larger companies with well–established market niches are far more likely to know whether their European sales potential would justify the efforts of getting the CE mark and to have the funding that is required to CE mark their products.

5. CE MARKING AND INTERNATIONAL TRADE

The problem with CE marking should be stated more precisely. As a stand–alone system, CE marking is a logical, elegant and successful solution to regulatory problems facing the European Union. There is nothing inherently protectionist about the design of the system. However, it is different from the product standards and conformity assessment systems generally used in the US. US problems with international trade are based on these differences between national regulatory systems, and not on the intrinsic qualities of the systems used on either side.

Our comments about the CE marking system represent, of course, only a small part of the whole story. The Europeans also have a long list of trade grievances against the United States. Many of the trade obstacles encountered by Europeans in the US have emerged because of the regulatory and purchasing policies adopted by American state governments (Directorate General for Trade, 2001) These problems have developed, not because either the CE mark system or US regulatory practices are consistently and intentionally protectionist, but because the US and EU have adopted very different standards and processes for product regulation.

Thus, the dispute over CE marking represents only one part of a larger issue, how best to promote international convergence in domestic regulatory policies and practices. This problem is exacerbated by the reality that most American and European regulatory authorities are not normally sensitive to international concerns. According to Stefan Micossi, former Director General for Industry:

> The North American paradigm of decentralized institutions and highly competitive markets is a far distance from the continental European model of a 'social' market economy with extensive government intervention, strong trade unions and a tradition of concerted management of social conflict and industrial adjustment . . . These differences have been recognized as forming a significant barrier to Transatlantic business. Inevitably, discussions have evolved from trade policy to cover domestic rules; from border measures towards the need to achieve effective access to each other's markets. (Transatlantic Business Dialog, 2000a)

This is a general problem, it is not confined to just the Europeans. As the TABD pointed out in a comment about the American system of product regulation:

> the American regulatory system has, in the past, been unresponsive to the pressures of globalization, concentrating solely on its role in consumer and worker protection . . . Some organizations strive to maintain control over the certification and standards–setting process, fearing that their respective jurisdictions could be usurped by the fulfillment of the TACS recommendations. (Transatlantic Business Dialog, 2000a)

Several tools have been developed for promoting the harmonization of national standards and certification requirements. International obligations are defined primarily by the Technical Barriers to Trade Agreement, one of the international conventions that have been negotiated through the World Trade Organization. The venues for negotiations over the international harmonization of national standards are provided by, among other groups, the International Standards Organization and the International Electrotechnical Commission in Geneva. The Europeans can point to their more active involvement in the international coordination of national standards and certification processes. American participation in the process of coordinating international standards has been weakened by conflicts among competing private interests in a decentralized US standards community (Office of Technology Assessment, 1992).

This leads to another point about trade disputes based on the development of the CE marking system. Trade issues involving differences in product requirements are not easily managed through the traditional channels and tools for international trade negotiations. The issues involved in these disputes have traditionally been regarded as matters of safety, health and environmental regulation that fall within the primary competencies of domestic governments. They are quite different from issues of tariffs, quotas, and intellectual property disputes that clearly fall within the jurisdiction of GATT and the WTO. Furthermore, the development of domestic regulations and regulatory agencies often involve a substantial level of decentralization and private sector involvement. Given these factors, it has been very difficult for international trade representatives to effectively negotiate for a more open system. As the TABD concluded, 'If government–to–government negotiations . . . are to succeed, the US government must play a stronger role in the regulatory sphere – government cannot negotiate terms over which it has no control' (Transatlantic Business Dialog, 2000b).

The difficulties experienced by trade negotiators on both sides in addressing the problems created by these differences emerge from the ways in which the two systems are administered. Both the CE marking system and the product standards systems in use in the US are quite decentralized. It is not clear that the trade negotiators have the authority on either side to amend national regulatory practices. It is clear in both regions that decentralized implementation leads to some loss of central control over policy.

Fortunately, the CE marking story provides a basis for hope as well as alarm. The International Standards Organization, an international agency based in Geneva, offers an alternative venue for reducing international differences in national product standards. With the support of governments on both sides of the Atlantic, regulatory agencies, private businesses and trade associations are becoming increasingly involved in lobbying for a world–wide reduction of national differences in standards and conformity assessment requirements. However, this approach has only been effective in a few industrial sectors and may be a limited model for addressing the general problem. It is not clear that governments would move on the issue without active business advocacy. The model may fail in industrial sectors where businesses are less enthusiastic about free trade.

6. WHY SHOULD WE CARE?

To quote the United States Trade Representative:

> Our work is based on economic principles that are sound in theory and proven by over half a century of experience; open markets and freer trade are good for Americans and our trading partners. In economic terms, market opening brings growth opportunities and rising standards of living – helping producers sell to

wider markets, sparking investment and technological, progress; offering consumers greater choice and quality; and helping workers find opportunities for higher wage employment. More broadly, as countries trade with their neighbors, they gain an interest in prosperity and stability beyond their borders, strengthening the chances for lasting peace. ('Vision Statement', United States Trade Representative, 2000, p. 6)

Product standards are not just an arcane specialty that can only interest the engineers and managers that have to deal with these requirements. We all have a significant stake in the outcome of the global standards wars. Standards are a significant element in the mix of issues that will determine whether the global economy remains open to the world or whether we drift towards the development of regional markets. Inconsistent standards can create barriers to free trade, the global adoption of similar standards can promote international trade.

The globalization of the US economy is evident. The value of US merchandise trade, the sum of US exports and imports of goods, has risen from $59 billion, or 6 per cent of the gross domestic product, in 1970 to $1 593 billion in 1999, or 16 per cent of the GDP. In US industries such as computers and electrical products, over 25 per cent of all US production is exported (US Census Bureau, 2002).

Most of the growth has occurred in the value of the goods imported into the US. The value of US exports as a fraction of the GDP has actually declined from 8 per cent in 1996 to 7.5 per cent in 1999 while the value of US imports has risen to 11 per cent of GDP (US Census Bureau, 2001). These statistics do not prove that CE marking is a major cause of lagging US exports, but they do suggest that lowering the barriers facing US exporters should be an important policy priority.

Free trade has been a backbone for global prosperity in the last half century (Baier and Bergstrand, 2001). Free trade allows manufacturers to effectively realize economies of scale. Car manufacturers, for example, have been faced with two intersecting trends. On one side is the reality of market saturation. Car manufacturers have strong incentives to make increasingly specialized cars that better meet the needs of narrower sectors of the consumer market. The proliferation of sports utility vehicles on the American market has been one example of this trend. On the other hand, new car development costs are continually rising as manufacturers are faced with ever more stringent market demands and environmental and safety requirements. The impact of these rising fixed costs on product pricing can only be brought down to an acceptable level by expanding sales.

These two trends of niche marketing and rising development costs can best be reconciled by going global. This allows manufacturers to realize sufficiently large sales despite pressures to develop more specialized products by marketing in a larger international economy. The result has been a series of international alliances and acquisitions in the automobile industry and the emergence of world cars based on single designs that are sold in many national markets.

Free trade also brings competition. The American car industry was seriously shaken by the emergence of the Japanese automakers on US markets in the mid 1970s. As a result of this challenge, the US market has become far more competitive. US car manufacturers have responded by producing higher quality cars that better meet the needs of the consumers. This competition is at the heart of what Schumpter (1950) calls the 'creative destruction' of competitive capitalism. Inefficient businesses that are driven out of the market provide room for their efficient competitors to grow. As a result, innovative small businesses in the United States can become big businesses in a surprisingly short period of time. In the recent past, companies such as Montgomery Ward, Ames, K–Mart and Atari were prospering and no one had heard of Wal–Mart, Target, Microsoft or Intel.

Free trade is also a major prop for peace. The basic idea goes back at least to Montesquieu (Hegre, 2000). As Polanyi (1944) pointed out, countries rarely go to war with their trading partners. World Wars I and II could only be launched after economic ties among the warring states had been cut. There is strong support for the basic thesis. See Blainey (1973), Rumel (1972), Barbieri and Levy (1999, 2001), Anderton and Carter (2001a, 2001b), Hegre (2000) and Dorsussen (2002) for an extended analysis of Polyani's idea.

This academic discussion has real–life implications. For the first time in the last two millennia, there has been general peace in Europe for more than fifty years. In this case, peace was made possible by the success of free trade and the European Union. A shared commitment to free trade has also made it easier for the United States, Europe and Japan to weather differences that could have led to more serious tensions in the past. One motive for the upcoming expansion of the EU is to promote prosperity, stability and peace in Eastern Europe.

The success of the EU in promoting economic integration in Western Europe can be measured by the international trade statistics. In 2000, the value of international trade for the fifteen member states of the European Union varied from a high value of 64 per cent of GDP for Belgium (reflecting, perhaps, the impact of the port of Antwerp) to a low value of 19 per cent of GDP in Italy. On average, the value of European international trade as a fraction of GDP was 32.8 per cent. This is substantially higher than the figures for the US economy. More importantly for our argument, most of the international trade by EU member states is with other EU members. On average, 62.1 per cent of all foreign trade was intra–EU. This trade constitutes over 20 per cent of the average European GDP. This is an impressively high level of economic integration (United Nations, 2003).

The economic ties between the US and EU economies are substantially looser. These ties are continuing to develop, but a relatively slower pace. In 1996, for example, the US merchandise exports to the EU were valued at $96.74 billion. This constituted 15 per cent of all US exports and 1.24 per cent of the US GDP. By 2001, US merchandise exports to the EU had grown to $179.1 billion. These exports represented 17.8 per cent of all US exports and 1.32 per cent of our GDP. In 2001, merchandise trade among EU countries was valued at $220.1 billion. The level of US–EU trade will have to grow substantially before the level of transatlantic economic integration approaches the intra–EU levels.

The international harmonization of standards and conformity assessment requirements has become an important element in the search for larger markets. Most governments have de–emphasized the importance of global negotiations through the WTO as the principle strategy for lowering tariffs. The effectiveness of multinational negotiations has been hampered by the diversity of interests, the relative intractability of the issues and the political backlash against 'globalization'.

Both the EU and the US are developing a series of deeper trade alliances in other areas. The Caribbean Basin Initiative provides free trade arrangements between the United States and most Caribbean nations. NAFTA, the North American free Trade Area, came into effect on January 1, 1994. The United States has also signed the Central American Free Trade Agreement and separate free trade agreements with Jordan, Israel, Singapore and Chile. The development of the Free Trade Agreement of the Americas, a proposed free trade zone covering the western hemisphere from Canada to Argentina, is a high priority for the Bush administration.

The European Union grew with the accession of ten new member states in May 2004. There is the possible accession of an additional two and possibly three countries soon hereafter. The EU has also negotiated free trade agreements with Mexico and Brazil. Although the GATT rules only sanction regional arrangements that create rather than divert trade, these regional free trade areas are likely to attract a disproportionate portion of future developments in trade, investment and political effort. If so, then the failure to continue the process of liberalizing US–EU trade may well lead to a weakening of the trade alliances on which the Western Bloc has been based.

The agreements supporting these alliances generally include major provisions governing the harmonization of standards and conformity assessment requirements. There are two major models that can be followed for standards and conformity assessment. On one side is the European CE marking model. The system has been developed through the administrative leadership of the European Union. It has been supported by a close working relationship with the International Standards Organization.

On the other side is the American system for standards development. Supporters argue that the US system is more likely to lead to technically superior standards. On the other hand, there is very little government involvement in the American system. US standards are developed in the context of a market rather than an administrative system, which is not easily adopted by other countries.

Which side is likely to prevail in this competition between dueling standards systems? The prevailing side will enjoy a significant advantage in the competition for global markets. Conditions in this rivalry are not frozen in time like a fly in amber. We should consider these national and regional arrangements for standards and conformity assessment as works in progress. Which system becomes the predominant model for the global market may depend on which side is better able to respond to the challenges posed by standards for world business.

Our goal is to understand how and why the CE marking system has developed in a particular way and to draw some preliminary conclusions about the probable effectiveness of the system in the global marketplace. The development of the CE marking system did not occur in a vacuum. It constitutes a specific response to a particular problem in the context of a distinctive set of regulatory expectations and political pressures. To understand how and why the system has developed in a particular way, we must first consider this context. In order to better understand the difficulties of coordinating standards and conformity assessment procedures developed in the EU and the US, we will later consider the distinctive characteristics of the American system as well.

To this American observer, the pictures that we will be painting are distinctive and distinctly different. To a large extent, the decision–makers in the EU are generally insulated from business pressures and the need to understand the business perspective. This reflects both tradition and the reality that national governments have a preponderance of power in the politics of the Union. As a result, the administration of the CE marking system depends heavily on governments programs. On the other hand, reforms are possible through the political process.

The American system is characterized by decentralized political authority, quasi–independent regulatory agencies and the strong influence of business in the process of government regulation. The result has been the development of a market based system for standards development. The standards may be technically superior, but the system is neither transferable nor easily susceptible to reform. As a result: the US is lagging in the competition for the international marketplace for standards.

Our review of these issues is limited to examining the impact of the European CE marking system for regulating product safety. Since this is a competitive world, we will also consider the impact of the alternative US system for standards development. This is a very a narrow slice of life.

Corporations and governments are also contesting the development and application of product conformity standards, especially in the area of high technology and information processing. These standards will effectively limit the types of products that can be used in a particular market. Many of these standards, such as those governing the specifications for high definition television, are based on emerging technologies. Control over the application of these standards is often tantamount to control over the commercialization of the underlying technologies. However, this is a story that will have to be told by someone else.

REFERENCES

Anderton, C. and J. Carter (2001a), 'The impact of war on trade; an interrupted time–series study', *Journal of Peace Research* 38 (4), pp. 445–57.

Anderton, C. and J. Carter (2001b), 'On disruption of trade by war: a reply to Barbieri and Levy', *Journal of Peace Research*, 38 (5), pp. 625–28.

Baier, S. and J. Bergstrand (2001), 'The growth of world trade; tariffs, transportation costs and income similarity', *Journal of International Economics*, 53 (1), pp. 1 –27.

Barbieri, K. and J. Levy (1999), 'Sleeping with the enemy: the impact of war on trade', *Journal of Peace Research*, 36 (4), pp. 463–79.

Barbieri, K. and J. Levy (2001), 'Does war impede trade? A response to Anderton and Carter', *Journal of Peace Research*, 38 (5), pp. 619–24.

Blainey, G. (1973), *The Causes of War,* New York: The Free Press.

'China's CCC mark: a guide for US exporters' (2003), at www.export.gov/ exportamerica/AskTheTIC/qa_ChinaCCC_0433.html.

Cranville, Roger (1999), Assistant Secretary for International Development, Pennsylvania Department of Community and Economic Development, personal interview.

Directorate General for Trade (2001), *Report on United States Barriers to Trade and Investment.*

Dorsussen, H. (2002), 'Trade and conflict in multi–country models: a rejoinder', *Journal of Peace Research*, 39 (1), pp. 115–18.

Egan, Michelle (2001), *Constructing a European Market: Standards, Regulation and Governance,* New York: Oxford University Press.

European Council (1985), *Resolution on Technical Harmonization of Standards.*

European Telecommunications Standards Institute (2002), 'One standard, one test, accepted everywhere', October 14 press release, at: www.etsi.org/frameset/home/html?/pressroom/Previous/2002/WorldStandards_Day.htm

Hanson, D. and M. McKinney (n.d.), 'Is CE marking a barrier for US exporters?', under review.

Harpstead, John (1998), 'Bills mount up for CE marking', *Electronics Business,* January 24 (1), p. 35.

Hegre, H. (2000), 'Development and the liberal peace: What does it take to be a trading state?', *Journal of Peace Research,* 37 (1), pp. 5–30.

International Standards Organization (2003), 'Definition of a standard', at www.iso.ch/en/aboutiso/introduction/index.html.

International Trade Administration (1999), *Small and Medium Sized Exporting Companies; A Statistical Profile,* Washington: US Department of Commerce.

Judd, R.W., Greenwood and F. Becker (1988), *Small Business in a Regulated Economy: Issues and Policy Implications,* New York: Quorum Press.

Laird, S. and A. Yeats (n.d.), 'Quantitative methods for trade barrier analysis'. Washington, World Bank, as quoted in M. Egan (2000), 'Bandwagon or barriers? The role of standards in the European and American marketplace', Center for West European Studies Occasional Papers, at www.pitt.edu/~wesnews/epp/egan.html.

Messerlin, P. (2001), *Measuring the Costs of Protection in Europe: European Commercial Policy in the 2000s,* Washington: Institute for International Economics.

Office of Technology Assessment (1992), *Global Standards: Building Blocks for the Future, TCT–512,.* Washington: U.S. Government Printing agenda: a European View', at www.tabd.com/resources/content/micossi.html.

Organization for Economic Cooperation and Development (1996), *Consumer Product Safety Standards and Conformity Assessment: Issues in a Global Marketplace,* France: OECD.

Polanyi, K. (1944), *The Great Transformation,* New York: Octagon Books.

Rumel, R. J. (1972), *The Dimensions of Nations ,* Beverly Hills: Sage.

Schumpter, J. (1950), *Capitalism, Socialism and Democracy* (3rd ed.), New York: Harper.

'SEMI expects EU's directives to be costly' (1997) *Electronics News, October 6, 43 (2188), 28.*

'SEMI study shows costs of CE marking' (1997) *Test and Measurement World,* November 17(12), p. 6.

Solomon, S. (1986), *Small Business USA*, New York: Crown.

Stern, J. (1997), 'The Japanese technical infrastructure: issues and opportunities', in John R. McIntyre (ed.) *Japan's Technical Standards: Implications for Global Trade and Competitiveness*, New York: Quorum Books.

Transatlantic Business Dialog (2000). 'A new paradigm for standards and regulatory reform sector–by–sector', at www.tabd.com/resources/content.stern.html.

United Nations (2003), *2001 International Trade Statistics Yearbook, Volume 1; Trade by Country*, New York: UN. Office.

US Census Bureau (2001), *Statistical Abstracts of the United States: 2001 (121st ed.)*, Washington DC: US Department of Commerce.

US Census Bureau (2002), *Statistical Abstracts of the United States: 2002 (122nd ed.)*, Washington DC: US Department of Commerce.

United States Trade Representative (2001a), 'European Union', *Annual Report on Foreign Trade Barriers: 2000,* Washington: USTR.

United States Trade Representative (2001b), 'National Trade Estimate – European Union', at www.ustr.gov/nte/1996/eu.html.

United States Trade Representative (1995), 'National Trade Estimate – European Union', at www.ustr.gov/html/1995_eu.html.

United States Trade Representative (1996), 'National Trade Estimate – European Union', at www.ustr.gov/nte/1996/eu.html.

United States Trade Representative (1999), 'European Union', in *Annual Report on Foreign Trade Barriers 1999*, Washington: USTR.

United States Trade Representative (2000), *Strategic Plan; FY 2000–FY 2005*, Washington: USTR.

Wilson, J. (ed) (1980), *The Politics of Regulation*, New York: Basic Books.

2. Background to CE Marking

1. INTRODUCTION

What has led to the emergence of these international conflicts over domestic product safety standards? What are the prospects for a resolution? If we are to address these questions, we have to consider the political and administrative circumstances in which the dueling standards systems have emerged. In this chapter, we will consider the factors shaping the development of the CE marking system. We will examine the context for the development of the American system in Chapter 6.

2. GOVERNMENT AND BUSINESS IN EUROPE

Product safety standards are almost universally developed through industry–government partnerships. Government can contribute the incentive and enforcement. Business is needed to contribute product safety experience and design expertise. The nature of these business to government partnerships will have a major impact on the development of the product safety standard programs.

The European Union is based on partnerships between national governments and the EU leadership. The nature of these partnerships determines the ways in which functions are allocated between Brussels and the national governments and the priorities of program managers at both levels. If we are to understand the development of the CE marking system, we also have to consider the nature of these partnerships between national governments and community leadership.

There are fundamental differences between the political systems of the Western European countries and the EU and the political process in the United States. In Europe, civil administration was generally developed as an agent of a centralizing monarchy. As a result, the status of the senior civil service is generally high and their influence in policy debates tends to be strong (Kickert and Hakvoort, 2000). Governments are responsible for providing leadership for a unitary state. Popular interests are to be represented through elections and the legislative process, see for example, (Schmitter, 2000). From this perspective, the involvement by business interests in government discussions could constitute an unwanted intrusion into the policy process and a corruption of democratic principles. In reality, governments that are concerned about public welfare have to be carefully attuned to the impact of public policies on private economic interests. As a result, business interests will be heard. However, there are national variations in the process of business representation.

In France, the government has traditionally exercised a heavy hand through the direct regulation of business activity. This reflects a combination of the dirigiste tradition that pre–dates the French Revolution and the more contemporary traditions of French revolutionary politics. In the late 1970s, for example, the Mitterrand government set out to 'strike an irreversible blow at the power base of capitalism' by nationalizing almost 250 major French corporations (Ardagh, 1990). For the remaining companies, decisions about market entry and exit, buying and selling, hiring and firing and new product development had to be approved by the government in Paris. In return, the French government has traditionally defended the interests of the corporate national champions.

The graduates of the *grandes ecoles* in France constitute the leadership elite in politics, government and the top echelons of private business. These graduates constitute a close knit cadre who see themselves as the natural leaders of both corporate interests and government in France (Suleiman, 1978). As a result, the distinctions between 'public' and 'private' interests are blurred as leaders from both sectors 'plan, negotiate, and implement the broad outlines of industrial policy' (Schlenker, 1987).

The senior civil servants in Germany, to use Frederich the Great's phrase, are viewed as the first servants of the state. In Germany, the basic policy of a 'social free market' is based on the assumption that an unregulated competitive economy might not be able to provide for the needs of society. There is a much stronger emphasis on orderly consultations among the 'social partners'; business, labor and government. Open competition is discouraged by such policies as an acceptance of 'fair pricing' by manufacturers, a ban on comparative advertising and the virtual absence of anti–trust enforcement. It is common for bankers, suppliers and customers to hold seats on the boards of directors of their major customers. For the larger corporations, board membership is split between stockholders (usually partner businesses) and delegates elected by the employees. The unions are also in partnership with business and government in the administration of the all–important employee training programs. As a result of these and other measures, German businesses are protected by this network of formal and informal relations among companies, banks, unions and government. At the national level, this led to the creation of a 'concerted action' program where the government would lead negotiations between business and labor on the outlines of a national labor compact (Wessels, 1987).

The hereditary aristocracy in Great Britain is surprisingly small and traditionally quite powerful. These characteristics reflect the widespread practice of primogeniture; the eldest eligible candidate inherits both the title and the wealth. The establishment, people who have ties of family and friendship with the aristocracy but who did not inherit either the title or the money, has traditionally been very influential in both business and government (Winchester, 1982). Money is always respectable but manufacturing has generally been viewed as a comparatively low status occupation. Except during the periods of state socialism, the direct involvement of government in business decision–making has been relatively infrequent. However, business interests are brought into government indirectly through the financial interests of the members of the establishment. Competitive pressures in the British economy have often been softened by the social ties and informal understandings among senior British managers. The Thatcher revolution has changed this pattern somewhat. Channels have been created to promote contacts between business interests and the government program managers (Willis and Grant, 1987).

Although these patterns are different, they have a common effect. Governments are largely responsible for directing the national economies. The largest companies, those whose activities have a national impact, are brought into the economic planning process. European companies have also been partly shielded from competition by government regulation and formal and informal ties.

These patterns have an effect on the development of the standards used to coordinate economic relations and to implement national product safety requirements. The development and enforcement of product standards and conformity assessment procedures has generally been seen as a government function.

In many cases, these traditional ties among businesses and between government and standards development organizations are reflected in contemporary systems for developing national product standards (Krislov, 1997). Most national standards development organizations are funded in part by their national governments. AFNOR, the leading French standards development organization, is widely regarded as an arm of the French government. In Italy, businesses are under a statutory obligation to use standards that represent the state of the art. Only the standards developed by UNI, the Italian standards organization, are presumed to meet this requirement. UNI technical committees and mirror committees are generally dominated by private sector representatives. However, the views of the

Italian government are influential in areas where the Italian government has an interest. Siemens, a leading German corporation, provides direct organizational support for DIN, the German standards organization. The British Standards Organization has a reputation for professionalism and political independence. In part, this is a legacy of the deregulation efforts of the Thatcher government. It is also consistent with the status of the 'establishment' as an elite independent of government.

One index of government influence is the level of public funding in the standards development process. Table 2.1 sets out the data as of 1986, at the beginning of the CE marking process.

Table 2.1. Public support for standards development in Europe and the US

Country	Lead SDO	Percentage public funding
France	AFNOR	41
West Germany	DIN	20
Italy	UNI	25
Netherlands	NNI	17
United Kingdom	BSI	17
Canada	CSA	89
Japan	JISC	100
US	ANSI	0

Source: Kruger (1989).

3. THE EUROPEAN COMMON MARKET

The creation of the common market has further limited the influence of the business community in program development and administration. The governments of the member states have emerged, reasonably enough, as the dominant voice in community politics.

The most important decisions concerning the European Union are generally taken by the Council, which is composed of delegations from the member states. The organizational responsibilities of the Council members will vary from issue to issue. When environmental issues are under consideration, the Council will consist of delegates who have national environmental responsibilities (the 'environmental council'). The heads of state from the member countries participate only when fundamental political decisions are being taken ('the Council of Europe'). The program managers in Directorate General Enterprise who are responsible for the CE marking system generally work with the 'Enterprise Council', which consists of representatives from the national agencies with similar responsibilities in the member states.

Formal meetings of the Council occur on a relatively infrequent basis. Between meetings, the work of the Council and relations with the other agencies of the EU is managed by COREPER, the Committee of Permanent Representatives. COREPER is organized into a series of committees. Directorate General Enterprise works with two COREPER committees on CE marking issues. They are the committee on competitiveness and the committee on transport, telecommunications and energy.

The Commission of the European Union is responsible for planning and administering the work of the Union. There are 20 commissioners, who are appointed by the member states. They are pledged to consider only the interests of the Community as a whole. The president of the Commission is appointed by the Council. The president is responsible for coordinating the work of the different directorates general. The Commission is presently organized into 19 directorates–general. The Director General for Enterprise and the Information Society, Erkki Liikanen, is responsible for the CE marking system.

The senior managers in the directorates general spend a lot of their efforts coordinating proposals with the Council through COREPER. Since the Council represents the member countries, this coordination also involves ongoing consultations with administrative and political agencies in the member states (Wallace, 1996). Most directorates general have made widespread use of advisory committees in the process of policy development and program administration. These committees provide opportunities for consulting with outside interests without having to go outside the organization.

Until relatively recently, the direct impact of the European Parliament in Community decision–making has been relatively limited. Despite the expansion of the role of the European Parliament under the Maastricht Treaty, the Parliament is still the weakest of the four major institutions of the European Union. According to one analyst, the European Parliament can be, at best, considered as a 'conditional agenda setter' (Tsebelis, 1995).

The 626 members of the European Parliament are elected directly for five year terms. Rather than organizing by nationality, the members of the European Parliament have lined up by party and ideology into eight broad blocs. Internally, the EP has not had the administrative machinery necessary to support strong policy analyses. However, the Parliament has been able to force the Commission and the Council to consider its views on the issues that are considered under the 'co–decision procedure'.

Three different decision processes are specified in the Treaty of Rome. Most issues involving the liberalization of the internal market are passed under the 'co–decision' process under article 251 of the Treaty of Rome. 'Co–decision' gives the Parliament a qualified right to veto legislation. However, legislative proposals must be initiated by the Commission. The Council can adopt a 'common position' on the proposal by qualified majority voting. If the Parliament either takes no action or approves the proposal, then the proposal is adopted. If the Parliament amends the proposal and the Council then votes to accept the amendments, then the amended proposal is adopted. If the Parliamentary amendments are not accepted by the Council, then a joint 'Conciliation Committee' is created to review the dispute. If the Committee develops a joint text and both Parliament and the Council approve it, then the measure is passed. Finally, if the Parliament initially rejects the Council's common position, then the Council can explain its position to the Conciliation Committee. Parliament can then reconsider the proposal. Unless the proposal is rejected by an absolute Parliamentary majority, the measure is still adopted.

The importance of the advisory committees in the Commission has led to extended debates over 'comitology', the policies governing consultations between the Commission and outside interests through the committee process (Sleunenberg and Schmidtchen, 2000). Comitology has become an issue in the struggles between the Council and the European Parliament over control over the Commission.

The Council defined the role of these committees in the 1987 Comitology Decision (European Council, 1987). There was nothing in the comitology decision that granted any authority to the European Parliament over these committees or required the Commission to report to the Parliament on the work of the committees. The Parliament then sued the Commission in the European Court of Justice and lost. Subsequently, the Parliament and the Commission came to a 'modus vivendi' in which the Commission pledged to keep the Parliament informed about the provisions and schedules for any major initiatives and proposals (European Commission, 1994).

The relations between the EU and the member states are equally complex. The members of the EU are legally obligated to make national laws conform with the requirements of the EU directives. However, the implementation of EU policy is tempered by the policy of 'subsidiarity'. During the negotiations over the Maastricht Treaty, many countries argued that increasing the authority of Brussels to regulate national concerns would lead to a dangerous concentration of power in the Community. To meet these objections, Jacques Delors, President of the Commission, stated that the EC would limit the exercise of regulatory authority only to 'appropriate levels where the states cannot act alone' (Goldstein, 1992/1993). As a practical matter, this principle of subsidiarity means that Community policies should be made through government–to–government negotiations in Brussels and that enforcement should be delegated as much as possible to regional, national and local entities (Wistrich, 1994). This pattern reflects the desire of political executives at the national level to preserve as much autonomy as possible while pursuing collective arrangements for mutual advantage.

In principle, the Commission is expected to provide long–term policy direction for the EU. In reality, this leadership can be uncertain. Both the Council and the Commission are heavily dependent on the policy interests of the political leaders in the member states. This can vary over time. Because neither the Council nor the Commission can provide consistent, long–term policy leadership, the member states cannot be sure that any compromises in one set of negotiations will be made up by gains on other issues.

Since the Commissioners are primarily concerned with sectoral bargaining and supporting their specialized national constituencies, coordination across directorates general on larger issues tends to be weak (Wallace, 1994). On the other hand, the sectors managed by the directorates general tend to cover a significant range of policy interests. At the national level, CE marking enforcement involves government agencies that are otherwise involved in regulating such areas as medicine, construction, mining, telecommunications, workplace safety, consumer safety and weights and measures. At the EU level, the product safety aspects of these issues is handled by Directorate General Enterprise.

Decisions in the EU tend to be made in comparative secrecy. Transparency in the EU, according to many observers, means that 'we will tell you what the policy is as soon as we decide'. On the other hand, the EU has been very aggressive in making the planning documents available for public scrutiny through the internet. Most of the official EU documents cited in this book have been downloaded from the various EU websites.

For business, decision–making in the EU can be characterized as a system of 'participation by invitation'. Commission proposals are first reviewed by the European Economic and Social Committee. The EESC is a 'consultative body of the European Union' that consists of representatives of the various economic and social components of organized civil society. The participants in the EESC are 'selected on the basis of their particular responsibilities and experience'. The EESC is organized into three groups. Most of the members of Group I come from the major EU–wide employers confederations and chambers of commerce with some ad hoc participation from sectoral industry organizations. Group II includes representatives from the national unions that are members of the European Trade Union

Confederation. Group III is the 'various interests group' (European Economic and Social Committee, 2003).

The author has not come across any evidence that the EESC has a sustained significant impact on EU policies or programs. Given the scope of the business interests included in Group I, it would be surprising if the EESC was able to take positions on the details of the CE marking system.

For the most part, the committees in DG Enterprise that are involved in CE marking consist of representatives from the national regulatory authorities assisted by subcommittees made up of technical experts drawn from industry. Business interests are often articulated in these advisory committees, but only at the discretion of the political members.

The Commission also prepares a 'business impact' statement for major new initiatives. However, these analyses are prepared under contract that has been let under a public tender. Many observers have questioned the adequacy of the business impact reports and their effects on decisions that may have already been made (Directorate General Enterprise, 2002). Trade associations may also receive funding from the Commission to prepare position papers on major initiatives and to participate in the development of the standards used to implement the CE marking system (European Commission, 2001).

This pattern has a clear impact on the regulation of industrial and consumer products in the EU. For the most part, the development of the CE marking system has been led by Directorate General Enterprise in consultation with their national counterparts. The national governments often bring the considerations of the major European corporations to the discussions. However, the ability of DG Enterprise to coordinate and review decisions that have been delegated to national and local agencies is correspondingly limited. The system has also been generally consistent with the interests and practices of the major European multi-national corporations.

This pattern also influences the evolution of policy in the other directorates general, in particular, Directorate General Environment. Different issues involve working with different national agencies and different interests. Business interests are often omitted from these policy coalitions. Since Directorates General Enterprise and Environment work with different interests in national governments, the level of policy coordination between the two directorates is generally weak.

4. CE MARKING AND THE COMMON MARKET

The Cold War between the USSR and the West emerged in full force with the Berlin Blockade in 1948, the Greek Civil War in 1949 and the Korean War in 1952. The need to develop an effective Western military alliance led to the organization of the North Atlantic Treaty Organization (NATO) in 1949. The success of the alliance would depend in part on the rapid development of the European economies. In 1950, the Communists had the strongest political movements in Italy and France. Given the magnitude of war devastation in Europe, demands for radical changes would be hard to fend off unless democratic capitalism could offer substantial improvement in the short term. Furthermore, the political unity of NATO could not be taken for granted. World War II was only one episode in a thousand–year struggle among the European powers for economic and political domination of the region.

The development of an effective common market was an essential tool for the emergence of a prosperous, economically integrated Europe. One of the key tools for promoting international peace and prosperity, as we discussed in the last chapter, is the vigorous development of international trade.

The European Economic Community was founded in 1957 with the ratification of the Treaty of Rome. The primary goal of the Treaty was to create an effective, comprehensive common market in Western Europe. The Treaty of Rome was to ensure the emergence of the 'four freedoms' on which the common market was to be built: freedom of movement for goods, services, capital and people.

The six original signatories to the Treaty of Rome were pledged to the development of policies to ensure the emergence of these freedoms. These included the elimination of internal tariffs, the development of a common external trade policy and the coordination of national tax policies around the principles of VAT. Intra–community tariffs were gradually reduced and finally eliminated on 1 July 1968. The struggle over non–tariff trade barriers within the European Community became more intense as direct trade barriers were eliminated.

The Treaty of Rome also set forth basic principles to govern anti–trust and anti–monopoly policies. The Treaty provisions governing intra-European commerce reflect a balance between the need to promote trade and the obligation to protect legitimate national goals. As currently codified, the basic provisions are:

> Article 23. The Community shall be based upon a customs union . . . which shall involve the prohibition between member states of customs duties . . . and of all charges having equivalent effect. . .

Article 28. Quantitative restrictions on imports and all measures having equivalent effect shall be prohibited between member states.

Article 30. The restrictions of Articles 28 and 29 shall not preclude prohibitions . . . on grounds of public morality, public policy or public security; the protection of health and life . . . the protection of national treasures . . . or the protection of industrial and commercial property. Such prohibitions . . . shall not . . . constitute a means of discrimination or disguised restriction on trade between Member States.

Articles 23, 28 and 30 do not spell out a clear trade policy for the Union. Rather, these provisions represent an invitation for the governing entities to settle the real issue; how to define the boundaries to what is prohibited under Article 28 and what is allowed under Article 30. Given the political and administrative dynamics of the EU, we would not expect this issue to be resolved until circumstances demanded Community action because all other options had been exhausted.

Article 176 on environmental regulation states that:

The protective measures adopted pursuant to Article 175 shall not prevent any member state from maintaining or introducing more stringent measures. Such measures must be compatible with this Treaty.

Article 176 raises the issue of defining the boundaries of trade–related measures, which are governed by the EU under Article 28, and environmental measures on which the member states are free to exceed EU requirements. We will discuss the potential collusion between trade–related and environmentally based EU product standards in Chapter 9.

Judged by the twin criteria of political unity and economic prosperity, the first 15 years of the European common market were a resounding success. The major European economies grew on average at 5 per cent per year between 1957 and 1973. Because of this sustained growth of the major European economies, concerns about the impact of product standards on intra–EEC trade tended to be muted.

France was the clear leader of the European Economic Community for the first 15 years of the common market. There were only five other members. Germany was still recovering from the moral and political shocks of the Nazis, the politics and governments of Italy were too chaotic to offer consistent policy leadership, and the Benelux countries were too small to consistently counter French influence. The clarity of these political realities made it easier for the EEC to develop in a reasonably coherent manner. The guiding French philosophy was simple; the EEC is an agreement among sovereign states. It has no inherent power. The administrators of the common market can only exercise authority to the extent that it has been delegated by a treaty signed by the member states (Newhouse, 1967).

The EU has tended to evolve during crises. The oil crisis of the early 1970s provided a major shock to the European economies. Between 1968 and 1973, world oil prices went from an average of $2.15 per barrel to a high of $40 per barrel. This increase had a major inflationary impact in Europe, which is heavily dependent on imported oil for energy. The oil shock triggered a cascade of events; the Bretton Woods Agreement was scrapped and the major governments of the world went to a system of floating exchange rates. Towards the end of the 1970s, the Iranian hostage crisis precipitated another spike in oil prices and stagflation in the EU (Wallace and Young, 1996; Coffee, 1995). The changing fortunes of the European economies also emerge in the data on growth, inflation and unemployment. Some details are provided in Table 2.2.

This dramatic drop in growth rates and increase in unemployment represented a crisis for the European common market that has led to the development of several new programs. Fixed exchange rates provide at least the promise of price stability across national boundaries in international trade. Price and cost predictability is essential for the development of an integrated regional economy. Floating exchange rates could seriously impede cross border commitments in the European Community.

In order to stabilize currency exchange rates, the Community adopted the European Monetary System, the Exchange Rate Mechanism and the European Currency Unit in 1978. Under the Exchange Rate Mechanism, the member countries were committed to defending exchange rate stability within the Community. The European Currency Unit ('ecu') was a fictitious accounting unit that was based on weighted averages of the different Community currencies at the official exchange rates. This 'basket' of Community currencies was then set free to float as a unit on international currency markets. The members of the EMS were pledged to maintain stable exchange rates among the EEC currencies in accordance with the basket (Fischer, 2000).

The dramatic rise in oil prices during the 1970s created inflationary pressures for countries such as Germany and Italy that were strongly dependent on imported crude. Other countries, such as the UK and Norway, found prosperity in exports from their off–shore oil operations. These differences created severe pressures on the European economies and the EMS (Coffee, 1995).

Table 2.2. Economic conditions in the EU

GDP: percentage change from previous year at constant market prices

Year	1961	1973	1981	1986	1995
France	5.5	5.4	1.2	2.4	1.8
Germany	4.6	4.6	0.1	2.4	0.6
Italy	8.2	6.5	0.8	2.5	1.8

Unemployment rate:

Year	1958	1973	1981	1986	1995
France	1.0	2.7	7.4	9.9	11.3
Germany	3.0	1.0	4.5	6.4	8.0
Italy	7.5	6.2	7.8	8.9	11.5

Source: European Union (2003).

Unfortunately, the EMS was not self–enforcing. Participating currencies could still be subject to balance of payments problems and pressures for currency devaluations. Belgium, France, Denmark, Italy and other EU members devalued repeatedly between 1979 and 1986. These devaluations effectively lowered the price of their exports on European markets and took market opportunities at the expense of the manufacturers in countries that had not devalued. This was one origin for the rising demand for domestic market protection. The economic stagnation of the 1980s and 1990s also led to the adoption of measures to protect domestic industries. Since raising tariffs was out of the question, many member states turned to the adoption of specialized product standards and conformity assessment requirements instead. This led to a long–term rise in the importance of inconsistent national product regulations as the source of intra–community trade barriers.

The growing impact of national requirements on intra–community trade was threatening to derail the Common Market. In response, the Commission sponsored the development of a series of economic studies on the costs of protection among the members of the common market. Volume 6 of the 'Cecchini Report' examined the impact of national technical requirements in intra–community trade (European Commission, 1988). As the Cecchini report made clear, either the members of the EC would have to develop policies to liberalize internal trade or the effectiveness of the common market would be seriously compromised.

Table 2.3. The rise of non-tariff trade barriers within the EU

Percentage of foreign trade in manufactured goods significantly affected by non-tariff trade barriers

Country	1966	1966–1986 change
Germany	12	+ 47
France	6	+ 55
Belgium – Luxembourg	21	+ 48
Netherlands	8	+ 50
Italy	9	+ 57

Source: Laird and Yeats (1988).

The EC would go through two other experiments in regulating national product standards before adopting the New Approach and the CE marking system. Initially, there was only one route to the harmonization of European product standards. The European Court of Justice could find that a national product requirement imposed an impermissible burden on intra–community trade. This approach was primarily applied to national markets that were protected on the basis of traditional methods of food preparation. The German Rheinheitsgebot (Beer Purity Law), for example, was enacted in 1517. It stated that beer sold in Germany could only be made from hops, barley, yeast and water. Most beer made outside Germany also includes wheat or rice. More importantly, only draft beer can be made in accordance with the Rheinheitsgebot. It cannot be pasteurized. As a result, beer sold in Germany could only have a shelf life of perhaps two months. This gave German breweries a tremendous advantage over foreign breweries in serving the German market. The EU Court of Justice ruled that the Rheinheitsgebot was a trade barrier that was inconsistent with Germany's obligation to free trade under the Treaty of Rome 1987 (European Court of Justice, case 176/84, 1987). The decision was based on the provisions of the FAO/WHO Codex Alementarous, which made it easier for the Court to overrule the German position.

The Commission turned to the European Court of Justice for relief under Article 28 from inconsistent national product requirements. The thinking of the court was summarized in the 1974 Dassonville case. *Procurer du Roi v. Dassonville* (European Court of Justice 1974, Case 8/74, ECR 837).

Involved a Belgian law requiring companies importing some types of hard liquor to produce a certificate of origin from the country of origin. The defendant, Dassonville, was prosecuted for importing Scotch whisky from France under a French certificate of origin.

The Court ruled that the prohibition in Article 28 (formerly codified as Article 30) applied to all measures that had the potential to restrict intra-Community trade. In other words, it was not necessary to show actual harm to invoke the article. However, restrictive measures would still be allowed if: a) the policy was intended to prevent unfair trade practices, b) the measure represented a reasonable means to achieve this goal, and c) there was no Community system for achieving the same goals. The court then struck down the Belgian law under this test.

In the Cassis de Dijon case, The European Court of Justice considered the permissible scope of state action under Article 28. A Belgium company wanted to sell Cassis de Dijon, with 15 per cent alcohol content, to the German state alcohol monopoly. The transaction was barred because German law required drinks labeled as "cassis" to have at least 32 per cent alcohol.

The Court held that the Community policy in favor of free trade should be upheld unless a member state could show compelling reasons why trade should be restricted. In effect, the burden of proof was shifted onto the member country proposing restrictions to show why the policy was needed to achieve legitimate state goals. In effect, each member state must accept the validity of regulations adopted in other member states that are intended to achieve the same goals, unless they can show good reasons for not accepting them. In order to implement a national regulation that could impede trade, a member state would have to show that the measure taken:

- Was intended to achieve one of the goals listed in Article 28
- Was based on a direct causal link between the regulatory goal and the
- measure adopted,
- Imposed restrictions that were proportionate to the importance of the goals to be achieved, and
- Was the only option, that is, there was no alternative means to achieve the same goal that would have a lesser impact on community trade.

The German regulation failed under the Cassis test and was struck down. (European Commission, 2000).

Despite the seemingly tight restrictions placed by the Dassonville/Cassis de Dijon cases on state action, the ECJ subsequently upheld a number of national measures based on legitimate national differences in factual interpretations, market conditions or policy goals. Countries could ban the addition of nisin in cheese (*Eyssen v. BV*, European Court of Justice, 1981) and vitamins to food products (*Sandoz Case*, European Court of Justice, 1983) because the scientific evidence for and against these measures was inconclusive. France could restrict the importation of German woodworking machines because of the differences in the safety training provided for equipment operators in the two countries (*Commission v. French Republic*, European Court of Justice, 1986). Denmark was allowed to impose a bottle recycling requirement in order to achieve legitimate environmental goals even though it imposed higher costs on foreign producers (*Commission v. Denmark*, European Court of Justice, 1988).

It was clear from this line of cases that the prospects for removing broad ranges of inconsistent national product requirements through the courts on the basis of Article 30 were slim. The Commission then began advocating greater cooperation among the member states on the basis of voluntary reciprocal recognition of the adequacy of product regulations at the Community state level (Egan, 2001, p. 109–13). Predictably, the regulatory agencies in the member states were generally hostile to this initiative. Advocacy groups, such as the Consumer Consultative Council, opposed the initiative as an unwarranted intrusion into the domestic affairs of the member states that had taken the lead in raising the levels of regulatory protection. (Consumer Consultative Council, 1981).

Litigation is a blunt instrument for creating a coherent and effective system of Community–wide product regulations. It was quite possible that the Court of Justice would find that a member state did have a sufficiently strong justification for a product regulation and the requirement would be allowed to stand. This would, however, impede the development of an alternative system that could achieve the same national goals without creating significant barriers to intra–Community trade.

By the early 1980s it was clear that the Community was approaching a crisis. Non–tariff trade barriers were threatening to derail the goal of achieving free trade in the internal market. However, there was no agreement on how the problem should be addressed. Disagreements over the authority of the member states to determine standards and conformity assessment requirements for products imported from third party countries was a frequent source of conflict. According to the American Chamber of Commerce in Brussels, American companies were facing widespread barriers from inconsistent product standards, border formalities and export licenses. France and Italy were cited as the worst offenders (*Financial Times*, 1983a). The French government responded by cataloging the difficulties encountered in entering German markets (*Financial Times*, 1983b).

The Mutual Information Directive of 26 April 1983 (European Council 1983) provided the legal basis for a comprehensive regulation of national product requirements that could create trade barriers. Under the Mutual Information Directive, member states and national standards organizations are required to notify Brussels before implementing new standards or regulations that could impede the internal free market. The Commission is authorized to issue a three–month 'standstill' order delaying the implementation of any measures that they believe have the potential to create trade barriers. This period is intended to give the Commission sufficient time to resolve disputes and develop community–wide policies. The effectiveness of the standstill program has been complemented by the enactment of the *Product Safety Directive* (European Council, 1959) and Decision 3052/95/EC. Under the Product Safety Directive, member states are required to inform Brussels any time a product is taken off the market because of safety concerns. The Directive requires the member states to notify the Commission when they take measures that restrict the circulation of goods but falls short of an outright ban.

These measures have not solved the problem of how to harmonize national product requirements. Countries frequently adopted regulations and standards without going through the notification requirement. The Commission often had trouble assessing the impact of the measures that were brought up for review. Many times, national measures affected the internal free market, not because they were inherently protectionist, but because they differed from equally reasonable policies in neighboring states (European Commission, 2003; European Commission, 2000; Weatherill, 1996). The evaluation of many of the proposals is complicated by the complexity of the underlying analyses (Pelkmans and Egan, 1992).

The European Commission then tried to develop EU–wide product requirements directly. Under this 'old approach' to EU product regulation, the standards were, in effect, developed by the Commission and written into the directives. The problems with the old approach became apparent in 1992 as the transportation sector was brought into the internal free market. Prior to 1992, trade in cars and trucks was exempt from the Treaty of Rome. For the most part, the national car companies dominated the national car markets. As the free market in cars approached, the car manufacturing countries tended to develop national automotive design and manufacturing requirements that could only be met by their national car companies. The EU would then develop a European standard covering the same aspects of product design and performance.

The European Commission does not necessarily have the in–house expertise to develop product standards in technical areas such as automotive design and manufacturing. As a result, the Commission would have to turn to outside experts to develop the technical requirements in the directives.

Developing a technical consensus that could bridge national differences in design philosophy could be a difficult task.

The convoluted system for political decision–making in the European Union has often provided national governments with opportunities to block Community decisions that countered national interests. National representatives could argue in Council for the primacy of their national requirements. The political compromises needed to overcome these differences could compromise the technical integrity of the original proposal.

This process often triggered a paper chase. A national government would issue a proposed standard regulating some aspect of automotive design or manufacturing. The Commission would then place a hold on the enforcement of a proposed automotive standard. A national government would then issue a new national standard regulating a different aspect of automobile design or performance. This, in turn, often led to another round of activity to develop European requirements.

Many directives governing transportation–related products were developed in partnership with UNECE, the United Nations Economic Commission for Europe (United Nations Economic Commission for Europe, 1995). The partnership with the non–political UNECE eventually provided the outside expertise needed to develop a reasonably comprehensive, consistent and effective system for regulating the design and performance of transportation equipment. Nevertheless, the old approach often led to the development of unnecessarily detailed regulations in many areas of car design and manufacturing.

The old approach to developing product safety requirements is widely regarded as a failure. Nevertheless, the old approach directives are still in force for transportation equipment, many foodstuffs and pharmaceuticals. However, the scope of these old approach directives is limited. Many traditional, low technology products not included under the New Approach are still covered only by national requirements.

In the late 1980s, it had become clear that more energetic measures were required to develop a true internal free market. This led to the development of the 'three hundred directives' that were intended to eliminate the barriers to a true internal free market. These directives covered a broad range of commercial activities and Community programs. Many directives addressed trade barriers created by inconsistent national regulations, especially in the pharmaceutical, agricultural and telecommunications markets. With this came a corresponding commitment to develop a broader, more effective alliance. These commitments led to the ratification of the Maastricht Treaty, and the creation of the European Union.

The logjam over product regulation was broken by the invention of the 'New Approach' to setting mandatory product standards. The 'New

Approach' to developing European product standards was outlined in *Council Resolution of 7 May 1985* (European Council, 1985). The New Approach and the associated CE marking system were based on the legal principle of subsidiarity. Product safety policies for the European Union would be made at the top by the European Union. However, the implementation of these policies is to be delegated to national and local levels. The administration of the CE marking system would rely heavily on the participation of national governmental agencies, standards developing organizations, commercial auditing and certification companies, and European industry. The ultimate responsibility for complying with the requirements of the system has been left to the product manufacturers themselves.

5. CE MARKING AND EU TRADE POLICIES

The European implementation of GATT/WTO trade obligations has often been relatively protectionist. As Messerlin (2001) has pointed out, EU tariff levels in the most protected industrial sectors have remained among the highest in the developed world. The EU has vigorously defended a protectionist Common Agricultural Policy. The EU anti–dumping regulations (European Council, 1996) authorize the imposition of countervailing duties on any product that is sold at a higher price in any other market. Messerlin (2001) concludes that EU anti–dumping measures are, in fact, pro–cartel policies.

This pattern may reflect the impact of national agendas on Community decision–making. France, in particular, has tended to use Community policies and institutions to promote national development priorities and industrial champions (Ambler and Reichert, 2001).

Some of these trade policies seem to reflect a proactive policy of social development. At the heart of the US–EU 'banana wars' has been the reluctance of the Union to cut back on high cost imports from former Caribbean colonies that are highly dependent on banana exports (Darling, 1999; Cooper, 2001). These paternalistic tendencies in external trade are matched with paternalist domestic labor policies, an acceptance of industrial subsidies and the broad acceptance of the principle of state aid for regional economic development (Messerlin, 2001).

In Messerlin's (2001) opinion, these protectionist tendencies in other aspects of EU trade and economic policies also emerge in the implementation of CE marking. The CE system has established a uniform system of product safety standards throughout the EU and associated countries. 'Uniformity' is not the same as liberalization. In his view, the implementation of the CE marking system has too often been based on the more restrictive national regulatory systems rather than the less restrictive systems.

Some would argue that these protectionist elements are not necessarily inappropriate. Gavin (2001) has argued that the goal of good government is to improve the quality of life and not just to promote economic development. Governments should act to address the social costs of free trade. In many cases, protectionist policies would involve placing limits on the four freedoms within the EU and a more protectionist emphasis on international trade policies.

However, Messerlin raises another possibility; the protectionist elements in EU economic policies are as likely to reflect the organization of the policy process as they are likely to be based on deliberate policy choices. The fundamental purpose of the Union has been to promote free trade within the Union by overriding local protectionist arrangements. Predictably, EU reform efforts are likely to meet local resistance. Messerlin sees the European Union as a relatively weak political institution, with limited legitimacy, resources and institutional history. Given these constraints, it would not be surprising to find the re–emergence of protectionist elements through the process of political bargaining that accompanies the development and implementation of a policy initiative. A tacit acceptance of protectionist elements in international trade policies could be a reasonable compromise for efforts to liberalize community trade.

Egan's (2001) account of the development of the CE marking system supports Messerlin's general thesis on several points. In her view, the EU was faced with a classic problem of regulatory mismatch: the tools available to limit the impact of national product standards and conformity assessment requirements on the internal market were not especially appropriate for achieving the desired goals. The 'old approach' to product regulation has been widely regarded as a failure. The Commission lacked the technical expertise needed to draft effective standards and the political resources needed to have them adopted in a reasonable period of time. The protectionist interests that had supported the development of restrictive policies at the national level were often able to derail the development of more liberal policies at the EU level. The solution developed by the founders of the CE marking system was to decentralize the implementation of the CE marking system to the point where there were few contentious points left in the 'New Approach' directives developed by the Commission. Industry groups and national governments were also given major roles in the implementation of the CE marking system.

REFERENCES

Ambler, John and Shawn Reichert (2001), 'France: Europeanization, nationalism and the planned economy', in Eleanor Zeff and Ellen Puso (eds), *The European Union and the Member States: Cooperation, Coordination and Compromise.* Boulder, Colorado: Lynne Reimer Publishers, pp. 29–58.

Ardagh, John (1990), *France Today,* Hammondsworth: Penguin Books, 44.

Coffee, Peter (1995), *The Future of Europe* Aldershot, UK and Brookfield, US: Edward Elgar.

Consumer Consultative Council (1981), *Opinion on the Consequences of the Judgment of the Cassis de Dijon Case,* ccc/29/31, Rev 4.

Cooper, Helene (2001), 'Dole fails to find much appeal in accord to end banana war', *Wall Street Journal,* 13 April, p. A12.

Darling, Juanita (1999), 'Human struggle for survival plays out behind banana wars', *Los Angeles Times,* 11 July, p. 1.

Directorate General Enterprise (2002), *Business Impact Assessment Pilot Project Final Report: Lessons Learned and the Way Forward,* Working Paper.

Egan, Michelle (2001), *Constructing a European Market*, Oxford: Oxford University Press.

European Commission (1988), *Technical Barriers in the EU: An Illustration by Six Industries,* Volume 6, *The Cost of non–Europe: Basic Findings* Luxembourg: The European Commission.

European Commission (1994), 'Commission proposal for a Council decision on the implementation of Commission power', 20 December, Official Journal L43.

European Commission (2000), *Report from the Commission to the Council, the European Parliament and the Economic and Social Committee on the implementation of Decision 3052/95/CE in 1997 and 1998* Brussels, 07.04 COM(2000) 194 final.

European Commission (2001), *Report from the Commission to the Council and the European Parliament on Actions Taken Following the Resolutions on European Standardization Adopted by the Council and the European Parliament in 1999,* COM(2001) 527 final.

European Commission (2003), *Report from the Commission to the Council, the European Parliament and the European Economic and Social Committee: The Operation of Directive 98/34/EC from 1999 to 2001* Brussels, 23.5 COM(2003) 200.

European Council (1959), *Product Safety Directive*, 92/59/EEC.

European Council (1983), *The Mutual Information Directive* 83/189 of 26 April, OJ NO L 108, as amended.

European Council (1985), *Council Resolution of 7 May 1985 on a New Approach to Technical Harmonization and Standards.*

European Council (1987), *Council Decision on Officially Established Advisory Committees, Management Committees and Regulatory Committees.*

European Council (1996), *Council Regulation 384/96 of 22 December 1995 on Protection against Dumped Imports from Countries not Members of the European Community.*

European Court of Justice (1974), *Procurer du Roi v. Dassonville*, Case 8/74.

European Court of Justice (1979), Cassis de Dijon case (*Rewe Zentral AG v. Bundesmonopolverwaltung fur Branntwein*), ECR 649.

European Court of Justice,(1981), *Eyssen v. BV*, ECR 409.

European Court of Justice (1983). *Sandoz Case*, 174/82, ECR 2445.

European Court of Justice (1986), *Commission v. French Republic*, 188/84, ECR 1986.

European Court of Justice (1987), *Rheinheitsgebot* EEC Case 176/84.

European Court of Justice (1988), *Commission v. Denmark*, ECR 1988.

European Economic and Social Committee (2003), *The EESC: A Bridge Between Europe and Organized Civil Society*, Brussels: EESC.

European Union (2003), *50 years of Figures on Europe: Data 1952-2001*, Luxembourg: The European Union.

Financial Times (1983a), 'France and Italy Operate Worst Trade Barriers', 22 September, p. 1.

Financial Times (1983b), 'Paris Catalogs the EEC Tariff Trip Wires', 1 March, p. 1.

Fischer, Thomas (2000), *The United States, the European Union and the Globalization of World Trade; Allies or Adversaries?*, Westport Conn.: Quorum Books.

Folsom, Ralph (1995), *European Law in a Nutshell, 2nd ed*, St. Paul: West Publishing.

Gavin, Brigid (2001), *The European Union and Globalization*, Cheltenham, UK and Northampton, MA, USA: Edward Elgar.

Goldstein, W. (1992/1993), 'Europe after Maastricht', *Foreign Affairs*, Winter, pp. 117-132.

Iritni, Evelyn (1999), 'EU may yield in banana fight After WTO backs US', *Los Angeles Times*, 20 April p. 1.

Kickert, Walter J.M. and Jan L.M. Hakvoort (2000), 'Public governance in Europe: a historical institutional tour d'horizon', in Oscar van Heffen, Walter J.M. Kickert and Jacques J.A. Thomassen (eds), *Governance in Modern Society: Effects, Changes and Formation of Government Institutions*, Dortrecht, Netherlands: Kluwer Academic Publishers, pp.

223–55.

Krislov, Samuel (1997), *How Nations Choose Product Standards and Standards Change Nations*, Pittsburgh: University of Pittsburgh Press.

Kruger, Lennard G. (1989), *Industrial Standardization: The Federal Role*, Washington, DC: Congressional Research Service, Library of Congress, p. 10.

Laird, Sam and Alexander Yeats (1988), *Trends in Nontariff Barriers of Developing Countries: 1966–1986*, Washington: The World Bank.

Laird, Sam and Alexander Yeats (n.d), 'Quantitative methods for trade barrier analysis', Washington: World Bank.

Messerlin, Patrick (2001), *Measuring the Costs of Protection in Europe: European Commercial Policy in the 2000s*, Washington: Institute for International Economics.

Newhouse, John (1967), *Collusion in Brussels*, New York: Norton.

Pelkmans, J. and M. Egan (1992), 'The politics of the green paper on the development of European standards', *Occasional Paper*, Brussels: Center for European Policy Studies.

Schlenker, L.H. (1987), 'France: the business state', in M.P.C.M. van Schlendelen and R.J. Jackson (eds), *The Politicization of Business in Western Europe*, London: Croom Helm, pp. 114–33.

Schmitter, Phillippe C. (2000), 'Decision–making and the representation of member states in a future euro–democracy: general principles and specific reforms', in Edward Best, Mark Gray and Alexander Stubb (eds), *Rethinking the European Union: IGC 2000 and Beyond*, Maastricht: European Institute of Public Administration, pp. 255–62.

Sleunenberg, Bernard and Dieter Schmidtchen (2000), 'The comitology game: European policy making with parliamentary involvement', in Oscar van Heffen, Walter J.M. Kickert and Jacques J.A. Thomassen (eds), *Governance in Modern Society: Effects, Change and Formation of Government Institutions* Dortrecht, Netherlands: Kluwer Academic Publishers, pp. 15–33.

Sulieman, Ezra (1978), *Elites in French Society t,he Politics of Survival*, Princeton: Princeton University Press.

Tsebelis, George (1995), 'Power of the European parliament as a conditional agenda setter', in Gerald Schneider, Patricia Weitsman and Thomas Bernauer (eds), *Towards a New Europe: Stops and Starts in Regional Integration*, Westport: Conn. Praeger, pp. 75–109.

United Nations Economic Commission for Europe (1995), *Agreement Concerning the Adoption of Uniform Technical Prescriptions for Wheeled Vehicles, Equipment and Parts which can be Fitted and/or be Used on Wheeled Vehicles and the Conditions for Reciprocal Recognition of Approvals Granted on the Basis of these Prescriptions; Revision 2.*

Wallace, Helen (1996), 'The institutions of the EU: experience and experiments', in Helen Wallace and William Wallace (eds*), Policy–Making in the European Union,* Oxford: Oxford University Press.

Wallace, Helen and Alasdair R. Young (1996), 'The single market: a new approach to policy', in Helen Wallace and William Wallace (eds), *Policy-Making in the European Union,* Oxford: Oxford University Press.

Weatherill, S. (1996), 'Compulsory Notification of Draft Technical Regulations: The Contribution of Directive 83/189 to the management of the internal market', *Yearbook of European Law,* p. 16.

Wessels, B. (1987), 'Business profits from politics', in M.P.C.M. van Schlendelen and R.J. Jackson (eds), *The Politicization of Business in Western Europe,* London: Croom Helm, pp. 134–55.

Willis, D. and W. Grant, (1987), 'The United Kingdom–still a company state?' in M.P.C.M. van Schlendelen and R.J. Jackson (eds), *The Politicization of Business in Western Europe,* London: Croom Helm, pp. 156-177.

Winchester, Simon (1982), *Their Noble Lordships,* New York: Random House.

Wistrich, Ernest (1994), *The United States of Europe,* London: Routledge.

3. A New Approach to Product Regulation

1. INTRODUCTION

In the next two chapters, we will discuss some of the issues that have emerged during the development of the CE marking system. If we are to understand these issues, we also have to understand the details of the system. In this chapter, we will therefore discuss how the system is organized, the general patterns of the directives that set out the specific legal requirements and the nature of the organizations that are involved in the implementation of the system. We will be looking for patterns rather than reciting all of the details.

2. THE EVOLUTION OF THE NEW APPROACH SYSTEM

The New Approach to developing a harmonized system of product safety standards in the European Union evolved over a twelve–year period. The Low Voltage Directive, which was adopted in 1973, was an important first step (European Council, 1973). Instead of relying on formal technical requirements developed by the Commission, the initial version of the LVD set out a series of safety goals. European standards development agencies were asked to develop the standards needed to implement these general requirements.

Several of the member states saw the LVD as an intrusion of the Commission and the European Standards Development Organizations (SDOs) into the development of product standards, an area that had been the responsibility of national standards organizations. There were intensive negotiations over the implementation of the LVD with the governments of Ireland, Denmark and Britain, which were applying for membership in the EU. Denmark was able to delay implementation of the LVD for five years until 1978. Italy refused to implement the LVD on the grounds that the directive was already covered by Italian law. In *Commission v. Italy* (European Court of Justice, 1977), the ECJ upheld the validity of using harmonized standards developed by private agencies to achieve Community goals. See also Hartley (1982).

There were the inevitable delays in developing standards for the LVD. During the interim, manufacturers generally used national standards to implement the requirements of the LVD. In *Frankovitch v. The Italian Republic* (European Court of Justice, 1991) the Italian government was sued for blocking the importation of electrical goods from Germany and Belgium on the grounds that they did not meet the standards developed by UNI, the Italian standards agency, to implement the LVD. The ECJ again ruled against the Italian Government, holding that the member states must accept products that met the minimum requirements of the LVD, even if compliance was achieved through different means. See Egan (2000) pp. 118–125 for a further discussion.

3. THE NEW APPROACH TO PRODUCT REGULATION

The legal framework for the CE marking system was set forth in the *Council Resolution of 7 May 1985 on a New Approach to Technical Harmonization and Standardization* (European Council, 1985a). The basic elements are simple:

- The harmonization of national law is to be limited to the essential requirements that a product must meet in order to be traded freely within the Community.
- The technical specifications needed to implement these essential requirements will be set forth through the harmonization of product standards
- Since these are product standards and not technical requirements, their use is voluntary and manufacturers will be free to use other means to meet the essential requirements.
- Products that are designed, built and documented in accordance with the harmonized standards will be presumed to comply with the essential requirements. Products that are not based on the harmonized standards will not be granted this presumption.
- The member states will be responsible for making sure that the products circulating in their territories comply with the New Approach.
- The national enforcement authorities will also be able to take any product that they regard as unsafe out of service under a 'safeguard' clause, regardless of whether it is CE marked or complies with the harmonized standards.

This New Approach to product safety regulation largely solves the problems that the EU had encountered with previous efforts at product regulation. Since the essential requirements were to be incorporated in harmonized EU legislation, the member states were required to incorporate the same set of requirements into national law. This avoided the difficulties encountered under the Standstill Directive with trying to develop compromises among different sets of national legislative requirements.

In general, the essential requirements set forth in the New Approach directives have either been statements of concern about specific types of product risks or a requirement that the design of a product must incorporate specific safety related elements.

By limiting legislative harmonization to the essential requirements, the New Approach has avoided the problems that have bedeviled the old approach to product safety regulation. Since these essential requirements are very general, the New Approach directives can apply to broad categories of products. The Commission does not have to develop specific directives for very specific types of products, such as car silencers.

Stripped of the technical details, the task of identifying regulatory priorities becomes far easier. A listing of the types of safety concerns that a product must meet can be developed more easily and in less time than a description of the steps that must be met to make sure that the product is, in fact, safe.

It is also far easier to obtain the approval of the European Parliament and Council for a list of safety concerns than for a description of detailed product requirements. It is hard to oppose a directive that generally requires manufacturers to make a safe product. The disputes over approaches and technologies that clogged up Council reviews of old approach directives don't emerge in the review of the far more general requirements in the New Approach directives.

The New Approach to product regulation is also far more consistent with the philosophy of subsidiarity than the old approach. The EU defines the basic regulatory goals and establishes the broad administrative framework for implementation. The tasks of developing and enforcing the specific requirements are then delegated to the national governments of the member states.

There are limits to the scope of the New Approach. The products covered by a New Approach directive should present similar types of hazards. It must be possible to differentiate between essential requirements and technical specifications. It must be possible to control the risks through the development of product or process standards. Finally, the New Approach was not extended to product areas in which effective Community regulations had been developed under the old approach. The New Approach does not apply, for example, to foodstuffs, pharmaceuticals and transportation vehicles and equipment (European Commission, 2000). The New Approach to product regulation is in force throughout the European Economic Area. The EEA includes a number of countries that are currently outside the EU. The EFTA countries, Iceland, Norway and Liechtenstein, are also required to adopt harmonized legislation (European Union, 1994).

Manufacturers covered by the New Approach must place the CE mark on the products they sell or place in service in the EU to show that they are in compliance. There are also a number of Global Approach directives that use the module system for conformity assessment but do not require the use of the CE mark. See, for example, The Packaging and Packaging Waste Directive (European Council, 1994). The Trans–European Rail Interoperability Directive (European Council, 1996a) and the Marine Equipment Directive (European Council, 1997).

Products covered by the New Approach must be in compliance with the essential requirements if they are to be placed on the market or put into service inside the EEA. Non–conforming products that were placed on the market or put into service before the relevant directives came into effect are also exempt from the CE mark system. However, used equipment that is first imported into the EU after the effective date of a directive is covered by the directive. Products that are neither placed on the market nor put into service are also exempt. This includes, for example, trade show exhibits. There is also a partial exemption for medical equipment that was designed and built specifically for medical investigations. (European Council, 1993a).

4. THE LEGAL CONTEXT

The major goals of the CE marking system are to reduce the risks associated with the use of workplace equipment and consumer products.

CE marking is not the only system for regulating product safety in the legal context of the European Union. The New Approach directives are complemented by other directives that also regulate workplace safety. The *Workplace Safety Directive* (European Council, 1989b) develops the general principles for eliminating workplace risks and informing and training workers on risk avoidance. The EU legislation sets the minimum requirements for workplace safety. Under Article 118A of the Treaty of Rome, member states are free to impose additional requirements. Workplace Safety is also a framework directive: it will be implemented through other directives that will focus on such areas as personal protective equipment, video display terminals, handling heavy loads and temporary work sites.

There are two product liability directives. The *General Product Safety Directive* (European Council, 2001) concerns responsibilities for damages caused to consumers by defective products and the *General Product Liability*

Directive (European Council, 1985b) covers a manufacturer's liability for defective products and components. According to the Product Liability Directive, a product is assumed to be defective if it, 'does not provide the safety which a person is entitled to expect, taking all circumstances into account'. However, this is not a settled policy. EU liability policy and the role of national tort law are still under review in the EU (Lovells, 2001).

EU liability policy is based on the principles of strict liability. A manufacturer is liable for injuries caused by his or her product, even if this defect was not foreseeable at the time the product was manufactured. A manufacturer's defenses to liability claims can include contributory negligence. The manufacturer can also claim that the 'state of the art' in product safety engineering was not sufficiently advanced at the time the product was manufactured to have uncovered the defect or to have prevented the injury (Hagigh, 1992).

These directives support the enforcement of the CE marking system in a number of ways. Meeting the CE mark requirements is likely to be a necessary, but not sufficient, condition for defending against a product liability claim. If a product does not meet the CE mark requirements, then any claim that the product safety level was equivalent to the state of the art is likely to fall on deaf ears, especially if the neglected requirements are addressed to the actual causes of the injury.

The 'state of the art' defense to product liability claims also means that it is not enough for a manufacturer to mechanically check off the CE marking requirements, s/he must also produce a product that is as safe as practicable. This highlights the importance of the risk assessment and compliance with the safety engineering hierarchy of 'design out risks, safeguards next and warnings last'. These provisions also highlight the importance of the safeguards clause that authorizes the surveillance authorities to remove unsafe products, even if they are CE marked.

The Workplace Safety Directive and the implementing legislation extends the responsibility for the safety of industrial products to the customer as well as to the purchaser. This is particularly important for the Explosive Atmospheres and Personal Protective Equipment directives, where the risk is as much associated with the conditions of product use as it is with the nature of the products.

Finally, the Cassis de Dijon decision that was discussed in Chapter 2 still has an impact on free trade within the EU. National law still has an impact on trade within the EU. Many goods are not covered by the CE marking system. Even when a New Approach directive has been promulgated, delays can occur in national transposition or in the development of the associated standards. Even where the CE marking system is in place, notified bodies and surveillance authorities tend to refer to national law and practice for the interpretation of ambiguous points.

In the Cassis de Dijon decision, the European Court held that the member states are to accept the validity of product standards and conformity assessment requirements developed by other states unless there is some clear reason for not doing so. In other words, the member states have the burden of proof in justifying the exclusion of products that meet the national requirements enforced in some other member state. This doctrine has moderated some of the situations that could have developed as a result of difficulties in developing and implementing the CE marking system (Hagigh, 1992).

5. A TOUR OF THE NEW APPROACH DIRECTIVES

A series of New Approach directives provide the legal basis for the CE marking systems. A directive is an order from the European Union to the member states to make their laws conform to the requirements of the Community. As far as the manufacturers are concerned, these directives are not self–Llamm27Lamm27enforcing. The New Approach directives only become binding law when they are 'transposed' into the national laws of the member states. Because of this, many of the provisions of the New Approach directives are addressed to the states that will have to transpose and enforce them, and not to the manufacturers of the products covered by the directives. The requirement that the member states transcribe the New Approach requirements has left open avenues for national differences in the interpretation and application of the CE marking requirements.

At present, there are 22 New Approach directives. These directives fall into a series of loosely related groups. The 'horizontal directives' cover a series of broadly applicable aspects of design, manufacturing, packaging and use for a wide range of products. The definitions used in these directives are, of necessity, relatively general. This group includes:

Machinery Safety	Directive 98/37/EC
Low Voltage Equipment	Directive 73/23/EEC
Electromagnetic Compatibility	Directive 89/336/EEC
Pressure Equipment	Directive 97/23/EC
Packaging and Packaging Waste	Directive 94/62/EC

The other 16 directives cover narrower classes of product attributes. Again, they can be grouped into broad categories of similar directives. The 'vertical' directives generally cover all aspects of a particular type of product. The medical device directives fall into this category.

Medical Device: General	Directive 93/42/EC
Medical Device: Active Implantable	Directive 90/385/EEC
Medical Device: In Vitro Diagnostic	Directive 98/79/EC

There is also a series of risk related directives. These include:

Explosive Atmospheres	Directive 94/9/EC
Personal Protective Equipment	Directive 89/686/EEC
Explosives for Civilian Uses	Directive 93/15/EC

The construction related directives constitute another informal group:

Construction Products	Directive 89/106/EEC
Lifts	Directive 95/16/EC
Cableways Installations	Directive 00/9/EC
Gas Fired Hot Water Boilers	Directive 92/42/EEC

The largest group of vertical directives refers to consumer use items. These include:

Toy Safety	Directive 88/378/EEC
Recreational Craft	Directive 94/25/EC
Radio Telephone and	
Telecommunications Terminal Equipment	Directive 99/5/EC
Non–Automatic Weighing Instruments	Directive 90/384/EEC
Appliances Burning Gaseous Fuels	Directive 90/396/EEC
Simple Pressure Vessels	Directive 87/404/EEC

We will begin our review of the New Approach directives by considering the provisions that are of greatest interest to manufacturers. The New Approach directives start with the recitation of the policy considerations that prompted the development of particular directives. Although these 'whereas' clauses, do not set forth requirements that are legally binding on the product or manufacturer, they can often provide insights into the issues or conditions that the directive was intended to address.

The first articles generally define the coverage of the directive, the exemptions from the directive coverage and the definitions of the terms used. The products covered by a directive are usually defined in general terms. For example, article 1.2(a) of the Machinery Directive defines a machine as an assembly of moving parts with an external power source that are linked for a common purpose (European Council, 1998). The Low Voltage Equipment Directive applies to any product that uses electrical currents with voltages in the range of 50 to 1000 volts AC or 75 to 1500 volts DC (European Council, 1973, article 1). The Electromagnetic Compatibility (EMC) directive (European Council, 1989a) applies to any product that either emits radio waves, static electricity or power line harmonics that could interfere with other products or is susceptible to interference from other products. The Pressure Equipment Directive applies to any piece of equipment designed to contain liquids or gases at a pressure of more than .5 bar (European Council, 1997, article 1.1).

The coverage of the New Approach directives are, in general, not exclusive. It is quite common for a product to be covered by two or more directives. However, directives covering specialized, high risk products, such as medical devices or equipment for use in explosive atmospheres, will generally pre–empt the applicability of other New Approach directives on a particular product.

The directives also specify the date when the requirements are to be enforced. The directives provide for a transition period in which either national or EU product requirements are applicable, at the choice of the manufacturer. This transition period provides the member states with the time needed to transcribe the requirements of the directive into national law and to develop the supporting administrative systems. It also provides the manufacturers with the time needed to comply with the new requirements.

The next piece of information in a New Approach directive that would interest a manufacturer is the list of 'essential requirements' that products covered by the directive must meet. These essential requirements are far too general to provide a useful basis for designing or manufacturing a product. For example, the essential requirements in the *Machinery Directive* include the following provisions:

> 1.2.2 (a) Machinery must be so constructed that it. . . can be adjusted and maintained without putting persons at risk when these operations are carried out under the conditions foreseen by the manufacturer.
> 1.2.2. (b) . . . [T]he manufacturer must apply the following principles in the order given: . . .
> [E]liminate or reduce risks as far as possible
> Take . . . protection measures in relation to risks that cannot be eliminated
> Inform users of any residual risks. . .
> 1.1.3. The materials used to construct machinery. . . must not endanger exposed persons' safety or health. Control systems must be designed and constructed so that they are safe and reliable. . .
> 1.2.3. It must be possible to start machinery only by voluntary actuation of a control provided for the purpose. (European Council, 1998)

For the most part, the essential requirements are far too general to be used as a guide for developing or evaluating a product. The Commission has therefore delegated the task of developing the standards that can be used to implement these essential requirements to three European standards development agencies, CEN, CENELEC and ETSI. CENELEC, the Comité Européen de Normalisation Electrotechnique, is responsible for developing "electrotechnical" standards. ETSI, the European Telecommunications Standards Institute, develops standards for telecommunications products. CEN is the Comité Europen de Normalizacion which develops standards for all other types of products. The relevant European national standards development organizations are members of CEN, CENELEC and ETSI.

The development of a harmonized standard begins when the Commission issues a mandate for standards development to CEN, CENELEC or ETSI. The mandate is for the development of a standard to meet specific essential requirements. The Commission also provides funding for the work by the standards development organizations done under the mandate.

All three organizations follow the same general procedure for developing the standards. The work of developing the harmonized standards is carried out by technical committees (TCs). Each technical committee is responsible for developing standards for a particular industrial area. The members of the technical committees are named by the national SDOs that belong to the organization.

The technical committee members are appointed as national representatives rather than as representatives of the companies that may be their primary employers. Generally, the positions taken by the members of the technical committees in standards development are controlled by their sponsoring national development organizations through the organization of national 'mirror committees' that follow the progress of committee work. In general, the members of the technical committees make decisions on a consensus basis.

Once a draft standard has been developed by a technical committee, it is released for public comment. To be considered, the comments on a draft standard must include both a critique of the draft and suggested alternative language. The technical committee that developed the draft is then responsible for developing technical critiques for the comments.

When the technical committee has completed the response to the comments, the revised draft standard is released for review by the membership of the standards development organization. If the members of CEN, CENELEC or ETSI vote to accept the draft standard, it is then forwarded to Directorate General Enterprise for review and approval. If DG Enterprise accepts the standard, a notice of acceptance in placed in the

Official Journal of the EU and it becomes a harmonized standard that carries the presumption of compliance with the essential requirement.

Under the terms of the organizational charters, the members of CEN, CENELEC and ETSI are also required to adopt the approved standard as a national standard. The responsibility for translating the standards into the different national languages is placed with the national standards organizations. CEN, CENELEC and ETSI only publish standards in French and English.

Since CEN, CENELEC and ETSI are not government agencies, manufacturers are not required to use the harmonized standards. The manufacturers are only required to meet the essential requirements. Any other standards can be used if the manufacturer can show that they meet these requirements. However, products that are built in accordance with the harmonized standards developed by CEN, CENELEC and ETSI are 'presumed to comply' with the essential requirements.

This presumption provides a strong incentive for manufacturers to use the harmonized standards. For products that are covered by the presumption, the surveillance authorities must have positive evidence of noncompliance before a CE mark designation can be challenged. No evidence of noncompliance is needed to challenge the CE marking status of products that have been designed and built with non–harmonized standards. Companies manufacturing products that are not covered by harmonized standards must therefore be ready to prove that their products meet the essential requirements. This can be a daunting task; there are no published guidelines on how compliance with these very general requirements can be proven. At best, a manufacturer using non–harmonized standards can use a detailed gap analysis to show that the standards used cover all of the points raised in the harmonized standards at an equivalent or higher level.

The conformity assurance requirements are the next set of materials in the New Approach directives that directly concern the manufacturer. These refer to the steps that the manufacturer must take to ensure that the covered products meet the essential requirements.

Council Resolution of 21 December 1989 on a Global Approach to Conformity Assessment (European Council, 1989c) sets forth the guiding principles for developing a comprehensive system of conformity assessment. See also European Council (1993b). The conformity assessment provisions in the directives cover the design and manufacturing processes of the product as well as product performance. The conformity assessment requirements are graduated to reflect the level of risk presented by the product. In general, the manufacturers of low risk products can self–certify compliance with the essential requirements. Only a few types of products are likely to cause death or major injuries if they malfunction. Very high risk products, such as a cardiac pacemaker, must undergo continuous, comprehensive reviews from the development of the initial design to the production and testing of individual products.

The various conformity assessment requirements have gradually been codified into a comprehensive, logical system for certifying product design and manufacturing that draws heavily from the ISO 9000 system of process documentation. There are eight basic modules or sets of conformity assessment requirements. The basic requirements for modules A to H are summarized below.

Module A: Internal control of production. The manufacturer can self – declare that the product design and the production quality assurance system conform to the relevant New Approach directives.

Module B: EC type examination. The manufacturer hires a notified body to review and approves the design of the product.

Module C: Type conformity. The manufacturer self–certifies the production quality assurance system.

Module D: Production quality assurance. The manufacturer must retain a notified body to review and approve the quality system for production, final product inspection and testing in accordance with ISO 9002.

Module E: Product quality assurance. A notified body must certify the adequacy of the manufacturer's quality control system for product manufacturing. This is equivalent to ISO 9003.

Module F: Product verification. The manufacturer must retain a notified body to test a sample of the final products on a statistical basis.

Module G: Unit verification. The manufacturer must retain a notified body to certify product conformity by testing all products.

Module H: Full quality assurance. The manufacturer must have an approved quality control system based on ISO 9001 that covers product design, manufacturing, final product inspection and testing.

The actual system is, of course, more complex. Many directives impose additional inspection or testing requirements in addition to the specified modules. With these additional requirements, there are over 24 alternatives instead of just eight.

Furthermore, the module A to H system was invented in 1993 (European Council, 1993b). Since then, the directives have followed the language of the modules more or less exactly. However, the New Approach directives were developed in 1985. The directives that were drafted before 1992 do not make reference to any particular system. The Commission is gradually amending the older New Approach directives to incorporate the modules. Until then, the task of reconciling the earlier and later versions of the conformity assessment system falls ultimately to the notified bodies and surveillance authorities.

The governing directives will specify which conformity assessment modules must be used with which types of products. The directives will generally lay out a series of rules that must be used to classify products into a series of categories. Different conformity assessment requirements will apply to products in different categories.

For example, Annex IX in the *Medical Device Directive* (European Council, 1993a), lists 18 rules that are to be used to classify medical devices into four categories. Under Rule 4, for example, all non–invasive medical devices that come into contact with wounds that can only healed by secondary intent are in Class IIb. Conformity assessment for class IIb medical devices must involve either module H or module B combined with modules D, E or F.

Most products under the New Approach, perhaps 70 per cent, are covered by self–certification under module A. In general, the directives requiring the use of more restrictive conformity assessment modules provide manufacturers with a number of alternatives. This may involve choices between a reliance on a certified quality assurance system under modules D or E and a reliance on a product inspection by notified bodies under modules F or G.

The review of a manufacturer's quality assurance system by a notified body under modules D, E or H is to be based on ISO 9000. ISO 9001 is the basis for module D, ISO 9002 is used for module E and module H requires the manufacturers to have in place the equivalent of a full ISO 9003 system.

Almost all of the New Approach directives follow the same general format as the Pressure Equipment Directive. There are extra features on a few of the directives. Manufacturers of products covered by the medical device directives, for example, have to report any adverse use incident reports to Directorate General Enterprise. Statistics on injuries caused by consumer products must be reported through the EU's Rapex database (European Council, 1992).

In addition to the New Approach directives and standards, the manufacturer may wish to consult with the 'guidance documents' that have been developed by DG Enterprise. For an example, see the *Guidelines on the*

Application of Council Directive 73/23/EEC (electrical equipment designed for use within certain voltage limits. (European Commission, 2000). The guidance documents have been developed in consultation with the notified bodies and provide guidance on the interpretation of the directives. Although they carry no legal weight, the guidance documents are becoming increasingly influential.

6. IMPLEMENTING THE NEW APPROACH

Companies manufacturing products that are covered by conformity assessment modules B to H will have to hire a notified body to carry out the required conformity assessment procedures. 'Notified bodies' are non-governmental organizations that have been approved by the national governments of the EU to conduct the conformity assessments for the manufacturers of CE marked products in accordance with the New Approach directives.

Bodies are generally notified only for specific aspects of specific directives. The closest analogies in the American context would be a certified public accountant or an ISO 9000 registrar. Although most notified bodies are highly specialized and fairly obscure agencies, there are some well-known names in the ranks, such as BSI, TUV and UL.

Although bodies are notified by the member states of the European Union, their authority is community-wide. All regulatory and enforcement agencies are required to accept the judgments of any notified body. Products only have to be reviewed once. Manufacturers of products requiring the services of a notified body can use any body with the necessary authority, anywhere in the EU. This 'one stop shopping' rule was a major advance over the old system, which often imposed repetitive certifications on products before they could be sold freely throughout the European Union.

The notification process is straightforward. The member states are responsible for ensuring that their nominees are technically qualified, have the resources needed to carry out their operations and are in compliance with the EN 17000 series of standards. These standards establish the qualifications that should be met by organizations that offer services as testing laboratories, inspection bodies or certification agencies. Under these standards, notified bodies are prohibited from also offering consulting services. There is an obvious conflict of interest when the group that recommends a course of action is also in charge of deciding whether that action was appropriate.

The member states forward the names of their nominees to the Commission. The Commission then assigns the notified body an identification number and adds the name of the organization to the list of notified bodies. In theory, notification can be withdrawn from a body if it fails to carry out the assigned duties properly or it fails to comply with the notification criteria. 'De–notification' would be the responsibility of the member state that was responsible for the original notification.

The New Approach directives generally state that the national governments can designate the conformity assessment bodies in accordance with the general standards set forth in Annex IV. These criteria are based on the provisions of the EN 17000 series of standards. The governments have to notify the Commission about the groups they have designated. These then become the 'notified bodies'. Some form of this clause is present in virtually every New Approach directive. A copy of the product instruction manual must also be included in the technical file. This is a very important document. In many cases, the manufacturer will be able to limit product risk and CE mark obligations by carefully defining the conditions for product handling, installation, use, maintenance, removal and disposal.

The EOTC, the European Organization for Testing and Certification was organized in 1990 on the basis of a memorandum of understanding signed by the Commission, EFTA, CEN and CENELEC. EOTC was charged with the responsibility for coordinating the activities of the notified bodies. EOTC has no legal authority, coordination is carried out by organizing member notified bodies into a series of sectoral committees. Each committee is concerned with conformity assessment issues in a particular industrial sector (International Trade Administration, nd). EOTC is also responsible for managing the Testing, Inspection, Calibration, Certification and Quality Assurance database. The TICQA Project was launched in 1991 to develop an inventory of the European organizations that are working in these fields.

7. THE MANUFACTURERS' RESPONSIBILITIES

The last elements in the New Approach directives that would immediately interest the manufacturers are the provisions regarding the documentation of CE mark compliance. The manufacturer of record is responsible for developing a 'technical file' (sometimes called a technical construction file) that documents the steps taken to comply with the CE mark requirements. The qualifier 'of record' is added to this sentence because the CE mark system provides a lot of flexibility in assigning basic responsibility for compliance. Almost any party in the distribution chain can stand in as the responsible party as long as the procedures and documentation that are requirements of the CE marking system are under the control of the manufacturer of record.

The person who places a product on the market or puts it into service is responsible for identifying the relevant CE mark directives, essential requirements and conformity assessment procedures. Usually, this is the manufacturer of record.

The required contents of the technical file are spelled out in the list of essential requirements of the relevant directives. In general, this includes:

- Product documentation, including drawings, schematics, descriptions and operating instructions.
- A list of the applicable directives and essential requirements.
- An analysis of the steps taken to ensure a safe product, including a list of the standards used, the results of any product testing, and, generally, a product safety analysis. The safety analysis is required to comply with the Machinery Directive standard, EN 1050. Similar standards are associated with other directives. Under EN 1050, the manufacturer must assess the probability and severity of the risks posed by the product in a number of areas, and then document the measures taken to reduce these risks. The CE mark system is based on a consistent design philosophy, serious risks must be designed out as much as possible and interlocks should be used to limit the most serious residual risks. Warnings can be posted against minor residual risks.
- Certificates of compliance from any required notified bodies.
- Two versions of the technical file may be prepared. They are conventionally called Part A and Part B. Part A includes the summarized documents relevant for the general design, manufacturing and testing of the document. Part B contains the full design calculations and complete reports as well as the documentation for individual pieces of CE marked equipment. The surveillance authorities would be given the Part A file if they were interested in verifying the use of the CE mark for a production series. The Part B file would be relevant to verify CE marking on a particular piece of equipment.
- The manufacturer of record must then draft a certificate of conformity for the product. In general, the certificate must identify the product and give the name and address of the manufacturer and authorized representative (if any). It must also list the governing directives. Finally, a responsible officer of the manufacturing company must attest that the product conforms to all relevant essential requirements in these directives.
- Finally, the manufacturer can place the CE mark logo on the product and ship it in good conscience. In some cases, the serial number of the notified body that attested to the conformity of the product must also be

included on the product identification plate. The requirements for product documentation are spelled out in the New Approach directives.

The technical file must be provided to the surveillance authorities on demand, generally within one working week. The manufacturer can appoint an 'authorized representative' – someone in the EU who will take responsibility for working with the surveillance authorities in the event that an issue of CE mark conformity arises. One responsibility is to hold the technical file and make it available to the surveillance authorities on demand. The manufacturer must have an authorized representative in the European Union for products covered by the medical device directives. For other directives, naming an authorized representative is optional.

A manufacturer only needs to have one authorized representative in the EU. If an authorized representative is located in, for example, London and someone in Dusseldorf questions whether a particular product complies with CE mark requirements, then the German surveillance authorities will generally forward the query to the British authorities, who will, in turn, contact the authorized representative. However, the Dusseldorf authorities are likely to take unilateral action if someone has been injured or the product seems to pose an immediate safety threat.

If a manufacturer has not appointed an authorized representative in the European Union, then the surveillance authorities are likely to approach the importer, distributor or customers with any questions about CE mark compliance. The party contacted may then be responsible for proving that the product is both safe and in conformity with the CE mark requirements. If this can't be done, then the importer, distributor or customers may be responsible for pulling the product off the market and out of service. In most cases, neither the manufacturer nor the buyers want the customers to assume this responsibility. Appointing an authorized representative, even if not required under the governing directives, is generally a good practice.

Enforcement is the last component of the CE marking system. Each participating government is responsible for appointing the 'surveillance authorities' that will be responsible for enforcing some aspect of CE marking system in their jurisdiction. The CE mark surveillance authorities are typically the regulatory agencies that would have jurisdiction over a particular type of product under national law. Thus, the health inspectorates are generally responsible for enforcing the medical device directives, the labor inspectors are responsible for CE marking on production machinery and the consumer affairs divisions generally have responsibility for CE marking on consumer products.

Except in France, customs officials rarely have primary responsibility for reviewing CE mark qualifications. However, they may be required to block the importation of goods that have been removed from the marketplace by other surveillance authorities for violations of CE mark requirements. In France, the customs authorities are authorized to independently review CE mark documentation for imported products. Other French authorities with jurisdiction in the areas of medical, labor and consumer affairs are also charged with surveillance functions in the domestic market.

The surveillance authorities are prohibited from impeding products that have been properly CE marked from being placed on the market or put into service in their jurisdictions. Products that have been built in accordance with the harmonized standards shall be presumed to meet the essential requirements in the relevant New Approach Directives. Member states must allow non–CE marked products to be shown at trade fairs, exhibitions, demonstrations, and so on, as long as the products are clearly marked as non–compliant and are not offered for either sale or use. National governments are allowed to develop collateral rules governing user safety, particularly with regard to workers, as long as they do not require further modifications of equipment that has been properly CE marked.

The New Approach directives generally include a safeguard clause. The safeguard clause authorizes the surveillance authorities in the member states to take products off the market or remove them from service if they are liable to endanger people, property or animals, even if they are properly CE marked. Member states have to notify the Commission when taking any action under the Safeguard Clause. The Commission will then consult with all parties, review the action, and make a determination as to whether the actions were justified. The Commission decision will call for an amendment of the CE marking requirements, require the member state to reverse the action taken, or some combination of the two. The Low Voltage Directive sets forth a simplified safeguard clause procedure. National safeguard initiatives are not reviewed by the Commission unless some other country challenges the action (European Council, 1973, article 9).

Enforcement of the CE marking system rests heavily on the honor system. For the most part, there is little positive inspection for CE mark violations. An investigation may be triggered by an incident in which someone has been injured or killed by a product, or by reports of non–compliant products from consumers, workers or competitors. Only Germany has undertaken systematic programs of workplace and store inspections for CE mark compliance. Even here, a complete inspection cycle will take from two to four years. Most surveillance actions are initiated in response to reports from third parties about products that may not comply with the CE mark requirements.

This is, in many ways, a remarkably decentralized system. As a practical matter, manufacturers have a lot of latitude in determining the level of energy they will devote to CE marking. No affidavits have to be filed with the authorities attesting to CE mark rigor and there is no central registry of CE marked products. Manufacturers may be able to ship products that are out of conformity for years without any adverse consequences. In many cases, issues about CE compliance concern the adequacy of the technical file. If so, the surveillance authorities are likely to give the manufacturer a few months to bring documentation up to requirements.

However, enforcement, when it comes, may well be retroactive and painful. The surveillance authorities are authorized under EU law to bar the sale of non–compliant products and to require the manufacturer to pull products that have already been sold off the market and out of service. Under national law, the surveillance authorities and courts are often authorized to impose civil and criminal penalties for fraudulent CE mark certification.

Other provisions of the New Approach directives concern the administrative systems that are to be developed at the EU level for review and enforcement. The directives generally authorize the formation of a standing advisory committee that will periodically review the implementation of the directive. Membership in the Directive Committee is drawn from representatives of relevant regulatory offices in the member states. An advisory subcommittee is almost always organized to provide technical assistance to the Directive Committee. These committees are covered by the 'comitology' policies discussed in the previous chapter.

The member states can, for example, raise questions about the adequacy of the harmonized standards for meeting the safety goals listed in the essential requirements. These issues are referred to the Standing Committee set up under Article 5 of the Mutual Information Directive (European Council, 1983). After consulting with the Standing Committee, the Commission is responsible for informing the member states whether a particular standard should be withdrawn from use. However, there are no deadlines for this determination. This committee considers issues regarding the adequacy of the harmonized standards for all of the New Approach directives.

8. CONCLUDING THOUGHTS

When we dig a little deeper though, these basic principles are neither as comprehensive nor as consistent as they may seem at first. These inconsistencies and omissions are important. They effectively transfer some degree of policy authority over CE marking to the national governments. Since CE marking is implemented and enforced at the national level, policy ambiguities expand the scope for local interpretation of basic policy provisions.

For example, coverage by the Explosive Atmospheres Directive and the Toy Safety Directive is not based on the nature of the product but on the environment of use or the probable reactions of children. When does a manufacturer become liable for incidents that may occur because the purchaser made proper use of the product but in the wrong environment?

For example, what is the difference between a personal protective device, which prevents harm, and a medical device, which relieves harm? What is the proper classification for a shoe insert that can prevent and/or relieve a fungus infection? Should both directives apply?

For example, does the application of the CE marking system to products that are 'placed on the market' or 'put into service' apply to individual products or to the production of a series of identical products? If it applies to a production run, then individual products that have been physically manufactured after the effective date of an otherwise relevant New Approach directive may be exempt from coverage as long as: a) the first product in the run was manufactured before the effective date of the directive and: b) there have not been any significant changes in the design or manufacturing of the products since then. This ambiguity provides a partial explanation of a common observation; many products that would seem to be covered by the system are freely sold in European markets without the CE mark.

REFERENCES

Directorate General Enterprise (2000), *Guidelines on the Application of Council Directive 73/23/EEC (electrical equipment designed for use within certain voltage limits).*

Egan, Michelle (2000), *Constructing a European Market*, Oxford: Oxford University Press.

European Commission (2000), *Guide to the Implementation of Directives Based on the New Approach and the Global Approach.* Luxembourg.

European Council (1973), *Council Directive of 19 February 1973 on the Harmonization of the Laws of the Member States Relating to Electrical Equipment Designed for Use within Certain Voltage Limit,* 73/23/EEC.

European Council (1983), *Council Directive 83/189/EEC of 28 March 1983 Laying down a Process for the Provision of Information in the Field of Technical Standards and Regulations.*

European Council (1985), *Council Directive 85/374/#EEC of 25 July 1985 on the Approximation of the Laws, Regulations and Administrative Provisions of the Member States Concerning the Liability for Defective Products.*

European Council (1985), *Council Resolution of 7 May 1985 on a New Approach to Technical Harmonization and Standardization.*

European Council (1987), *Council Directive of 25 June 1987 on the Harmonization of the Laws of the Member States Relating to Simple Pressure Vessels.*

European Council (1988), *Council Directive of 3 May, 1988 on the Approximation of the Laws of the Member States Concerning the Safety of Toys*, as amended by Directive 93/68/EEC.

European Council (1989a), *Council Directive 89/336/EEC of 3 May 1989 Concerning the Approximation of the Laws of the Member States relating to Electromagnetic Compatibility.*

European Council (1989b), *Council Directive 89/391 of June 12, 1989 Concerning Workplace Safety.*

European Council (1989c), *Council Resolution of 21 December 1989 on a Global Approach to Conformity Assessment.*

European Council (1992), *Council Directive 92/59/EEC of 29 June 1992 on General Product Safety.*

European Council (1993a), *Council Directive 93/42/EEC of 14 July 1993 Concerning Medical Devices.*

European Council (1993b), *Council Decision of 22 July 1993 Concerning the Modules for the Various Phases of Conformity Assessment Procedures and the Rules for Affixing and Use of the CE Conformity Marking, which are intended to be Used in the Technical Harmonization Directives.*

European Council (1994), *European Parliament and Council Directive 94/62/EC of 20 December 1994 on Packaging and Packaging Waste.*

European Council (1996a), *Council Directive 96/48/EC of 23 July 1996 on the Inter–operability of the Trans–European High–Speed Rail System.*

European Council (1996b), *Council Directive 96/98 of 20 December 1996 on Marine Equipment*; OJL 46 of 17/02/1997.

European Council (1997), *Directive 97/23/EC of the Parliament and of the Council of 29 May, 1997 on the Approximation of the Laws of the Member States Concerning Pressure Equipment.*

European Council (1998), *Directive 98/37/EC of the European Parliament and Council of 22 June 1998 on the Approximation of the Laws of the Member States relating to Machinery.*

European Council (2001), *Directive 2001/95/EC of the European Parliament and the Council of 3 December 2001 on General Product Safety.*

European Court of Justice (1977), *Commission v. Italy* Case 133/76, ECR 1449.

European Court of Justice (1991), *Frankovitch v. The Italian Republic*, ECR 94.

European Union (1994), *Agreement on the European Economic Area of 1 January 1994.*

Hagigh, Sara (1992), 'Hundreds of new product standards will apply to sales in the EC after 1992', *Business America,* 113 (1), p. 16.

Hartley, T. (1982), 'Consumer safety and the harmonization of technical standards; the Low Voltage Directive', *European Law Review*, pp. 55–62.

International Trade Administration (n.d), 'Testing and Certification in the Single European market', *Standards setting in the European Union*, at www.stat-usa.gov/miscfiles.nsf/TO/631DF2FEF04A2748852566BF00 66C634? Open.

Lovells (2003), *Product Liability in the European Union: A Report for the European Commission.* European Commission Study MARKT/2001/ 11/Dt.

4. From Directives to Standards

1. INTRODUCTION

The European Union is a work in progress. The political realities and administrative processes that shape the development and administration of EU programs have continually been under revision. In the next two chapters, we will take a retrospective view of the realities that have shaped the development of the system until the turn of the century. Chapter 9 will examine the ways in which the new realities of the EU are affecting the future of European product regulation.

2. DEVELOPING THE DIRECTIVES

The New Approach directives are drafted by Directorate General Enterprise and Information Society. Policy guidance is generally provided by an advisory committee made up of the government representatives from the member states. This committee is generally assisted by a subcommittee of technical experts, also recruited from the regulatory offices of the member states.

Proposals for new directives are generally forwarded first to the EESC and then to the relevant policy committee in COREPER, the standing administrative organization that coordinates the work of the Council (DEsite, 2003). COREPER is responsible for preparing the work for the Council, and is divided into two parts. Part 1 (COREPER 1) includes the deputy permanent representatives to the Council who are involved in employment, social policy, health and consumers, competitiveness, transport, telecommunications and energy, agriculture and fisheries, environment, and youth and culture. The work of COREPER involves more than the passive management of the Council agenda. There are over 250 committees and working parties recruited from the civil services of the member states that provide technical assistance to the COREPER members (EU Presidency, 2004).

The draft directives are generally open for discussion and amendment during the consultations with COREPER and the Council. Once COREPER and Directorate General Enterprise agree on a draft text, the draft is submitted to the Commission as a whole for review and approval. At this stage, the major discussions are likely to concern jurisdictional issues and potential conflicts with initiatives in other directorates general rather than the policy details of the proposal.

Once approved by the College of the Commission, the draft is submitted to the European Parliament for review under the co-decision process discussed in Chapter 2. The project managers at Directorate General Enterprise tend to resist amending draft directives after they have been submitted to Parliament. Unless there is an appreciable risk that Parliament will reject the Council/Commission draft by an absolute majority, the Council/Commission draft is likely to stand.

In this process, program managers in Directorate General Enterprise will generally be concerned about coordinating their efforts with the national government policy officials. There are three institutionalized avenues for these discussions, the in–house policy advisory committees, the technical subcommittees and the COREPER subject committees. These discussions tend to be mutually reinforcing. The COREPER administrators will work closely with the relevant national delegates to the Council. In turn, these delegates are likely to work closely with the policy officials in the relevant national government offices.

From time to time, DG Enterprise has subsidized trade associations, especially environmental and small business advocates, in order to demonstrate that these points of view are represented in the discussions over the CE marking system. The Commission has provided support for the European Association for the Co-ordination of Consumer Representation in Standardization, the European Trade Union Technical Bureau for Health and Safety, The European Office of Craft, Trades and Small and Medium Sized Enterprises and the European Environmental Bureau (European Commission, 2001). However, their input has largely been limited to the development of position papers in specific issues. Their involvement usually stops when Commission funding ends. This pattern is much more in the spirit of invited participation than the robust involvement of interest groups at all stages of policy development that is common in the US.

In part to overcome the lack of business input into the policy development process, DG Enterprise commissions the development of a 'business impact assessment'. However, this process has come under criticism. Frequently, the charge is given either to an academic researcher or to a European consulting firm. In neither case is the researcher directly involved in the businesses and business processes coming under regulation. Finally, there are no known criteria or procedures for assessing the adequacy of the final report. In the words of the Commission:

It is widely acknowledged that the existing BIA system has not always worked . . as a tool to be used. . . . only in the drafting process in order to minimize potential negative impacts on business. Instead BIAs are often carried out as ex-post 'paper exercises' on already finalized proposals. . . . [M]any BIAs are not backed up by objective information and impacts on business are rarely quantified. (Directorate General Enterprise, 2002, p. 4)

This process of contracting out for a business impact assessment on a draft directive also highlights the potential isolation of the Commission from the European business community. The process of developing the business impact assessment, including the range and number of industries consulted, is under the control of the Commission and the contract developer. The report is not, in general, a public document and there are no formal channels for public comments on the evidence and conclusions in the report. In fact, some have argued that the choice of a contractor to develop the business impact assessment has been in some cases affected by a desire for the contractor to come to a particular set of conclusions.

The Commission has made a series of administrative recommendations for improving the quality and usefulness of the business impact assessments. It is not clear that these will have the desired effect unless there is the political will to develop a more effective system (European Commission, 2002).

Other directorates have similar alliances and shared perspectives with different sets of national regulatory authorities. Environmental regulation, for example, is also likely to have an impact on the design, manufacturing, use and disposal of products. However, environmentalists are more likely to push for reductions in existing levels of pollution and to advocate improvements in present levels of product performance. Thus, environmentalists generally share the broad goal of forcing the development of new technologies. The managers of Directorate General Environment are more likely to view businesses as adversaries, to insist that technical requirements should be set to force the development of new technologies and that legal mandates and prohibitions should be used to ensure business compliance.

The managers at DG Enterprise have little incentive to discuss issues with other directorates general that have little to contribute to the political interests of DG Enterprise. The relations between DG Enterprise and DG Environment are important and often competitive. Article 6 of the Treaty of Rome states that environmental considerations must be incorporated across the broad range of EU legislation. In order to carry out these responsibilities, DG Enterprise has organized an environmental committee. In turn, the committee has been used to support the argument that DG Enterprise can and should be responsible for both the safety and environmental aspects of the

New Approach directive. However, this environmental commitment often seems to be inconsistent with the political alliances between DG Enterprise and the member state governments.

Directorate General Internal Market would be a logical partner for resolving policy conflicts among the different directorates general. Their lack of involvement in regulating the turf wars generally reflects the weakness of the presidency of the Commission. The president of the Commission is responsible for coordinating the activities of the different directorates. The heads of state in the 'Council of Europe' are the natural allies for the president. However, the current political realities of the EU are likely to have a major impact on the support given by the heads of state to the president of the Commission. The economic dislocation of the late 1990s and the erosion of the internal free market gave Jacques Santer, then president of the Commission, a powerful hand in the initial development of the CE marking system. The success of CE marking and the comparative tranquility of the EU over the last 15 years have impeded the ability of Romano Prodi, the current president, to mobilize the national governments and the other directorates general behind major new initiatives in the CE marking system.

This is a fairly closed system. It reinforces the tendency for the commissioners to be sensitive to the political interests of the national governments that appoint them. It does not provide a strong basis for coordinating the competing interests of the different directorates general. As a result, business is not commonly involved in the development of new directives. Business participation in the development of directives is sporadic, at best. DG Enterprise may be viewed within the Commission as the voice of business in the development of EU regulations. However, it is not generally viewed that way from the perspective of business.

Despite the closed nature of the system, business concerns are often a major consideration in the development of the CE marking system. Participation though is generally by invitation of the national authorities. Siemens may talk to the German government through DIN, and the German government will talk to the Commission and the Council. Program managers in DG Enterprise may also solicit public business backing for a proposal from time to time when faced with entrenched political opposition that has been based on economic arguments. Again though, this is representation by invitation.

This pattern of invited representation is at the heart of the policy struggles over CE marking inside the Commission and the Council. Proposals for developing new directives are usually initiated when a member state is able to convince a majority of the other member state governments that regulatory restraints in other member states are impeding expansion and economic development. The development of a new directive usually starts the process of shifting control of regulatory policies in a particular area from the national authorities to the EU.

This shift in power from the national to the Community level is generally resisted by the national regulatory authorities. As we have seen though, the decentralized nature of the CE marking process has restored substantial control to the national level in the development of the standards, the work of the notified bodies and the management of the surveillance authorities.

The Commission and Council provide the venues for these Community debates over the competing demands for liberalizing the internal market versus regulatory autonomy at the national level. The nature of these debates generally has a strong effect on the policy outcomes. The program managers in DG Enterprise will spend a lot of time lobbying the national regulatory authorities to gain support for new regulatory proposals. National regulators are more likely to support a proposal if they are at least able to advance their points of view in the development of the directive and maintain their jurisdictions in the program administration. This has resulted in a tendency to define the scope of the New Approach directives to match the jurisdictional scope of the national regulatory authorities.

For example, the CE marking system was originally based on the assumption that, as much as possible, each directive would cover all safety related aspects of a particular product. In reality, there are at least four horizontal directives that potentially cover the same set of products. Under the original vision for the CE marking system, the EU would combine the requirements of the Machinery Directive, Low Voltage Directive, Electromagnetic Compatibility Directive and the Pressure Equipment Directive in a single proposal. However, developing three directives leads to a better match between the CE marking system and the jurisdictional interests of the regulatory agencies in the member states.

The major EU countries, France, Germany and the UK, have the broadest representation and most influential voice in the Council and therefore the Commission. National governments tend to pay attention to their leading national businesses. New directives therefore tend to emerge when the major corporations in the leading countries are willing to lobby vigorously for a further liberalization of the internal free market in their markets.

One example is the development of the Toy Directive. European production in the toy industry is dominated by a few large companies such as Danish Lego, German Playmobil, British Spears and Waddington and the French Monnert that enjoy high brand recognition. However, there had been a proliferation in the types of technologies of toys, which raised concerns about the adequacy of national regulatory systems for toys. All European toy companies faced substantial competition from imports. This encouraged industry support for the development of unique national standards and conformity assessment requirements that would both improve consumer safety and help preserve national markets.

The European toy market was divided by a substantial number of conflicting standards and conformity assessment requirements. For example, German standards were the most stringent, Belgium had voluntary standards and Portugal and Luxembourg had no regulatory requirements. Germany, Austria and Finland enacted safety requirements for toys as a part of their general consumer product legislation. Ireland and Britain had developed specific regulations governing specific types of hazards associated with toys. However, these national requirements also limited the extent to which European toy companies could participate in the broader European market (Egan, 2000).

The development of comprehensive EU–wide regulatory policies for toys provided an alternative strategy for ensuring product safety and promoting free trade within the Community. As a result, there was support in the industry for the development of a Toy Directive. Program managers in Directorate General Enterprise initiated discussions with toy experts, manufacturers and consumer organizations in 1976.

The Toy Directive was one of the first ventures in what would later become the New Approach. This was the first time that the Commission delegated the development of the implementing standards to CEN and CENELEC. The Commission had hoped to introduce a Toy Directive by mid-1978. The proposed draft would cover general toy safety, mechanical properties and flammability issues. Toxicity, an issue that was especially important to the Germans, would be considered in a later proposal.

However, the national regulatory authorities resisted the loss of regulatory control. Parliament criticized the draft directives on the grounds that they were too cumbersome, that the TCs that would be responsible for developing the harmonized standards were likely to be dominated by the toy manufacturers and that the use of voluntary standards gave the toy manufacturers too much latitude to erode Community safety requirements.

Development of the Commission draft directive was delayed until July 1980. This proposal tried to address the regulatory concerns of the member states. It was, as a result, quite complex. Furthermore, the technical foundations were in question. There was no scientific consensus on what constituted acceptable levels of toxicity in the materials used in manufacturing toys.

There was little support for the new proposal. The toy industry trade associations generally opposed the new draft on the grounds that it threatened to strangle the industry through over regulation. Although the proposal called for the use of voluntary standards to enforce regulatory requirements, CEN expressed reservations because of the differences between the technical requirements in the draft directive and the toy standards that had already been adopted. Several committees in the European Parliament considered the new draft. The Economic and Monetary Affairs Committee refused to consider the proposal on the grounds that there was no consensus for a proposal this complex. The Commission tabled the proposal in 1981. It was then withdrawn in 1986.

A new Toy Directive was proposed a few years later that was based more firmly on the New Approach. The Commission also proposed tougher certification requirements for toys and a more stringent market surveillance system. Nevertheless, the Danish representatives opposed the new proposal during the second parliamentary reading on the grounds that it delegated too much authority to CEN and that member governments would be prohibited from imposing more stringent requirements at the national level. Denmark was then allowed to retain stricter toy requirements and the Toy Directive came into force in 1 January 1990. For an extended discussion of the development of the Toy directive, see Egan (2000, pp. 169–174).

Another example, the development of ATEX, the Explosive Atmospheres Directive, was the result of complaints by French businesses that the German system for workplace regulation was limiting their sales to German companies. The ATEX directive applies to equipment that is used in explosive atmospheres. It differs from most of the other New Approach directives in that product coverage is defined by the terms of product use rather than by the intrinsic nature of the product.

The circumstances leading to the development of the Explosives Atmosphere Directive are equally complex. In Germany, the use of machinery is regulated in part by the *Berufgenossenschaften* (BG). The BGs are a series of mutual assistance societies that provide workers' compensation insurance for the member companies. In order to receive the insurance, the members must also follow the BG rules on workplace safety. These safety rules had a significant impact on machine design. Although the BG rules did not affect what types of machines could be used in a factory, they did address the requirements that the machine must meet before the workplace employer could be insured under the BG policies.

French exporters argued that the BG workplace safety rules constituted a trade barrier for their exports to Germany. Since these policies fall in the area of 'labor relations' rather than 'free market', EU requirements constitute a minimum requirement for national governments. Under the Treaty of Rome, member states can always enact measures that exceed these minimum requirements. However, if these same measures could be presented as internal free market issues, then the German government would be required to implement the EU requirements exactly.

The French government therefore pushed for the adoption of the ATEX directive to force the adoption of similar rules by all EU member states. The extent to which the German BGs could develop more restrictive rules would be significantly limited. As a result, the political battles surrounding the development of the ATEX directives and implementing standards continued well after the final adoption of the directive. The scope of these implementation wars is suggested by the very long (nine-year) implementation period.

As a result of the political battles that led to the development of ATEX, it is inconsistent with the rest of the CE marking system in a number of areas. The product coverage for most of the directives is defined in terms of the nature of the product and the purpose for their uses. Coverage under the ATEX directive is defined for the most part in terms of the environment in which a product is to be used.

ATEX only covers those aspects of product design and use that are relevant for safety issues in explosive environments. Products covered by the ATEX directive are also likely to be covered by, for example, the Machinery Directive, Low Voltage, EMC and/or Pressure Equipment Directive. However, there is no mechanism for ensuring that the standards that are used to implement the other directives are consistent with use in explosive atmospheres. In fact, some of the standards used to implement the Low Voltage Directive may be inconsistent with the ATEX requirements.

This issue is implicitly addressed by a shift of emphasis in ATEX towards the evaluation of product safety in comparison with the best technology available on the market. However, this has a further impact. The presumption that products developed in accordance with the harmonized standards comply with the essential requirements laid out in the New Approach directives is potentially inconsistent with the best practicable technology requirement. Since the development of the ATEX standards is controlled by CENELEC and CEN, there is no way to be sure that the harmonized standards used for the other directives are developed on the basis of the best practicable technologies for ensuring safety in explosive atmospheres.

The passage of the ATEX directive did not eliminate the impact of the BGs on product usage. In one instance, a British company was passing out free samples of a new and better type of silk screen printing ink. German printing companies generally refused to accept the samples because they were inconsistent with the BG workplace insurance requirements. BGs were refusing to provide work compensation insurance for companies that were using the ink because they had not completed their general internal review of printing ink and worker risk. As a result, the British ink manufacturer was temporarily shut out of the German market.

There are other consequences to a reliance on business lobbying through national governments to provide the impetus for developing new CE mark directives. The Commission is also not likely to initiate new proposals if the national champion industries in the leading countries are opposed to any further liberalization of their internal markets.

For example, Annex II of the Low Voltage Directive (European Council, 1973), explicitly excludes household electrical plugs and sockets from coverage. There are significant national differences in plug design and performance standards. In the larger countries, these markets are generally served by national manufacturers. Since there is little demand by the leading plug manufacturers for easier access to other European markets, these products have been excluded from harmonization efforts.

For example, the steel companies in the leading European countries are generally more interested in protecting national markets than in expanding exports to other European countries. Article 11 of the Pressure Equipment Directive (European Council, 1997b) contains a provision for the 'European approval of materials' for metals that will be used to contain pressure. The notified bodies are responsible for the review and approval of these materials. The decision is not based on conformity with a harmonized standard defining the requirements for materials to be used in pressure vessels. In fact, there are few such standards. National metal standards are generally drafted to favor the materials manufactured by national companies. The development of harmonized standards defining required metal characteristics would end this tendency towards market protection. The notified bodies are therefore free to use national standards in their review and approval of pressure–bearing materials.

The next step is for DG Enterprise to create an administrative structure that will support the development of the directive. For most directives, this will consist of a 'directive committee that consists of representatives from the relevant surveillance authorities of the member states. The directive committee is usually assisted by a technical subcommittee that includes experts from the private sector. There is a widespread feeling that the tekkies should be on tap, but not on top. More technical committees have been created for the more specialized directives. There is, for example, an 'Expert Working Group' for the ATEX directive and a 'working party' for the Lifts Directive.

More elaborate administrative arrangements have been developed for some of the more contentious directives. The scope of the Construction Products Directive (European Council, 1989) for example, goes beyond the usual parameters of ensuring product safety. The CPD also addresses mechanical resistance and stability, hygiene, protection against noise, energy economy and heat retention. The implementation of the CPD takes place in the context of regional differences in climate, local building traditions, protected markets, national differences in building codes and strong traditions of local regulation. There are very few EU standards for construction products. Instead, construction products are to be submitted to designated national bodies for 'European technical approval'.

DG Enterprise has therefore directed EOTC to create a new organization, the European Organization for Technical Approvals. The task of EOTA is to provide EU–wide coordination for the process of granting technical approvals at the national level. CEN is also engaged in the heroic task of developing regional building codes that can support the development of specific construction product standards.

DG Enterprise is a primary intermediary between EOTA and CEN on one hand and the member states on the other. Because of the importance of these relations, a construction products 'unit' has also been organized within DG Enterprise.

The last step in the process is the transposition of the directives into national law. The directives are not self–enforcing. Legally, they represent orders from the EU to the member states to incorporate the directive provisions into national law. The speed and manner in which the directives are transposed into national law has an effect on how they are interpreted by the notified bodies and surveillance authorities. Overall, Sweden has been able to incorporate new directives into national law in seven months. In contrast, the transposition delay for France has averaged 18 months (European Commission, 2000, p. 7).

In part, the delays in transposition reflect national differences in culture and the governing legal regimes. In the UK, for example, directives are enforceable as national law as soon as they come into effect. Transposition then becomes an issue of reconciling the new directive with other statutes. In Germany though, new directives have to be incorporated into national law through the enactment of new legislation. In Germany, the Lander (states) are responsible for enforcing most New Approach directives. The Lander therefore must be involved in the transposition process. Transposition must also involve both the enabling legislation and the detailed regulations that control implementation. These factors have contributed to the relatively long time that is often required to transpose EU directives into German national law (Lankowski, 2001).

Transposition of Community directives in the French government is managed through negotiations among the Council of State, lead ministry, the Secretariat–General of the Government and the Secretariat–General of the Interdepartmental Committee (SGIC). The SGIC is responsible for consulting with the governments of the other member states to assess transcription strategies and implementation issues (Sauron, 2000).

Some directives are more troublesome than others. For example, the Toy Directive came into full force on 30 June 1989. The Commission then set 1 January 1990 as the target date for complete national transposition. Even so, the Toy Directive had not been transposed by four of the twelve member states by January 1992 (Hagigh, 1992). Since the Toy Directive was not legally binding in the countries that had not transposed it into national law, these delays left toy manufacturers in a condition of uncertainty and created new trade barriers within the common market.

In the long term, transposition is a moot point. In *Costa v. ENEL* (European Court of Justice, 1964) the European Court of Justice held that only the EU interpretations of the directives are legally binding. To enforce this principle though, the Commission would have to file and win a suit before the ECJ. This is a long and costly process.

3. DEVELOPING THE HARMONIZED STANDARDS

Since the membership of CEN, CENELEC and ETSI is primarily drawn from the national standards organizations, their work is affected by the relations between the SDOs and the national governments. This relationship will have an impact on the process of recruiting the members of the technical committees and working groups who will carry out most of the work in standards development. It will also have an impact on the independence and priorities of the national mirror committees that monitor and direct their work.

The European SDOs are chartered by their governments. As a result, there is only one SDO in a given industrial sector in the EU member countries. However, this relationship varies from country to country. In countries such as the UK, there are few other ties between the government and the national SDOs. BSI, the British Standards Institute, has one of the strongest reputations for combining political independence and technical sophistication. At the other extreme, AFNOR, the leading French SDO, is generally regarded as an arm of the French government. The Italian pattern is more typical. Under Italian law, products must meet state–of–the art levels of safety. Compliance with Italian product standards is presumptive evidence of meeting this requirement. The Italian SDO,s UNO and ENI, are independent from the government unless they are considering issues in which the government has an interest.

The relations between CEN and CENELEC and the Commission are governed by the *General Guidelines for Co-operation between CEN and CENELEC* (European Commission, 1984) and the *Council Resolution of 18*

June 1992 on the Role of standardization in the European Economy (European Council, 1992).

At times, the mandate from DG Enterprise for the development of a new standard has been drafted in a way that shifts responsibility for resolving political conflicts from DG Enterprise and the development of the essential requirements and towards the standards development organizations. For example, DG Enterprise resolved a dispute on whether the emissions regulated under the EMC directive should include the generation of line current harmonics by referring the issue to CENELEC under a standards development mandate.

The recipient SDO will then have to decide whether to accept the mandate. The funding from the mandate does not cover the salaries of the TC members who will actually develop the standard. If the mandate is accepted, the management of, for example, CEN, will pass the task of developing a new standard to one of the organization's technical committees.

The mirror committees often play a role in the work of the technical committees and working groups. Seemingly intractable fights may be resolved overnight through telephone calls between the relevant mirror committees. As a result, the process for standards development may be far from transparent.

The chairs of the technical committees may ask the surveillance authorities in the major countries for their reaction to the draft standards. The goal is to make sure that they would not threaten to invoke the safeguards clause for products conforming to the proposed standard. The mirror committees are not always in a position to ensure national acceptance. The extent to which the mirror committees are able to coordinate their decisions with the national surveillance authorities may depend on the currents of national politics.

The draft standard and the TC report are then forwarded to the members of CEN, CENELEC or ETSI for a vote on whether or not to adopt the draft as a standard. If adopted, the draft will also have to be transcribed by the member standards organizations as national standards. The draft standard will therefore have to be forwarded to the Commission under the 'standstill' provisions of the Mutual Information Directive program discussed in Chapter 2.

Once approved, the new CEN, CENELEC or ETSI standard will be forwarded to the Commission for review, approval and publication. Once published, it becomes a harmonized standard that carries the presumption of fulfilling the essential requirements. The process of review and publication provides opponents with a last chance to block the acceptance of an unwanted standard. Member states have, from time to time, threatened to use their powers under the safeguards clause to pull products off the market that have been manufactured in compliance with the new standard. This has happened several times with the standards developed for the Packaging and Packaging Waste Directive. The sponsoring standards development organization is then likely to reconsider the offending standard.

The process of developing the harmonized standards can also provide the participants with a second chance to contend issues that they failed to carry during the original development of the directives. For example, the passage of the Toy Directive did not end the struggle for regulatory control. The German government has required manufacturers of plastic toys to also comply with the toxicity requirements developed for plastic cooking implements. In response to complaints from the British Toy and Hobby Association, the German government began lobbying to have the CEN adopt the German requirements as an integral part of the harmonized standards developed to implement the essential requirements of the Toy Directive.

Standards development is an expensive process. It can take several years to develop a new standard. Since the members of the TCs and working groups are usually unpaid volunteers, their salaries and expenses are generally covered by their employers. Considering the number of people involved in the TCs and working groups, the magnitude of their commitment and the time required to develop a standard, the costs can be substantial As a result, the managers at CEN, CENELEC and ETSI are generally reluctant to accept mandates unless they have industry support for the standards development effort.

The source of the support will have an impact on the way in which the standards are developed. The business interests that led the member states to advocate the initial development of a new directive are often willing to support the development of the standards needed to implement the directive. The national interests that support the development of both the directives and standards often leave an imprint on the nature of the standards. For example, British interests promoted the development of the Gas Fired Appliances Directive. The standards developed to implement the GFA directive are quite similar to the BSI equivalents. German interests advocated the development of the Personal Protective Equipment directive and the resulting standards resemble the DIN standards.

The Vienna Agreement between CEN and ISO and the Dresden Agreement between IEC and CENELEC (American National Standards Institute, 1996) add another dimension to this process. CEN and CENELEC have agreed to adopt international standards whenever appropriate. CEN and CENELEC will first offer the task of developing the new standard to ISO and/or IEC. Only if ISO or IEC reject the invitation for new standards development will CEN or CENELEC proceed to develop the standards.

The options of using ISO or IEC standards to meet a DG Enterprise mandate or of shifting the task of standards development to the international level can be very attractive. At the very least, this will cut the costs of developing a new standard very substantially and may also cut the time required as well. In many cases, this international approach is followed. Over 70 per cent of the CENELEC standards are identical with their IEC counterparts. An additional 15 per cent of the CENELEC standards are based on the IEC originals (ANSI, 1996, p. 28). The frequency of international cooperation in standards for CEN is far lower.

From time to time, CEN has encountered technical problems developing standards. The CEN TC developing standards for the Toy Directive was dominated by employees from the major toy manufacturers. They did not have the technical expertise needed to respond effectively to the German emphasis on toxicology requirements (Egan, 2000, pp. 175–7). Given the abstract nature of the essential requirements, many of the key policy decisions were taken in the standards development process. The standards were to be developed through the technical committees by technical experts from the regulated companies. There was little opportunity for the regulatory agencies to participate in the process. However, the toy manufacturers were generally comfortable with their national regulatory requirements. The proposals considered by the technical committees often mirrored the alternatives advocated by the national regulatory agencies. Because of these conflicts, the process of developing the harmonized standards needed to implement the Toy Directive has gone very slowly. This has, in effect, shifted responsibility for interpreting the essential requirements of the Toy Directive back to the notified bodies and surveillance authorities at the national level.

Controversies have also emerged in the development of the standards for the three medical device directives. In part, this reflects the strategy that was used in drafting the medical device directives. The directives are generally written under the assumption that the product safety is primarily an engineering issue, and not a medical issue. The Pharmacological Directive (European Council, 1965) defines a 'pharmacological product' as one that operates via pharmacological, immunological or metabolic means. Medical products that are primarily used to deliver single doses of a medicinal substance are also covered by the Pharmacological Directive. Only the mechanical aspects of the medicinal substance/medical device combination are to be covered by the medical device directives (European Commission, 1994).

In reality, many medical products are beginning to take on medicinal characteristics that are not effectively regulated by the medical device directives or the harmonized standards implementing them. The closest the medical devices come to acknowledging this situation is in the essential requirement of the Medical Device Directive that products covered by the directive must effectively perform the functions of a medical device in accordance with the intent of the manufacturer. This requirement does not offer an effective basis for developing standards governing medical devices with medicinal functions, such as a plastic matrix for growing collagen in the shape of a human ear, cochlear implants or implantable artificial hearts.

As a result, Britain and France have been cooperating in the development of an additional set of requirements governing medical devices. These 'common technical specifications' govern the design, performance and evaluation of the medical products with medicinal properties as an addition to, rather than as a substitute for, the harmonized standards.

Literally thousands of standards have been developed to implement the New Approach directives (see Table 4.1). This has been a major task requiring substantial commitments of time and money. The Commission has not always been happy about the results of standards development. DG Enterprise conducted a though review of the standards development process in 1998 (European Commission, 1998). DG Enterprise was concerned about the long time it takes for CEN to develop the standards needed to implement a new directive. According to the Report, an average of 75 months passed between the initial drafting of the mandate and the final transposition of a CEN standard by the national standards organizations. For CENELEC, the time required for standards development ranged between 24 and 48 months. The time needed for ETSI standards was only 28 months.

These delays posed problems for the New Approach. Mandates to develop new standards were usually issued after a directive had been approved. A long lead time in development meant that few harmonized standards would be available when the directive was in full force. Directive interpretation would then be left to the discretion of the notified bodies and surveillance authorities.

In part, the shorter lead time needed for CENELEC and ETSI standards reflected the nature of the products they were considering. In general, it is easier to achieve a Community consensus on a new standard than to find a compromise among a series of established national standards. Since electrotechnical and telecommunications technologies are developing rapidly, CENELEC and ETSI are more likely to have the luxury of developing new standards.

Table 4.1. Standards developed for the New Approach directives

Directive		Number of standards
Low Voltage	73/23/EEC	603
Machinery	98/37/EEC	450
Personal Protective Equipment	89/686/EEC	259
Medical Devices	93/42/EEC	252
Radio Telephone Terminal Equipment	99/5/EC	185
Electromagnetic Compatibility	89/336/EEC	112
Pressure Equipment	97/23/EEC	102
Construction Products	89/106/EEC	100
Recreational Craft	94/26/EC	58
In Vitro Diagnostic	98/79/EC	43
Implantable Medical Devices	90/386/EEC	40
Explosive Atmospheres	94/9/EC	38
Toys	88/378/EEC	23
Simple Pressure Vessels	87/40/EEC	12
Lifts	96/16/EEC	7
Cableways	00/9/EC	2
Packaging and Packaging Waste	94/62/EC	2
Weighing Instruments	90/384/EEC	1
Gas Fired Appliances	90/396/EEC	0

Source: estimates from data in European Commission (2003a).

The Commission made a series of recommendations on ways to speed up the standards development process. These include the wider use of electronic communications, improving communications with the Commission, establishing deadlines for national transposition and a greater use of independent research. A recommendation that CEN and CENELEC should be merged was rejected. Recent mandates for standards development have tied financing to compliance with a schedule for standards development.

The effectiveness of these measures is not clear. The staff employees of CEN, CENELEC and ETSI provide support services for the technical committees, working groups and chairs that actually develop the draft standards. The people actually involved in standards development are, for the most part, volunteers who are supported by their employers and responsive to their national mirror committees. Pressuring the SDO staff is not always an effective way to speed up the pace of TC work.

A lack of standards for directives covering broader categories of products strongly suggests the problems in developing a consensus. This is the case for the Toys, Construction Products and Personal Protective Equipment directives. On the other hand, the few standards for the Lifts, Cableways and Recreational Craft directives effectively summarize a large volume of accepted international standards.

Once a standard has been developed, accepted and published, the drafting standards development agency is responsible for informally monitoring the use of the standard and for developing periodic updates and amendments. The program managers at CEN, CENELEC and ETSI may meet with the leading notified bodies and surveillance authorities in order to determine whether changes may be needed.

For example, it was very difficult to test a product for susceptibility to electromagnetic radiation under the original versions of the EMC standards. The test conditions were not well defined. A thorough test house could generally force a failure by testing the product under ever more strenuous circumstances. It became common practice for manufacturers to negotiate with test houses over test conditions and pass rates before testing was begun. These problems have been largely resolved in the last few years.

The problems associated with standards development tend to be more severe for CEN. It is less of a problem for CENELEC and ETSI because they are more likely to transcribe ISO and IEC standards rather than develop separate European standards. To a large extent, this reflects the greater interest by the major manufacturers in these sectors in international trade. Technology is developing rapidly in these areas. As a result, CENELEC and ETSI are more likely to be developing new standards than reconciling national differences in established standards. This difference also reflects the greater degree of current standards development at the international level. It is often cheaper and easier to rely on international standards development, especially since the European countries often provide a majority of the participants in the standards development process both at the TC and ISO/IEC approval levels.

Directorate General Enterprise has been facing a renewed emphasis on environmental issues and increased competition from Directorate General Environment. In 1985, there was a palpable sense of crisis about the future of the internal market and the European Union. The President of the Commission, Jacques Santer, was therefore able to use his considerable influence to advance the position of DG Enterprise and promote the development of the CE marking system. CE marking was a cornerstone for the development of the 300 directives, 1992 project and Maastricht

Convention. The role of the European Parliament was limited. As a result, there was little internal opposition to development of the CE marking system.

There is now a much stronger focus on environmental issues in the on-going development of the CE marking system. The political influence of the Greens has increased substantially both within the European Parliament and at the national level, particularly in Germany. The role of Parliament was expanded substantially in the 1992 Maastricht Agreement. For the first time, a vote against a draft directive in Parliament could force a reconsideration of the proposal by the Council in consultation with the Commission. These three factors, the lessening sense of crisis about product standards and the free market, the lack of strong leadership in the Commission and the emergence of the Greens in Parliament, have led to a new environmental emphasis in the more recent New Approach directives.

Neither the program managers in DG Enterprise nor their allies in the national regulatory agencies have much interest in sharing authority with other public or private groups, especially in the environmental sector. Instead, there is a strong incentive to minimize the need to coordinate with other directorates general by maintaining as much control as possible over all aspects of a particular program.

Turf wars have been handled by DG Enterprise with the mantras: 'one directive for all aspects of product regulation' and 'CE marking for product development, environmental and labor legislation for how the products are to be used'. The national product safety regulators have generally provided strong support for this position in the Commission, the Council and at the national levels. These turf wars have left visible imprints on the development of the New Approach directives.

If the mantras were taken seriously, then the New Approach directives would be as concerned with the environmental as the safety aspects of products sold in the EU. In reality, DG Enterprise and its allies in the national governments seem to have difficulty balancing the competing requirements of business competitiveness, product safety and product pollution impact.

The Commission report also argued that the participants in the European standards development organizations should represent a wider range of Community interests, including small businesses, environmental, consumer and labor concerns. This is a major shift in the roles assigned to the three European SDOs. In the past, the mandate from the Commission was expected to define the policy goals of the draft standard. The major function of the technical committees was to bring private sector engineering and safety experience to this task. In contrast, the provisions of the report implicitly shift responsibility for balancing environmental, safety, consumer and business interests to CEN, CENELEC and ETSI and their technical committees. These are basic policy issues.

Environmental issues have also posed problems in standards development. The European Environmental Bureau (EEB), with funding from DG Enterprise, participated in the CEN TC developing standards for the Packaging and Packaging Waste Directive (PPWD). The results were disastrous. From the perspective of the EEB, the purpose of the PPWD was to push industry towards a more responsible use of packaging. In general, the industry members of TCs see their task as codifying the best engineering practices. The EEB representatives resigned in protest when it became clear that the conflicts between the two camps could not be resolved (European Environmental Bureau, 2000). Since then, the EEB has rejoined CEN as an institutional member. They are now in a position to evaluate the acceptability of a standard and to vote on approval without having to participate in standards development.

This process gives the few large, well supported, national standards development organizations that name most of the TC members substantial influence over the process. The national standards development organizations that are primarily responsible for staffing the working groups may also be in a position to influence the deliberations of the group through the energetic use of mirror committees. Participants in the process have reported that seemingly intractable disagreements may disappear overnight, probably in response to back channel negotiations among the major participating standards organizations.

This process tends to introduce a bias in favor of the legacy standards developed by the major European SDOs. Many of the harmonized standards are based on standards that have already been developed by BSI or DIN, or to a lesser extent, AFNOR. This bias reflects both the technical competence and political importance of the major SDOs in the work of CEN, CENELEC and ETSI. It also reflects the importance of the major countries in the standards developed by the SDOs in the smaller European countries at the national level.

International convergence of standards developed for medical devices, computers and telecommunications equipment can be attributed to other factors. These industries are characterized by rapid changes in technology and a widely shared reliance on international markets. New standards are always being developed. There is widespread support in the industry for the development of standards with international support. It is far easier to develop standards that are consistent with international practices than to harmonize inconsistent standards that have been widely used in industry for years. Because of these factors, the problems of international harmonization and development delays are far more pressing on CEN than on CENELEC and ETSI.

Specifications for steel and many construction products constitute the most serious areas of resistance to international harmonization. The problems emerge at the EU level. The PED contains a provision requiring a manufacturer to either obtain notified body approval for the specifications of pressure bearing metals or to only use metals manufactured by companies that have an approved quality control system in place. DG Enterprise put this provision into the PED rather than chartering CEN to develop standards defining steel quality. It was widely believed that CEN would not be able to develop a European set of steel specifications because of resistance from the national steel corporations and their government sponsors who were fighting to defend national steel markets.

The task of developing specifications for building materials was also taken away from CEN because of anticipated industry and government resistance. Instead, the specifications are to be incorporated into a series of regional building codes. The Construction Product Directive came into force in mid–1991. The building codes needed to implement it are only now being developed. See also Saunders (1993).

Two critical factors affecting the level of support for global convergence are: a) the importance of international markets in the industry and b) the extent to which there are existing national standards which are significantly different from their US counterparts. It is likely to be easier to agree on new standards than to reconcile differences among existing standards that are widely used in industry.

For example, companies are likely to have fewer problems with the differences between US and EU standards in recreational craft. Ship design and construction has been regulated for over a century. International convergence in the regulation of shipping was first promoted by private insurance carriers such as Lloyds and Veritas. International conventions governing ship safety and environmental performance are developed and administered by the International Maritime Organization. These requirements are enforced at the national levels by organizations such as the Coast Guard and the American Bureau of Shipping. CEN and CENELEC drew on this rich international legacy when developing the harmonized standards to implement the Recreational Craft Directive.

The linkage between CEN and ISO can also complicate the process of standards development in CEN. Companies interested in protecting local markets are likely to promote the development of distinctive EN standards. Corporations seeking broader markets are likely to prefer the adoption of ISO standards. The difference in perspective may depend on whether a company is a producer or a consumer of the products that are subject to the standard. As we have seen though, the producers tend to dominate standards development in CEN.

The role played by the Commission and DG Enterprise in these dramas varies from issue to issue. The Commission has promoted the development of a 'Global Approach' to product regulation. This closely resembles the New Approach with one critical difference; the specific criteria the manufacturers must meet are spelled out in the directives rather than in the harmonized standards. This shift away from a reliance on CEN to develop the required standards is intended in part to make sure that the requirements are based on ISO standards. It also reflects DG Environment's reluctance to hand, DG Enterprise led the fight to kill the ISO project.

The role of CENELEC and ETSI in the development of European harmonized standards is having an impact on the process of national standards development in the EU. Between 1999 and 2001, the number of electrical standards being developed at the EU level rose from 594 to 673, while the number being developed at the national level dropped from 36 to 16. In contrast, the impact on the development of non–electrical standards has been far less apparent. On average, almost 70 per cent of the standards were still being developed at the national level, most of them in the areas of foodstuffs, aeronautics and construction products (European Commission, 2003).

Many European standards organizations have been placing a greater focus on the lucrative business of certifying products to private quality and/or performance standards. BSI has been promoting the kitemark, DIN has the BS standards. Many national standard organizations have also been cutting back on the development of national standards to focus primarily on their roles in supporting the national mirror committees. BSI, the national standards body for the UK, and CIE and ENI, the Italian standards bodies, are in this category.

In some cases, this change of emphasis has led to the national standards development organizations serving as the champions of national commercial interests in the European standards development process. Some of the national standards organizations, AFNOR in particular, have become virtual advocates for the commercial policies of their national governments. In other cases, the national standards organizations have refused to allow the participation of US companies that have a strong presence in the EU to participate in either the CEN/CENELEC delegations or the supporting mirror committees on the grounds that they do not represent European interests.

The environmental perspective is also emerging in the development of the 'Global Approach' directives. The European Union has embraced the New Approach as the preferred strategy for public regulation, where appropriate.

The result has been the development of a 'Global Approach' to regulation that incorporates many, but not all, of the New Approach inventions.

A minor difference between the Global Approach and the New Approach is the omission of the CE mark logo. A major difference is a preference for mandated regulatory standards instead of relying on the independent work of CEN, CENELEC or ETSI. The Packaging and Packaging Waste Directive, for example, requires the member states to develop packaging waste regulations and management programs. The Noise Directive mandates the use of EN ISO 3744 or 3746 under prescribed test conditions for evaluating compliance with the directive. The proposed Removal of Hazardous Substances lists the materials that are to be banned and their minimum concentrations. This preference for state action probably reflects both disillusionment with the traditional standards development processes and a preference for direct state regulation.

REFERENCES

American National Standards Institute (1996), *American Access to the European Standardization Process,* New York: ANSI.
DEsite (2003), 'DEsite; COREPER', at drcwww.kub.nl/instructie/eu.en/T21. html.
Directorate General Enterprise (2002), *Business Impact Assessment Pilot Project, Final Report: Lessons Learned and the Way Forward,* Enterprise Working Paper, March, 4.
Egan, Michelle (2000), *Constructing a European Market,* Oxford: Oxford University Press.
European Commission (1984), *General Guidelines for Co-operation between CEN and CENELEC and the European Commission.*
European Commission (1994), Medical Devices; Guidance Documents, EDDEV 2 1/1.
European Commission (1998), *Report From the Commission to the Council and the European Parliament: Efficiency and Accountability in European Standardization Under the New Approach,* COM(1998) 291.
European Commission (2000), Single Market Scorecard, Number 7, November, 7.
European Commission (2001), *Report from the Commission to the Council and the European Parliament on Actions Taken Following the Resolutions on European Standardization Adopted by the Council and the European Parliament in 1999,* COM(2001) 527 final.
European Commission (2002), *Communication from the Commission on Impact Assessment,* COM(2002) 276 final.

European Commission (2003a), *Report from the Commission to the Council, the European Parliament and the European Economic and Social Committee: the Operation of Directive 98/34/EC from 1999 to 2001,* COM(2003) 200 final.

European Commission (2003b), New Approach directives and standards, at http://www.newapproach.org/Directives/DirectiveList.asp.

European Council (1965), *Council Directive 65/65 EEC of 26 January 1965 on the approximation of provisions laid down by law, regulation or administrative action relating to medicinal products.*

European Council (1973), *Council Directive 73/23/EEC of 19 February 1973 on the Harmonization of the Laws of the Member States Relating to Electrical Equipment Designed for Use Within Certain Voltage Limits.*

European Council (1989), *Council Directive of 21 December 1988 on the Approximation of Laws, Regulations and Administrative Provisions of the Member States Relating to Construction Products.*

European Council (1992), *Council Resolution of 18 June 1992 on the Role of Standardization in the European Economy.*

European Council (1997a), *Directive 97/23/EEC of the European Parliament and of the Council of 29 May 1997 on the Approximation of the Laws of the Member States Concerning Pressure Equipment.*

European Council (1997b), *Council Resolution of 18 June 1992 on the Role of European Standardization in the European Economy,* C173 of 9.7.

European Council (1998), *Directive 98/34 Laying Down a Procedure on the Provision of Information in the Field of Technical Standards.*

European Council (2000), *Directive 2000/14/EC of the European Parliament and of the Council of 8 May 2000 on the Approximation of Member States Relating to the Noise Emissions in the Environment by Equipment for Use Outdoors.*

European Court of Justice (1964), *Costa v. ENEL* (Case 6/64, ECR 585).

European Environmental Bureau (2000), *CEN at Work: How the Requirements of the European Packaging and Packaging Waste Directive (94/62) are Bypassed by CEN Standards,* EEB Publication, 2000/15.

European Union Presidency (2004), COREPER I at www.eu2004.it/ meeting.asp?sNavlocator+5,13&list_id=58.

Hagigh, Sara (1992), 'Hundreds of new product standards will apply to sales in EC', *Business America,* 113 (1), p. 16.

Lankowski, Carl (2001), 'Germany: A Major Player', in Eleanor Zeff and Ellen B. Puso (eds.) *The European Union and the Member States: Cooperation, Coordination and Compromise,* Boulder, CO: Lynne Riemer Publishers, pp. 89–113.

Saunders, Mary (1993), 'A single EC market for construction products?', *Business America,* 114 (2), p. 21.

Sauron, Jean-Luc (2000), *The French Administration and the European Union,* Paris: La Documentation Française.

5. From Notified Bodies to Surveillance Authorities

1. INTRODUCTION

How do we know the product actually complies with the requirements of the directives and implementing standards?

There are four guarantors of conformity assessment in the CE marking system. When the manufacturer signs the declaration of conformity, s/he is creating a legally binding pledge that the product conforms to the requirements of the relevant directives. The product may require testing. By signing an affirmative test report, the manager of the laboratory is attesting that the product met the standards to which it was tested. If the product presents an unusually high level of intrinsic risks, then the manufacturer may be required to hire the services of a notified body. The notified body will then check the product for conformity with the CE marking requirements. The ultimate arbiters of conformity are, of course, the surveillance authorities.

In this chapter, we will be analyzing the functioning of the notified bodies and surveillance authorities and how they affect the implementation of the CE marking system.

2. THE CONFORMITY ASSESSMENT PROCESS

Conformity assessment procedures under the New Approach cover product design, manufacturing and product testing. Product design is covered by modules A (self–declaration), B (type examination) and H (design dossier). Modules C, D, E and F cover production and/or testing. Module H covers everything.

The notified bodies are responsible for conformity assessment under the modules that do not allow for self–declaration. Collectively, notified bodies perform three general types of tasks. They can carry out a module B type review to make sure that a product has been designed and developed in accordance with the relevant directives. They can also be hired to review and approve a manufacturer's consistency control system for modules D, E and H that are based on ISO 9001, 9002 and 9003. Finally, they can inspect products for conformity with the essential requirements under modules G and H. This system has been developed in accordance with a 1993 decision of the Council (European Council, 1993).

Module B has the greatest impact on the administration of the CE marking process. Under module B, the notified body is required to review the design for a product to determine whether it conforms to the essential requirements of the governing directives. Virtually all products that require a notified body are covered by module B. Modules C, D, E, F and G complement rather than replace the use of module B.

3. THE NOTIFIED BODIES

Notified bodies are authorized by the competent authorities of their national governments to carry out these functions. On an informal basis, notified bodies are also likely to provide consulting services for the local surveillance authorities. Since CE marking is their only business and they are paid to be expert, notified bodies often have more ready access to technical expertise. A close relationship between a notified body and the local surveillance authorities can benefit manufacturers. Client companies are likely to be very pleased with their notified bodies if they are able to resolve issues raised by the surveillance authorities with a telephone call.

The national 'competent authorities' are responsible for making sure that applicant bodies are qualified before they are notified. According to Decision 93/465/EEC, the competent authorities in the member states should make sure that the candidate organizations meet the following requirements:

- They must be legal entities established under the laws of the notifying states
- They should be accredited under the EN 17000 series of standards
- They must have access to the necessary personnel and equipment
- The personnel must be technically competent
- They must demonstrate professional secrecy and integrity
- They must be independent from and impartial towards clients
- They must be insured

The EN 17000 series of standards cover accreditation, assessment and operational requirements for certification bodies, test houses and inspection bodies (European Commission, 2000).

In general, the notified bodies have substantial latitude in determining what constitutes an acceptable implementation of the essential requirements. In reality, there are significant differences in the technical sophistication and procedural rigor of notified bodies in different countries. This has posed one of the most significant challenges to the integrity of the CE marking process. The program managers of the notified bodies may not consider the CE marking system from the same perspective that is likely to be adopted in Brussels. Program managers at the EU Commission level are public officers who generally have to balance the competing demands from 15 member states. This is likely to lead to a broader, more international perspective on issues relating to the internal free market. As government agents, they are more likely to consider the impact of issues on their mandate to promote the internal free market.

In contrast, the notified bodies are private companies with strong ties to their national markets and to their national surveillance authorities. They are more likely to look at the common market from a commercial perspective, with a concern for marketing and revenue maximization. These factors can lead to a more parochial outlook.

There are also significant differences among notified bodies. These differences have an impact on the administrative uniformity of the CE marking system and can lead to a degree of forum shopping as manufacturers search for the notified bodies that will give them more favorable reviews. Manufacturers that want to make a long–term commitment to major European markets are likely to prefer to use rigorous, well–respected notified bodies. 'Bucket shops' that want to flood the European markets with cheap products and then disappear, are likely to seek out less demanding notified bodies.

National differences among notified bodies may reflect differences in the technical sophistication of the national economies. Notified body inspectors require highly specialized technical skills to make sure that products comply with the essential requirements in directives such as Explosive Atmospheres, Civilian Explosives, Medical Devices, In Vitro Diagnostic Medical Devices and Active Implantable Medical Devices. These skills may not be readily available in the smaller or less developed economies.

National differences among notified bodies may also reflect differences in local industry usage, government policies and surveillance authority priorities. For example, the British notified bodies are more likely to accept pressure vessels built in accordance with the ASME Pressure Vessel and Boiler Code as long as the manufacturer has explained how s/he has also complied with the additional requirements of the PED harmonized standards. In part, this reflects the close commercial ties with the US and the importance of US investments in the UK and British investments in the US. In contrast, the French notified bodies are likely to reject any product that is not built in accordance with all available harmonized standards and to insist that only European (preferably French) standards are used if harmonized standards are not available.

National differences in the operation of notified bodies may also reflect differences in market interests. For the most part, large country notified bodies can prosper by serving their domestic markets. A reputation for rigor in CE mark conformity assessment may keep marginal products out of local markets. The notified bodies from the smaller countries may be less rigorous in their design reviews. To an extent, this may reflect the reality that small country notified bodies have to attract business from other countries if they are going to be viable in the marketplace.

The balance between procedural conformity and technical expertise in the notification process has been struck differently in different countries. The French notified bodies tend to place a stronger emphasis on conformity with the formal procedural requirements in the conformity assurance modules while the Germans tend to look more for in–depth expertise and product quality. This issue emerges, for example, in the assessment of a manufacturer's quality control systems.

The larger countries, Britain, France and Germany, generally impose high standards for the notification process. Notification processes in the larger countries are coordinated through SOGOG, the Senior Officer Government Official Group. The Dutch competent authorities have considered coordinating their notification decisions with SOGOG.

The British competent authorities have a relatively strict regime for notifying and coordinating notified bodies. Companies interested in an appointment as a notified body must first be accredited under the EN 17000 standards by the United Kingdom Accreditation Service. In cooperation with the UKAS, the competent authorities have developed guidance documents that set forth national policies and procedures for implementing different directives. DG Enterprise is not involved in this process. British notified bodies are also required to meet quarterly with the competent authorities.

In general, the French government maintains close relations and tight control over French notified bodies, especially for the medical device directives. One notified body, GMED, was originally organized as an agency of the French Ministry of Health. Although GMED has been 'privatized', it has retained close ties to the government. There is a similar situation in Germany. TUV is a major notified body in Germany. Before notification, TUV was responsible for managing a number of official German inspection programs. The influence of the government on Italian notified body policies may be more pronounced in areas that directly affect government regulatory policies.

The rigor of the notification process and the level of notified body coordination process outside of France, Germany and Britain can be, at times, relatively lax. In part, this may reflect local business practices, the nature of the national markets for notified body services and the limits to local technical expertise.

Notified bodies are likely to have the greatest range for interpreting the essential requirements when conducting a module B type review. A module B review can be a very straightforward matter if the design is based on a robust risk assessment, harmonized standards are used to address all relevant essential requirements and the technical file is complete and well organized. In many instances, the manufacturer will not be so fortunate. Harmonized standards may not be available to cover all of the essential requirements. Products exported to the EU may have been designed and built to other, non–European standards. In some cases, the directives almost require the notified bodies to exercise their independent judgment. This includes, for example, the provisions of the Pressure Equipment Directive which calls for European approval of materials and the European Technical Approvals under the Construction Product Directive. Since there are no relevant standards defining acceptable materials attributes, the notified bodies have to exercise their own judgments.

More specialized issues arise in connection with modules D, E and H. The directives defining the modules state that companies covered by modules D, E or H must have internal quality control systems that are 'based on' ISO 9000. The notified bodies have the task of certifying these manufacturers' quality control systems.

This makes sense. By implementing the 1995 version of ISO 9000 a company will have to develop a system for documenting that company procedures are followed consistently. Although it makes little sense as a quality control measure, ISO 9000 can be used to show that a company is consistently making bad products. However, certifying a program for consistency checks is a useful way of ensuring that a manufacturer consistently follows approved design and manufacturing processes. It can also generate a paper trail on manufacturing processes that may be useful for assessing the causes of defective products.

A few issues involving the review of consistency review programs for CE marking purposes have emerged. According to the Council decision (European Council, 1993), a manufacturer's implementation of module D, E or H requirements should be 'based on' ISO 9000. What does 'based on' mean? To the French, it is likely to mean that the manufacturer must have an ISO 9000 system in place that has been approved by a European registrar.

German and British notified bodies are more likely to ask whether the manufacturer has implemented an effective quality and consistency control system. Although a certified ISO 9000 system would not be required, it could shorten the notified body review and approval process.

All notified bodies will be faced with the problem of making the shift from ISO 9000:1995 to ISO 9000:2000. The 2000 amendments have introduced major changes to the ISO 9000 system. To an extent, these changes are not compatible with the ways in which the system is being used in modules D, E and H. The major emphasis in the 1995 and earlier versions of the standard has been on describing business procedures and developing documentation that they have been followed. Effective quality control programs are usually based on continual improvement rather than on unvarying consistency. As a result, the standard has frequently been criticized as failing to provide an effective basis for quality improvement.

The 2000 version of ISO 9000 adopts the continuous improvement perspective. Companies using ISO 9000:2000 to meet their module D, E or H requirements would have to periodically review their relations with their customers, suppliers and employees as well as their internal business processes. They would have to document how they have identified issues through these reviews, how they have been addressed and how conditions have improved. ISO 9000:2000 then becomes an agent for change rather than a guarantor of consistency.

Several managers associated with different notified bodies have expressed concern over the shift to ISO 9000:2000. Many people said they would be reluctant to force companies to review and improve their relations with the workers, suppliers and customers as a part of a product consistency program. There is another, lesser concern. ISO 9001, 9002 and 9003 mapped directly onto the module D, E and H requirements. ISO 9000:2000 is not broken down into hyphen 1, hyphen 2 and hyphen 3 versions. DG Enterprise is expected to develop a guidance document that would describe how ISO 9000:2000 could be selectively applied to meet the different requirements of the three modules (European Commission, 2000, fn. 94, p. 33). As of the date on which this is being written, the long–awaited guidelines have not been published.

The Commission has recognized that the coordination among the member states in the notification and supervision of conformity assessment bodies should be improved.

Since the inception of the New Approach directives, with few exceptions, there has been no systematic exchange of information between Member States concerning the criteria and procedures applied at national level for the assessment and surveillance of notified bodies. This lack of transparency has encouraged suspicions about uneven levels of implementation which, in turn, undermine the confidence that is essential if the mutual recognition and acceptance of certificates issues by notified bodies is to function smoothly . . . Certain differences between the systems leading to the notification of conformity assessment bodies, and the possibility to demonstrate the abilities of those bodies by other means, have lead to a lack of confidence among some stakeholders. (European Commission, 2001)

The Commission has identified a need for improvement in supervision of notified bodies and the coordination of the surveillance authorities. Again;

> Some concerns about the uniformity of implementation across Member States and across sectors have been voiced. Therefore, the main priorities . . . are to establish guidance . . . on the . . . criteria and procedures that Member States apply to assess and monitor notified bodies. (Directorate General Enterprise, 2003)

There are, in theory, procedures in place to review the performance of the notified bodies and, if necessary, to de–certify them. Clients who believe that their notified bodies have not provided fully professional services can send a complaint letter to the certifying competent authorities. The competent authorities are not held accountable in their responses to complaints. In fact, no notified body has ever been de–certified. However, at least one major notified body came close to losing accreditation, and thus the notified body status, for a failure to effectively police client sterilization procedures.

The Commission does not have either the authority or, often, the political flexibility needed to monitor and coordinate notified bodies. Their heavy weapon, to sue the notifying government in the European Court of Justice for failing to carry out state obligations under the governing directives, is so unwieldy as to be largely useless.

It also became clear that Directorate General Enterprise did not have the legal tools for effectively regulating the newly appointed notified bodies. To address this gap, the Commission financed the development of EOTC, the European Organization for Testing and Conformity. The EOTC was charged with responsibility for developing criteria for notified body operations and with the organization of notified body consultation groups.

The EOTC initiative has not worked out as well as hoped. The organization had no legal basis for requiring notified bodies to either belong or obey. The EOTC managers started by trying unilaterally to impose relatively rigid rules on the member bodies. Within a few years, most of the notified bodies from the major market countries had resigned and the organization almost collapsed. Notified bodies from the UK, France, Germany and Italy are no longer affiliated with the organization. The Commission has also cut funding for the EOTC.

The EOTC has been reborn as a smaller, less intrusive agency. It only represents the notified bodies of the smaller countries. For the notified bodies that are members of the organization, The EOTC now coordinates the development of voluntary, self–regulating groups. For these groups, participation in EOTC serves to provide assurances of technical competence and administrative integrity for companies and surveillance authorities in the major market countries.

The notified body groups must meet EOTC standards for technical competence and legal responsiveness. The groups are then free to work out common responses to issues of common concern involving the interpretation of CE mark requirements. Although these decisions are not formally bound by the Administrative Council (AdCo) guidance documents, the groups are not likely to deviate far from DG Enterprise orthodoxy. The EOTC has also taken a lead in organizing and marketing public meetings and training sessions on CE marking and in providing technical assistance on CE marking issues to accession countries under contract.

The relatively chaotic conditions in the notified body community during these early days had several consequences. A number of industry experts have reported that the more sophisticated and rigorous notified bodies and surveillance authorities simply ignored questionable judgments made by the less rigorous notified bodies. Acceptance of a product by a notified body in, hypothetically, Portugal did not mean that the German authorities would allow the product to be traded freely in their country without a second review from a German notified body. This had a significant effect on the demand for the notified body services. In order to avoid a messy public fight in the European Court of Justice, the governments of Germany and Portugal agreed that the Germans would provide training and technical support for their Portuguese counterpart. As a result, the Portuguese notified bodies now have a reputation for strict adherence to the directive requirements.

Informal methods for coordinating the notified bodies have also been developed. DG Enterprise is developing a mechanism for notified bodies in the larger countries EU–wide. The Directorate sponsors the organization of informal AdCos, or administrative councils. The members of the AdCos are the major notified bodies that do not participate in the EOTC groups. The members of the AdCos also work out common solutions to shared CE mark issues.

DG Enterprise is now publishing the results of these deliberations as 'guidance documents'. The guidance documents typically describe a situation involving the interpretation of a New Approach directive, harmonized standard or other CE mark requirement, the interpretation of the situation and the interpretation that the AdCo has adopted. Guidance documents have been published for 12 out of the 21 New Approach directives. These guidance documents have no binding legal weight. However, they have become influential sources of guidance in coordinating the decisions of the notified bodies.

The generally close working relations between the notified bodies and the surveillance authorities also create pressures for international convergence in notified body activities. Most manufacturers are interested in a long–term market presence. They have a strong incentive to use notified bodies that have the credibility to effectively discuss conformity issues with surveillance authorities in a wide range of European member states. Only the 'bucket shops', non–European companies that want to flood the European market with cheap, non–conforming products and then disappear, are likely to have a strong interest in a lax review of CE mark requirements. Over the long term, the bucket shops will not provide a significant portion of the total market for notified body services.

These market considerations promote the interests of the larger, better respected and more diversified notified bodies at the expense of smaller, regional and more specialized bodies. Larger manufacturers are likely to prefer one stop shopping by using notified bodies that can work on a wide range of products with the surveillance authorities in a wide range of European countries. Complex products are often covered by a number of directives and different sets of notified body requirements. Clients tend to avoid potential conflicts among different notified bodies by using bodies that are notified for all applicable directives. Businesses that expect to sell products in a number of European countries also have an incentive to select notified bodies that have strong relations with the surveillance authorities throughout most of the EU. The American company, Underwriters Laboratory, is now affiliated with notified bodies in five EU countries and can cover virtually all directives. BSI and TUV seem to be following the same pattern. We expect to see the emergence of a system that is dominated by a few notified bodies with a presence in most major countries that have been notified for all directives.

4. THE SURVEILLANCE AUTHORITIES

The surveillance authorities, the last component of the CE marking system, have also evolved in unexpected directions. The member states were given wide latitude in the designation of their surveillance authorities for the different directives. With this latitude came significant differences in the enforcement strategies.

Overall, enforcement has been relatively light (Atkinson, 1998). In the words of the Commission:

[T]here is no assurance that levels of enforcement do not vary throughout the Union. This undermines the credibility of the New Approach and could lead to a *de facto* refragmentation of the Internal Market.

Some Member States have a 'proactive' approach to market surveillance, while others adopt a 'reactive' strategy . . . For some directives, some Member States do not have a well–defined strategy. In some Member States, severe financial restrictions mean the effectiveness of market surveillance is limited (European Commission, 2003, pp. 14–5).

In most countries, CE mark enforcement is based on a 'management by exception' approach. In general, products are not reviewed for CE mark compliance unless a safety incident involving the product has occurred or a report has been filed with the authorities charging non–compliance. These reports of product non–compliance are often filed by workers, consumers or competitors. In fact, American companies are often the most aggressive in charging their competitors with importing products that do not meet CE mark requirements. Once a decision has been made to ban trade in a product for violations of CE mark requirements, then the customs agencies of the member states are notified with orders to prevent further importation of the product.

This widespread laissez–faire attitude towards CE mark enforcement is consistent with another phenomenon that American exporters often note; there are many products made by smaller manufacturers in the EU that are still not CE marked. These gaps in compliance may reflect several factors. Before 1992, only products sold in more than one EU member country had to be CE marked. 'National' products could be sold under national standards. Old habits die hard. Furthermore, it is not completely clear that products sold before the CE marking system came into being, and that have not been modified since then, are not exempt from the new rules. CE marking obligations attach 'the first time' a product is placed on the market or put into service. It might be argued that the 'first time' applies to the first in a series of identical products, and not to each individual product.

This laissez–faire attitude towards inspection reflects a common pattern; surveillance responsibilities are generally given to the government agencies that had equivalent authority before the CE mark system was developed. Thus, the local equivalents of departments of labor are generally charged with inspecting CE marked products in an industrial environment, health departments review products used in a medical environment and consumer product safety departments enforce CE marking in the context of retail sales.

However, there are differences in the competencies required to inspect for shop floor safety and to assess products for compliance with CE mark requirements. Traditional inspection programs generally focus on finding safety issues on the shop floor, in hospitals or stores. Inspectors may compare observed conditions with a check–off list of required conditions. If an accident occurs, the inspectors are generally responsible for finding out the causes. These are different skill sets than what is required to test a product for compliance with the harmonized standards. Competencies in CE mark inspections are likely to require a higher level of general engineering skills, a significantly greater level of product specific competencies and a good working knowledge of the harmonized standards, required tests and other CE mark requirements.

In some countries, this initially laissez–faire policy towards CE mark inspection tends to be coupled with a more draconian approach to enforcement once an injury has occurred. Under the EU rules, the surveillance authorities are authorized to remove all offending products from the market, force products to be removed from service and to bar future importations. Under the rules of the EU though, CE mark requirements have to be transcribed into national law. This opens the prospects for national, as well as Community–wide, penalties for CE mark violations. In Italy, for example, it not uncommon for the courts to impose jail sentences and stiff fines on the company officials who signed the declaration of conformity on a product that caused physical injury or death.

A few countries have adopted different strategies for CE mark surveillance. In France, for example, surveillance functions are shared between the customs service and either the department of labor, the department of health or the department of consumer affairs, depending on the market. The French customs service defines its role as ensuring that there is complete documentation on CE mark compliance for relevant imported products. However, the scope of the requested documentation may exceed what is customarily expected for a well manicured technical file. The customs authorities have has been alleged to request, for example, a detailed report on EMC test conditions, from the original test house and in French. The prospects of successfully appealing an administrative request from a French customs official for more CE mark documentation are limited.

By involving the customs service in the CE mark surveillance system, the French officials are better able to head off the mass importation of products that have been fraudulently CE marked. This has been an issue, as we will discuss later, with the importation of low cost toys, tools and consumer products from the Far East. However, it also means that imported goods undergo two levels of surveillance while French domestic production is only subject to domestic surveillance.

There is a different pattern of CE mark surveillance in Germany. Germany has a long tradition of public–private cooperation. TUV, for example, had been charged with responsibility for inspecting German cars.

German manufacturers are also required to belong to the BG system of workman's compensation insurance. In the past, the BGs were also responsible for workplace safety inspection.

These arrangements were changed with the introduction of the CE marking system. In order to become a notified body, the ties between TUV and the government were cut. TUV has been, in effect, privatized. The authority of the BGs to inspect for workplace safety has been cut back. Although they still monitor for the maintenance of safe conditions in the workplace, authority to inspect workplace equipment for CE mark conformity has been delegated to the various Lander. Although the Bundesfinanzministerium is charged with the overall coordination of the CE mark inspection system, the operational judgments are strictly left to the Länder inspection offices. There is some coordination in the system though; different Länder have developed in – depth expertise in different directives. In order to lower administrative costs, the Länder inspection offices tend to refer the more complex CE marking issues to the Land surveillance authorities with the relevant areas of expertise.

Another aspect of German exceptionalism in CE mark surveillance is their emphasis on pro–active systems of product inspection. Over a three– or four–year period, the equipment used in every German workplace and hospital, and the consumer goods in every German distribution channel will be reviewed for CE mark compliance. This system is supplemented by the more common pattern of responding to allegations of non–conformity. In Germany though, the close ties between Länder CE mark inspectors and the workplace safety inspectors from the BG workman's compensation insurance clubs makes this reporting system more efficient than customary.

The rigor of the German CE mark surveillance system often has an effect on a manufacturer's choice of a notified body. It is important for a manufacturer to use a notified body whose judgments will be accepted by the surveillance authorities if a question should ever arise. Given the rigor of German product reviews, companies that plan to sell significant quantities of their product in Germany are often best advised to use a German notified body.

German exceptionalism has also been manifested in the 'user inspectorate' provisions of the Pressure Equipment Directive (PED). In order to meet German arguments that the CE mark system represented a step backwards from the prior German safety standards, the PED authorized major industrial complexes to use their own, more stringent safety requirements. Products sold to authorized user inspectorates are not CE marked, even though they will have met a more stringent set of safety requirements. However, a user inspectorate can put the CE mark on used equipment sold to third parties if they can document CE mark compliance.

User inspectorates can be organized under the Pressure Equipment Directive in any European country with CE marking. However, the system was originated in response to German pressure and is the most highly developed there.

5. THE SAFEGUARDS CLAUSE

Under the rules of a CE marking system, the surveillance authorities can pull a product off the market and out of use on three grounds.

First, the product did not conform to the CE marking requirements, it was not CE marked or it was improperly CE marked. If so, then the product can be pulled from the market. Charges could be filed against the manufacturer under local law. Information on national prosecutions for violations of CE mark requirements are not readily available. However, it is commonly believed that the German and French authorities have been the most aggressive in prosecuting non–compliant manufacturers.

There are clear drawbacks to the process if the goal is to remove dangerous products from the marketplace. It generally involves judicial proceedings in which the defendant manufacturer may have significant rights. If the product is imported, it may be difficult to get jurisdiction over the defendant. Even if the defendant is brought to court, the resolution of the issue may involve unsettled legal questions about the interpretation of the directives and complex factual questions about the interpretation of the requirements.

If the product conformed to CE mark requirements and harmonized standards, but the standards are not adequate to protect public health, then the surveillance authorities can pull the product off the market on a temporary basis. However, DG Enterprise has to be notified about the action and informed about the justifications given for it. DG Enterprise is then responsible for assessing the adequacy of the standard in question. If the standard is found to be inadequate, then it will be withdrawn and work will be initiated to develop a replacement standard. Once the standard is withdrawn, then the conformity of all products built to that standard is called into question. See, for example, articles 6 and 8 of the *Pressure Equipment Directive* (European Council, 1997).

In reality, this option has rarely been used. Discussions as to whether a particular standard is adequate or inadequate have usually turned into broader debates over the provisions of the directive and the decisions made in the process of standards development.

The 'safeguard clause' provides the third basis for pulling a product off the market. Even if a product conforms to all CE mark requirements, and the effectiveness of the implementing standards is not questioned, a surveillance authority can still remove it from the market and out of service if it presents a clear and immediate safety hazard. The surveillance authority then has to notify the Commission about the action taken. Brussels, in turn, will notify the competent authorities in the other member states. In theory, the manufacturer of the product that has been removed from the market must have a right of appeal under local law.

In reality, the safeguard clause has been used frequently against products where the major issue concerns CE mark compliance and not immediate threats to public safety. When a product is removed from the market under the safeguard clause, the surveillance authority is acting under administrative authority derived from EU law rather than legal authority based on national law. The safeguard clauses in a number of the New Approach directives require the surveillance authorities to provide an appeals process. These are rarely effective. To challenge the legitimacy of the removal, the manufacturer would have to file suit against the offending surveillance authority in the European Court of Justice. This can be a lengthy and expensive process.

To review a decision by a surveillance authority to remove a product under the safeguard clause, Directorate General Enterprise generally refers the issue to the relevant AdCos. The de facto resolution of the issue comes when a guidance document 'clarifies' the interpretation of the relevant provisions of the governing directives. Again, this can take time.

The language of the safeguard clause in the New Approach directives suggests that the decision on whether the surveillance authorities have acted properly will be made and enforced by the Commission. In reality, this is a relatively hollow threat if the surveillance authorities choose to stand their ground. The only leverage the Commission has to force a reversal by a recalcitrant national agency would be to file suit against the offending government in the European Court of Justice. This is a slow process that can be costly in terms of money and political capital. This could also be a hard issue for the Commission to litigate. Any litigation would be likely to involve a factual issue; was the product in question unreasonably hazardous? The local authorities have the benefit of subsidiarity and are likely to have better access to technical expertise and the specific facts in the case.

In some situations, the surveillance authorities can also take the more extreme step of interpreting coverage of the relevant directives in a way that does not cover the product in question. The product then falls under national law, where it is likely to be non–compliant. The major example of this process, the Dormont Case, will be discussed in Chapter 7.

Several observers have reported that the clause has been more vigorously utilized by the French surveillance authorities, especially against Italian and German products. Some of the reported cases include;

- Banning the sale and use of battery powered laser pointers that had been approved by British notified bodies;
- Banning the sale and use of German luminaria on the basis of a suspected fire risk;
- Banning the sale and use of an Italian printing press that relied on Optical–electronic interlocks instead of using a failsafe mechanical system.

Since then, the French position has been incorporated into the harmonized standards that implement this essential requirement in the Machinery Directive.

- Barring the importation of an Italian washing machine that incorporated a heating element for the water supply.

The French authorities argued that the heating element serves to sterilize the system as well as to heat the water. Therefore, the machine should have been covered by the Medical Device Directive.

These actions may have reflected the state of the European economy in the late 1980s. The European Union had been in a recession since the mid–1980s. The French government had been following an expansionary economic policy that was creating inflationary pressures. The Italians devalued in 1985. This move significantly lowered the cost of Italian products on French markets and the Italian market share began to expand rapidly. France devalued the following year and the threat from Italian imports abated (Apel, 1998). From this perspective, the wave of safeguard clause cases initiated by the French may have reflected their need to stabilize their internal markets in the face of new Italian competition.

In recent years, the majority of safeguard cases have been used because of issues covered by the Low Voltage Directive. In part, this reflects the special rules governing the safeguard clause under the Low Voltage Directive. See Table 5.1.

Table 5.1. Safeguard actions by directives during 2000

Directive	Number of actions
Low Voltage	342
EMC	72
Gas appliances	17
Toys	4
Personal Protective Equipment	3
Machinery	2

Source: Directorate General Enterprise (2001).

The Commission only has to respond to a surveillance authority initiative under the LVD safeguard clause if some other state disagrees with the action taken. For the other directives, the Commission has to determine whether a safeguard action was appropriate, regardless of whether or not other states disagreed.

The tendency to invoke the safeguards clause under the LVD may also reflect the nature of electrical risks and the provisions of the directive. Products covered by the LVD that are built to the harmonized standards, IEC standards, CEE rules or equivalent national rules can be self–certified under module A. As a result, few machines are reviewed by notified bodies under the terms of the LVD. However, a poorly wired machine can create dangerous and unforeseeable risks for anyone who is in contact with it. This is in sharp contrast with, for example, mechanical risks, which tend to be local and highly visible.

6. HOW WELL IS THE SYSTEM WORKING?

Has the CE marking system provided a level of product safety that is at least as high as the prior system? This question is not settled. Some have argued that the overall standard of product safety under the CE marking system is significantly lower than it had been under the earlier national systems.

One problem has been the willingness of outside exporters, especially from East Asia, to flood European markets with unsafe products and then disappear. CE, some wags argue, stands for 'Chinese Exports'. This has been a particular problem with cheap imported toys and hand–held power tools. By the time the surveillance authorities have been placed on notice and have had an opportunity to review the products, they have generally been distributed too widely across the European Union for a recall order to be effective. Judicial procedures against the manufacturers, importers and/or authorized agents are ineffective if they can't be found and brought before the court.

This problem has led to discussions as to whether all exporters to the EU should be required to maintain an authorized representative with sufficient assets to ensure they can be held accountable for CE mark compliance. This problem is also one of the reasons given by the French for giving the French customs limited surveillance authority functions. The customs authorities would be the first government function to find out about a sudden surge of low cost imports from a suspicious source.

There are two official EU–wide databases that are intended to track safety discrepancies. The member states report all safety incidents involving consumer products through the RAPEX system. RAPEX was organized to implement the Product Safety Directive. It has been adopted for use with the CE marking system. Unfortunately, the accuracy and effectiveness of the RAPEX system has been handicapped by the lack of accurate and complete information from the EU member states. There are significant problems with different event definitions, inconsistent data formats and incomplete reporting. German officials, for example, are unhappy with the RAPEX system. It seems to show that their level of consumer protection is significantly lower than in the rest of Europe. They dismiss these findings with the observation that only Germany collects comprehensive information and reports it accurately.

There are similar issues with the medical device reporting system. Under the terms of the three medical device directives, manufacturers of CE marked medical devices are required to pass any information about medical incidents involving their products to their national regulatory authorities. The British have developed a somewhat different system; the reports are to be made by the doctors, clinics and hospitals that use the devices. This shift in policy has resulted in the development of a database that is both more accurate and more useful. A close analysis of the British data has shown that the conditions of use have a major impact on the level of risk presented by a medical device. The route to safer products may well be via better training and restrictions on use, and not through improvements in the medical products themselves.

Is the CE mark accepted in the European marketplace? Again, reviews are mixed. On one hand, many manufacturers are reporting that their European buyers are insisting on the CE mark, even if the product is not technically covered by the system. This is particularly true for companies manufacturing non–power household goods or components. Manufacturers may then look for some basis for claiming CE mark coverage in order to have their products accepted in the marketplace.

On the other hand, the implementation of the CE marking system has not significantly reduced the demand in many markets for other voluntary quality or safety markets. The French have tried to outlaw the use of any other marks on the grounds that they could be confused with the CE mark. The market support for other marks was too great and the effort failed. The CE mark is not well regarded in Germany as anything more than a legal requirement for placing goods on the market or putting them into use. Unless the identification number of a notified body is placed next to the CE mark logo, the product is assumed to have been self–certified by the manufacturer. In general, a product may also need a GS, VDE or other German safety and quality mark before anyone will buy it. The 'kitemark' has been successfully developed and marketed by BSI in virtually all EU countries outside Germany.

The demand for products bearing other safety marks reflects a widespread belief that many Germans regard the CE mark as offering a lesser degree of safety protection than the earlier German national regulatory system. Only products with the numerical designation of the reviewing notified body on the CE mark logo merit any trust. As a result, many Germans, both individuals and companies, insist that the products they buy also bear the German voluntary quality marks. Whether these requirements are truly 'voluntary' is sometimes open to question. In a few cases, the mandatory BG insurance system has refused to extend coverage to workplaces that use CE marked products that have not met the higher German quality standard requirements.

On the other hand, there does not seem to be any significant opposition to the CE marking system or credible calls for major revisions. The Commission placed a questionnaire on possible revisions to the CE marking system on the internet. The government of the UK developed a national response to the questionnaire on the basis of consultations with British stakeholders. The British reply supported the current system of conformity assessment modules, rejected any requirement for filing the technical file with an authorized representative or notified body, and generally supported the present system for market surveillance. The British government did call for tightening up the process for notifying and coordinating notified bodies. The present system for managing the safeguards clause was also criticized. Given the complexity of the CE marking system, these are relatively modest and predictable criticisms of the system.

REFERENCES

Apel, Emmanuel (1998), *European Monetary Integration: 1958–2002,* London: Routledge.

Atkinson, Dan (1998), 'Forgers toy with safety and EU plays possum', *The Guardian,* Manchester, 12 March, p. 24.

Directorate General Enterprise (2001), *Consultation Document Prepared by the Directorate General for Enterprise on the Review of the New Approach,* 13 December, Annex III.

European Commission (2000), *Guide to the Implementation of directives Based on the New Approach and the Global Approach* Luxembourg: European Commission.

European Commission (2003), *Communication from the Commission to the Council and the European Parliament: Enhancing the Implementation of the New Approach Directives,* Brussels 7.5.COM(2003) 240 final.

European Council (1993), *Decision Concerning the Modules for the Various Phases of the Conformity Assessment Procedures and the Rules for the Affixing and Use of the CE Conformity Marking,* 93/465/EEC.

European Council (1997), *Directive 97/23/EC of the European Parliament and of the Council of 29 may 1997 on the Approximation of the Laws of the Member States Concerning Pressure Equipment.*

6. The American System

There is a clear need in the United States for greater attention to standards. US Office of Technology Assessment (1992)

1. INTRODUCTION

The CE marking system is creating problems with international trade, not because it is an unreasonable solution to a very real problem, but because it is significantly different from the American system. To understand the processes that have contributed to these problems, we have to look at the larger contexts. Although fingers may be pointed at the differences in standards and conformity assessment requirements, the underlying problems have emerged because of the differences in the political climates and regulatory systems in the two regions.

To understand why CE marking may prove to be a stubborn barrier to further trade liberalization, we have to compare the contending systems of product regulation in the US and EU. The trade barriers, in short, reflect differences between two reasonable, but different, approaches to product safety and do not arise from any intent to clog the arteries of commerce. The convergence of the two systems will probably require changes in both. We should therefore look at the administrative responsiveness of the US system as well as the scope of the differences with the European practices.

2. AMERICAN REGULATORY SYSTEMS

The starting point for our comparisons is a discussion of the differences in the political contexts of standards development in Europe and the United States. The differences between the patterns developed for standards development and product regulation in the United States and European Union are a reflection of the major differences in the political contexts in which these systems have been developed.

The American political system is dominated by private interests, including business interests. The US system is characterized by a strong Congress and a comparatively weak president. The president cannot introduce legislation and his power to veto legislation he opposes is limited. The activities undertaken and funds spent by the executive must be approved by Congress. Regulations can only be issued under authority granted to the president (or cabinet) in legislation passed by Congress. The president may be obligated to spend funds approved by Congress for specific programs, even if he does not support the programs or expenditures.

Political parties are comparatively weak and interest groups are strong. Election outcomes are significantly influenced by the comparative successes of the candidates in fund raising. Most political funding comes, directly or indirectly, from organized interest groups (Beck, 1997, ch. 12). In this environment, business groups can expect to have the right to be heard on all major issues affecting their industry.

It is not uncommon for a president of one party to face a Congress that is controlled by the opposing party. When this happens, bureaucratic managers are likely to be more concerned about the support of key Congressional leaders than worry about the support of the White House.

Policy implementation at the Federal level is strongly limited by the scope of Congressional authorization. Under American constitutional law, the mandates for regulatory agencies at the Federal level have to be set by statute. The courts have generally been reluctant to recognize implied regulatory powers. As a result, the provisions of regulatory legislation are ultimately set by Congress, not the executive branch. Legislation policies are set through bargaining between the president and Congressional leaders. Unless the president has a close working alliance with Congressional leaders, his control over legislation can be surprisingly limited.

Most legislation delegates the authority to issue implementing regulations to the responsible agencies. New regulatory policies can be set through regulation, subject to two limitations. The regulations must fall within the scope of the enabling legislation, and the regulations must have been developed in accordance with the terms of administrative law. However, the degree of presidential control over regulatory initiatives depends on the scope of his control over the responsible agency.

The weakness of the presidency and the power of Congress have led to a system where regulatory powers are split between bureaucratic agencies and independent regulatory commissions. The president has less influence over the management of the independent regulatory commissions. The bureaucratic agencies include:

- The Occupational Health and Safety Administration
- The Environmental Protection Administration
- The Food and Drug Administration

The independent commissions include:

- The Federal Communications Commission
- The Consumer Product Safety Commission

The independent regulatory commissions are generally managed by a bi – partisan board. The president's right to appoint board members is limited by a system of fixed terms, a statutory requirement for political balance and the need for Senatorial approval. The president's latitude in making the nominations is somewhat limited. Congressional leaders often regard the independent regulatory commissions as 'theirs', in contrast to the cabinet agencies, which belong to the president. When nominating new members to the commissions, the usual principle is that a majority of the regulatory commission must be from the party that controls the Senate and a minority on the board should be nominated by the party out of power.

The American system is also based on the development of a strong, on–going system of legal checks on the activities of the regulatory agencies. Both presidential agencies and independent regulatory commissions are subject to two statutes, the Administrative Procedures Act (5 USC 550, et seq.) and the Freedom of Information Act (5 USC 1000, et seq.). These laws are at the heart of the American system for regulating public bureaucracies. The APA mandates transparency and accountability in regulatory decision–making. With this comes an enhanced degree of agency autonomy.

The Administrative Procedures Act sets firm guidelines for decision–making in regulatory commissions. Under the APA, government agencies can regulate by either issuing regulations or by adjudicating disputes under existing regulations. Our interest here is in the development of new product standards by a regulatory agency, which are likely to be issued in the form of new regulations.

Before an agency can issue a new regulation, a notice of proposed rule making must be published in the Federal register and interested parties must have an opportunity to comment on the proposed rule. A record must be kept of the proceedings. Although the agency does not have to respond to individual comments, the final rule must be based on 'substantial evidence in the record as a whole'. A Federal court, the Court of Appeals for the District of Columbia, has jurisdiction over cases brought by private citizens charging that a government agency has not lived up to the requirements of the APA (Hall, 2002).

The Freedom of Information Act (FOIA) provides a relatively high degree of transparency for outside groups in this process. The FOIA simply states that the public must have access to all government documents unless the issuing agency can show that they are covered by at least one of a limited list of exceptions. Documents that are developed in the course of program planning or evaluation are routinely made available to the public on request (Bridges and Village, 1992). However, the US government lags far behind the Europeans in making them available for free on the internet.

These factors have led to a system where policies are made piecemeal by quasi–independent agencies. The American regulatory environment is characterized by organizational fragmentation and relatively weak policy integration. Most regulatory issues are considered independently from other policy issues. On the other hand, the importance of interest groups, especially business interests, in the American political system tends to slow any rush to regulate. New regulatory policies tend to emerge when public pressure and/or social events make the need for regulation clear.

These factors have an impact on the weak coordination of regulatory policies in the US. The US system does not support the development of a centralized clearinghouse for regulatory policies, a function performed by DG Enterprise in the EU. The differences between the two systems can be illustrated by a comparison of the coverage of the New Approach directives and the jurisdictions of US regulatory agencies, see Table 6.1.

Table 6.1. US regulators and the New Approach directives

New Approach Directive	US regulator
Machinery	OSHA (some)
Low Voltage	OSHA, FCC
Electromagnetic Compatibility	FCC
Pressure Equipment	OSHA (some)
Packaging and Packaging Waste	Unregulated
Noise	OSHA (some)
Medical Devices	FDA
In–Vitro Diagnostic Medical Devices	FDA
Active Implantable Medical Devices	FDA
Construction Products	States (some)
Lifts	States (some)
Cableways	States (some)

Personal Protective Equipment	OSHA (some)
Explosive Atmospheres	Bureau Mines (some)
Civilian Explosives	Treasury
Simple Pressure Vessels	OSHA (some)
Recreational Craft	Coast Guard
Radio and Telephone Terminal Equipment	FCC
Non–Automatic Weighing Instruments	States (some)
Gas Fired Appliances	CPSC (some)
Toys	CPSC

Source: Author's notes.

It would be difficult to develop a comprehensive equivalent to the CE marking system in the United States. If applied to the US the CE marking system would cut across the regulatory boundaries of the Food and Drug Administration, the Federal Communications Commission, the Consumer Product Safety Commission, the Occupational Health and Safety Administration, and the Environmental Protection Administration. One program would not fit all of their different regulatory agendas.

These provisions have several effects on the development of technical regulations by US Federal regulatory agencies. On one hand, they ensure independence, transparency and a measure of public involvement in the process. On the other hand, it is very difficult for a president, or any one in the executive branch to coordinate regulatory decisions across agencies or to change the pattern of incremental policy development in any one agency. Not only is presidential authority over the independent regulatory agencies limited, agency policies are also buttressed by a dense network of legislation, court decisions and prior agency policies.

Major changes in regulatory policy usually involve the use of a blunt instrument, the passage of new legislation that significantly changes the scope and process of agency decision–making. Efforts to deregulate the transportation industry, for example, eventually led to the abolition of both the Interstate Commerce Commission and the Civil Aeronautics Board.

Federalism further complicates the American regulatory landscape. Presidential power over the development of regulatory policies and product standards at the state level is even weaker than at the Federal level. The Tenth Amendment explicitly states that all powers not formally delegated in the Constitution to the Federal authorities are reserved for the states or for the people. As a practical matter, the regulation of construction codes and, to a lesser extent, workplace safety is largely in the hands of the states.

Article 3.2 of the Constitution gives Congress the power to 'regulate the commerce among the several states and with foreign nations'. The scope of this 'commerce clause' was greatly expanded in the civil rights decisions of the 1960s. However, it has not been used often to overturn patterns of state business regulation. To overturn a state regulation under the commerce clause, a lawsuit has to be filed. For the suit to succeed, the courts must find either that the state requirement unduly interferes with interstate commerce or that it is inconsistent with the express terms of a federal regulatory program.

The commerce clause has been used to overturn state product regulations from time to time. In *Bibb v. Navajo Freight Lines* (359 US 520, 1959), the Supreme Court struck down an Illinois state law that required all trucks on state roads to use a type of mud flap that was manufactured by an Illinois company. In *Kassel v. Consolidated Freightways* (450 US 662, 1981), the Court invalidated a state law that regulated the maximum length of trucks. The Supreme Court ruled that North Carolina could not prevent produce dealers from handling apples shipped in containers that listed the Washington state apple grade classification (*Hunt v. Washington State Apple Advertising Mission* 432 US 333, 1977). Similarly, Arizona could not force food brokers handling locally grown cantaloupes to use only state marked containers (*Pike v. Bruce Church, Inc.* 397 US 137, 1970). Litigation, however, is a difficult approach to changing state technical requirements. See Massey (2001) and Bland (1993).

The process of product regulation in the United States is further complicated by a system of strong courts and a vigorous tort bar. The availability of contingency fees and broad rights of pre–trial discovery, coupled with a willingness to accept class action suits and punitive damages, has encouraged plaintiffs to sue manufacturers for injuries caused by product defects.

As a result, the product liability insurers often have a strong incentive to reduce tort claims by mandating the application of product safety standards as a condition for insurance coverage. Organizations such as the National Fire Protection Association have focused their efforts on regulating building codes and construction products. Underwriters Laboratory, which was also founded by a consortium of insurance companies, focuses primarily on electrical and fire safety for consumer and industrial products. These standards tend to be developed and applied to specific categories of standardized products that are potentially risky and/or widely used, such as materials and components.

All of the parties that are involved in bringing an unsafe product to market can be held jointly liable under US tort law for any injuries or damages. As a result, the distributors of consumer products and industrial components have an interest in making sure that the products they handle are safe. This is often managed by insisting that the products they carry meet industry standards and/or are certified as safe by respected certification agencies.

This system has consequences for the regulation of product safety. In general, the dominant business groups in the US political system prefer not to be regulated. As a result, the scope of government product regulation is generally limited to situations in which the need to protect the public welfare is manifest. Many products are essentially unregulated. Instead, public complaints about defective or unsafe products tend to be resolved through litigation between individual consumers and manufacturers. However, larger manufacturers of high risk products often accept public regulation, both as a defense against the costs and uncertainties of litigation and to discourage the emergence of new competitors. The on–going sagas of the US tobacco and asbestos litigation provide illustrations of these processes at work.

These factors have contributed to the development of a fragmented system for product regulation. Regulatory requirements in the US can be vigorous for products such as medical devices in which the long term probabilities of adverse public attention and expensive lawsuits are high. Regulation is likely to be more gentle for products such as telecommunications equipment, in which public attention is likely to be limited and the threat of expensive product liability lawsuits is comparatively minor.

Many smaller manufacturers of products that are not subject to direct regulation may not have to consider conformity to technical requirements or the use of standards in the design and development of their products. Many smaller companies specialize in manufacturing one or two versions of a particular product for a single customer. These 'job shops' often design and build products without any serious reference to the use of standards. This does not mean that their designs are not safe. In most cases, product safety standards and technical requirements have been incorporated into their products through the use of approved materials and components. On the other hand, it does mean that many smaller manufacturers are unfamiliar with the use of standards and compliance with conformity assessment requirements. A simple lack of familiarity with the general use of standards and conformity assessment procedures is a major source of difficulty with CE marking for many smaller manufacturers.

Even where a product is covered by, for example, UL certification, the process for review and approvals is different from the system used in the EU. Organizations such as UL and ASME are involved in both standards development and in conformity assessment. UL controls the use of the UL logo; companies are not permitted to use the UL logo until their products have been tested and their production systems have been evaluated by UL. Because UL controls the process, the criteria that the company must meet and the procedures are clearly specified by UL. This is substantially different from the CE marking system where the manufacturer is ultimately responsible for complying with the broad requirements set forth in the directives. This difference between the two systems in the level of responsibility on the manufacturer has also created problems for US manufacturers.

3. DEVELOPING STANDARDS IN THE US

Inadequate support for the standards setting process will have detrimental effects. US Office of Technology Assessment 1992.

The differences in the regulatory climates of the United States and the European Union have an impact on the ways in which standards are developed and enforced in the two regions. There are several major differences between the US and EU systems of standards development. One difference is the number of organizations involved in standards development and the range of their activities. In Europe, standards development is generally dominated by one or two lead standards organizations. The emergence of CEN, CENELEC and ETSI at the European level has led to a significant shift in the activity of national standards development organizations. At the national level, there are few independent or subordinate standards development organizations. Few standards are developed for general use, for example, outside of DIN in Germany, BSI in the UK or AFNOR in France.

In contrast, the American standards development system is characterized by a proliferation of independent standards development organizations. Most American standards organizations have their roots firmly in the private sector, where they were organized to meet a wide range of business interests. There are over 300 members of the American National Standards Institute. Although most US standards are developed by ten leading SDOs, most of the ANSI members are involved in standards development in some capacity.

The development of standards and conformity assessment programs was pioneered in the United States, Great Britain and Germany at the beginning of the twentieth century for a number of reasons.

Public safety provided a major impetus for the development of product standards in the United States. Boiler explosions posed a major risk for the transportation of goods and people in the mid–eighteenth century. This led to Federal inspection of the materials used to make boilers that powered river steamers in interstate service. This forced a degree of standardization on a frequently unwilling industry. The American Iron and Steel Institute, which was organized in 1852, was the first trade association to develop standards (Zuckerman, 1997). The effectiveness of firefighting efforts during the Great Baltimore Fire of 1904 was impeded by inconsistent standards. The threads on the hoses used by out–of–town fire companies were not compatible with the threads on Baltimore fire hydrants (Hemingway, 1975).

Competitive forces in the emerging markets of the industrial revolution also contributed to the development of standards in the US. Auto manufacturers, for example, needed ways to summarize requirements for materials and components. The car companies also shared interests in lowering costs through the mass production of standardized components. The steel industry resisted further standardization in order to protect company markets. The professional engineering association for the automobile industry, the Society of Automotive Engineers, developed the needed product standards. The car manufacturers were able to force the steel industry to accept the standards through their purchase contracts. As a result, the car manufacturers could force the steel companies to compete for the fight to sell the same product, as defined by the specifications in the steel standards. By 1921, standardization is estimated to have led to a 30 per cent cost reduction in ball bearings and electrical equipment and a 20 per cent drop in the cost of steel. (Hemingway, 1975).

These same interests led to standardization in the railroad industry. The legacy of these efforts is visible today. ASTM International (formerly the American Society for Testing and Materials), was organized in 1898 as the product testing department for the Pennsylvania Railroad (Krislov, 1997).

The development of the engineering profession led to the rapid growth in research on the parameters determining product performance and durability. Engineers faced with the task of designing, for example, a new radiator or a new wheel have a strong incentive to draw on the lessons learned from past radiator or wheel designs. Research and development issues also emerged as the rapid expansion of the railroad industry and rising boiler pressures led to increased risks of boiler explosions. These factors led to the need to expand and formalize the training and practice requirements for engineers. This led to the organization of the American Society for Mechanical Engineers in 1880, the Institute of Electrical and Electronic Engineers in 1884 and the Society of Automotive Engineers in 1905. Not surprisingly, all three societies also became involved in developing standards for their respective professions.

The Federal government has also pushed for the development of standardization in the US. The US Office of Weights and Measures was organized in 1882. This led to the formation of the National Bureau of

Standards (now the National Institute for Science and Technology) in 1901. President Hoover, a trained engineer, pushed for the development of standardization as a tool for promoting cost reductions and economic development. (Hemingway, 1975, p. 88; Krislov, 1997).

World War II provided an additional incentive for the organization of standards development organizations. New standards had to be developed by the military to meet the rapid pace of technological development and the unique durability and quality requirements of modern warfare. The US government has been responsible for the development of over half of the estimated 94 000 standards that have been developed in the US. The US Department of Defense and the General Services Administration have developed the bulk of these standards for procurement purposes (Zuckerman, 1997, p. 30).

In more recent times, American trade associations have taken the lead in developing compatibility, performance and safety standards in specific industries. The list includes such groups as:

The American Petroleum Institute
American Iron and Steel Institute
Aerospace Industries Association of America
National Electrical Manufacturers Association
National Concrete Masonry Association
Toy Manufacturers of America
United States Cutting Tool Association
Telecommunications Industry Association
Electronic Industry Alliance

The list of public standards development organizations in the US also includes a number of professional associations. This list includes groups such as:

American Academy of Ophthalmology
Institute for Electrical and Electronics Engineers
American Association for Quality
American Society of Mechanical Engineers
(American National Standards Institute, 2003b)

Many of the compatibility standards that are widely used in the US have been developed by private manufacturers. For example, computer software standards such as MSdos, CPM and UNIX were developed by computer and telecommunications companies for private and, in some cases, public use. These companies are generally not members of ANSI.

This proliferation of independent standards development organizations in the US has an impact on the American pattern of conformity assessment. Each association has tended to develop a separate set of conformity assessment requirements that are based on the specific interests of the industry and the nature of the task. Since there is no automatic public enforcement of standards conformity assessment requirements, American SDOs have to develop their own means for enforcement. Where standards conformity commands a market premium, American SDOs have been able to sell the right to use their logo for use on conforming products. Manufacturers that need to have the UL logo on their products can contract with Underwriters Laboratory for product review and approval. UL will provide their clients with the relevant standards. This will be followed up with product tests, process inspections and periodic audits. If the products comply with the UL standards, then Underwriters Laboratory will give permission for the manufacturer to use the UL logo.

There is also a wide variance in the commercial interests of American SDOs. For most trade associations, standards development is only one element in a broad mix of services that are provided to the association members. Most trade associations are funded in large part by fees and membership dues. They do not, in general, depend heavily on revenues from the sale of standards to support the organization.

Other organizations, such as UL and ASME, have lucrative programs for certification and conformity assessment. Controlling the development and use of their standards is generally an important consideration for these organizations, since these set the requirements for certification and conformity assessment.

However, some American organizations are very dependent on the sale of standards to cover their budgets. ASTM International, for example, develops standards in a very wide range of products and attributes, including the classification, testing and evaluation of materials. This is a critical function. The development efforts of other organizations are often based in part on the work of ASTM in defining materials characteristics. Since ASTM International does not have a separate membership base or funding from services, it relies heavily on the sale of standards for organization funding.

The American National Standards Institute (ANSI) is the umbrella organization for the development of standards in the US. ANSI has been designated by the US Department of Commerce as the US representative at the national and international levels. ANSI is the US member for ISO and IEC. Most US members of ISO technical committees are recruited through ANSI.

ANSI does not develop standards. However, it can review and accept members' standards for inclusion in the ANSI standards portfolio. ANSI standards can then be forwarded to Geneva for consideration and adoption as an international ISO or IEC standard. However, ASTM International, ASME and IEE also maintain separate representation at the international level.

The largest source of income for ANSI comes from the sale of member standards that have been forwarded and accepted as ANSI standards as well. ANSI members that are dependent on revenues from the control or sale of standards have a strong incentive to keep them in–house. As a result, the relations between ANSI and the member organizations may, from time to time, become relatively competitive (US Office of Technology Assessment, 1992).

4. INDUSTRY, GOVERNMENT AND STANDARDIZATION

In a sharp contrast to the European pattern, the relations between government and SDOs in the US are both tenuous and tangled. Although President Hoover was an enthusiastic advocate of standards development and standardization, the effort largely died out by the Depression. Government efforts in standards development was then revived for the purposes of government procurement during World War II.

A few Federal agencies are directly concerned with standards development in the US. NIST, the National Institute for Science and Technology in the US Department of Commerce, is concerned with standards development at several levels. NIST is involved directly in metrology research. The results of NIST research have a direct impact on the precise definition of weights and measures in the US. It is also the US agency that is the most closely involved in efforts to promote the development of US industry. NIST has also chartered ANSI as the official US standards representative. However, NIST does not have a broad international advocacy role.

The United States Trade Representative is charged with negotiating and monitoring government–to–government trade related agreements. The USTR is involved whenever standards become an issue in international trade agreements. However, the office is not involved in the broad range of private sector activities in which standards are more likely to become an issue.

A major point of entanglement between private standards developers and public agencies in the United States emerges in the increasing tendency for Federal agencies to use private standards for public regulation and government procurement. The annual procurement budgets for the US Department of Defense and the General Services Administration are massive. In 2002, the two agencies spent an estimated $60 billion on public procurement. Traditionally, both agencies have developed proprietary standards for the procurement process that are designed to meet specific and unique government needs. To meet these needs, the two agencies have developed an estimated 40 000 standards as a part of their government procurement programs.

However, the costs associated with standards development can be substantial. While the use of specialized standards may lead to procurement of goods with unique qualities, the process of developing specialized standards is lengthy and expensive. Furthermore, the use of unique standards limits market choices, raises the costs of procurement and complicates the process of producing conformity products.

The Department of Defense and the General Services Administration began using private standards in an effort to lower procurement costs and expand the pool of potential vendors. The National Technology Transfer and Advancement Act (NTTAA, Public Law 104–113 of 7 March 1996) directs Federal agencies to use private standards for public purposes and to participate in standards development whenever feasible. Specific agency obligations are spelled out in OMB Circular A–119 (Office of Management and Budget, 2000). The Interagency Committee on Standards Policy coordinates Federal agency participation in standards utilization and development activities.

The overall impact of the NTTAA on Federal standards utilization has been significant. According to the 2000 Annual Report, US Federal government agencies used 5453 private voluntary standards for public purposes during the 1999–2000 fiscal year. Government agencies participated in 885 private consensus standards development bodies. On a closer examination though, the use of consensus standards has been largely limited to areas in which government standards have not yet been developed. According to the *Fourth Annual Report* (Office of Management and Budget, 2000) private consensus standards have been used as replacement for 537 existing public standards. However, the Department of Defense was responsible for 509 of these substitutions. The major regulatory agencies, such as the Federal Communications Commission, the Occupational Safety and Health Administration, the Consumer Product Safety Commission and the Environmental Protection Administration have been reluctant to use private standards in place of existing requirements.

The Consumer Product Safety Commission, for example, regulates the safety of consumer products and toys. The CPSC has developed regulatory standards for very few products. Instead, they rely heavily on industry self – regulation. However, they seem to be ambivalent about the process. Although CPSC representatives regularly sit on the technical committees (usually in ASTM International) that are developing relevant standards, they rarely vote on the draft standards. This approach provides the CPSC with greater latitude in deciding whether or not to adopt a particular standard as the basis for product regulation once the standard has been released for public use in final form. The Occupational Safety and Health Administration (OSHA) has also relied on standards developed in the private sector instead of developing public requirements.

The use of private standards for public purposes has an effect on the process of standards development. Many standards development organizations have offered membership to government agencies and have recruited government representatives for participation on the relevant technical committees. However, public participation has been relatively limited. Twenty six government agencies are listed as members of ANSI. At the Federal level, the list includes such agencies as:

Environmental Protection Administration
Food and Drug Administration
National Institute for Science and Technology
US Department of Energy
US Coast Guard
US Department of the Interior
US Maritime Administration
US Department of Veterans Affairs

The source of this list is the ANSI website (www.ansi.org). Notably absent from the list of ANSI members are regulatory agencies such as:

Consumer Product Safety Commission
Occupational Health and Safety Commission
Federal Communications Commission

The relations between government regulators and the US standards development organizations are also tangled in the area of building codes and the development of construction product standards. Construction products have to be consistent with building codes; building codes, in turn, are enacted by state and local governments. In most instances, state and local building codes are based on model codes. There are three model building codes that are widely used in the United States. The codes have been developed by the Southern Building Codes Congress, the Building Officials and Code Administrators Association and the International Conference of Building Officials. Other groups such as the National Fire Prevention Association have developed model codes that address specific issues such as fire and electrical safety. Local codes are usually based on one of the model codes, with variations to reflect local needs and political realities.

The regional building code councils are the major customers for the building product certification organizations, not the manufacturers of the products. A building product certifier that is able to maintain a reputation as the most rigorous review organization is likely to be approved in the largest number of jurisdictions and will, in effect, have a captive market. Organizations such as UL and Factory Mutual (an insurance company) have been able to meet competition from new certifying organizations by continually raising the level of technical sophistication of their product reviews. The construction product manufacturers may not resist these efforts to raise industry safety standards. Higher manufacturing costs are often counterbalanced by limitations to competition from raising the barriers to market entry. Many of these standards development and conformity assessment organizations have also earned a reputation for being slow, expensive and difficult.

Underwriters Laboratory has perhaps 65 per cent of the market for the safety certification of stand–alone electrical equipment in the United States. UL approval includes all aspects of the process from initial standards development to final conformity assessment. In effect, a manufacturer provides UL with a product and a check. UL will test the product for compliance and review the company's quality control operations. If both pass, the UL will then sell the logos to the company for use on the approved products. UL will periodically test product samples and inspect the factory to make sure that UL standards are maintained. Companies will hire UL to certify their products because the OSHA, many state labor departments and most insurance companies mandate the use of UL approved products.

Building codes may be adopted at the state, county or municipality levels. A customary pattern is to start with a model code and amend it to meet local construction and political requirements. The choice of a specific building code can have a significant impact on the interests of product manufacturers, trade unions and construction companies. It is not uncommon for product manufacturers, construction firms and building trade unions to lobby for special provisions in the regional building code.

The American standards establishment has been hit by a series of legal challenges in the last 30 years. In the early 1970s, the Federal Trade Commission raised the question as to whether the customary process of standards development constitutes an illegal restraint on trade. In effect, the process of standards development involves the close collaboration of representatives from a relatively small number of major manufacturers for the purpose of defining product attributes that are expected to be adopted industry–wide. The National Fire Prevention Association successfully argued that the industry representation was needed because they had the data and expertise and that the process involved the virtual representation of far wider range of community interests.(Dixon, 1978).

More recently, the Fifth Circuit Court of Appeals has challenged the system for using private standards for public purposes in *Veeck v. Southern Building Code Congress* (2002 US App. LEXIS 10963). The Texas towns of Ana and Savoy had mandated the use of a building code developed by the Southern Building Code Congress for new construction. Veeck had placed parts of the code on the internet and the Southern Building Code Congress sued him for copyright violation.

The Court ruled in Veeck's favor. The model Code had become the equivalent of a law when it was adopted by the two towns since it provided the basis for evaluating construction permits and inspections. There can be no private property rights in a public law. As a result, Southern Building Code Congress has lost their copyright interests in the model code. The US Supreme Court has refused to hear an appeal, so the Veeck case stands as Federal law. The long–term consequences of the Veeck decision for the development of building codes and construction product standards in the US is not clear.

The anti–competitive implications of this policy have been addressed by opening up the market to products that have been certified in accordance with any acceptable set of standards and conformity assessment requirements. This has led to a market environment that encourages a meticulous review of products and the continuing development of technically sophisticated standards.

5. THE FUTURE OF US STANDARDIZATION

There are other factors that may compel changes in the American system. The proliferation of standards–setting groups and the development of international standards through ISO and the IEC has weakened industry support and funding for developing standards at the national level. These factors point to a continuing problem with the coordination, financing and representation of the standards development community in the United States.

Standards development is a very expensive process. The costs are generally borne by the employers of the members of technical committees that are actually engaged in the work of standards development. TC participants may have to devote perhaps a quarter of their time for several years developing a new standard. The travel costs associated with standards development are often significant. Many companies are unwilling to make this investment unless they have an immediate need for the development of a new standard or the revision of an existing one.

The interests of the standards development organizations have a strong impact on these dynamics. Virtually all of them have a strong interest in maintaining the independence and viability of their organizations. However, the ways in which these interests will be translated into policy preferences will depend on their market interests. SDOs, such as ASTM International, that are only engaged in the standards business have a strong interest in promoting the creativity and viability of the American standards establishment. However, their ability to cooperate is often limited by competition for revenues from the sale of standards.

The SDOs that are backed by insurance companies, trade associations or professional organizations are generally less dependent on revenues from the sale of standards or the certification of compliance with existing standards. However, the power of their organized constituencies can also make it difficult for them to cooperate with other groups to promote the common good.

Behind these problems lies a more fundamental problem: American business and government agencies can generally select from a wide range of American standards. The portfolio of standards that are available for public use (for a fee) in the United States is sufficiently diversified that companies and government regulators are generally able to find something that fits their needs. If existing standards are not exactly right, then companies may modify them until they become more useful. As a result, managers have less incentive to participate vigorously in the standards development process. Since the costs of standards development are generally spread across many companies, individual companies may feel that their reluctance to participate will have little impact on the system as a whole. As a result, American businesses and government agencies have little incentive to support the on-going task of standards development and modernization.

The policy of using private standards to achieve public regulatory goals has helped give some order to the highly decentralized American system of conformity assessment. Laboratories and test houses are free to open their doors to the public without having to meet any licensing requirements or demonstration of technical competences. However, several laboratory accreditation systems have been developed in order to meet the need for competent review of compliance with public requirements. The leading private group is A2LA, the American Association for Laboratory Accreditation. NIST, The National Institute of Standards and Technology in the US Department of Commerce, is sponsoring NVLAP, the National Voluntary Laboratory Accreditation Program. Both A2LA and NVLAP require accredited laboratories to be certified to the ISO 17000 series of standards. These are the same basic requirements that the European notified bodies have to meet.

6. SOME OBSERVATIONS IN LIEU OF A CONCLUSION

In short, the distinctive features of the US standards development establishment are shared by three factors; the weakness of ANSI, the importance of the industry constituents to the ANSI member organizations, and the competing commercial interests of the member organizations. Ties between government policy–makers and the US standards establishment are weak. ANSI is largely powerless. The standards development organizations are mindful of the regulatory agencies that adopt private standards for public use. However, the regulatory agencies often lack the technical expertise and/or the manpower needed to have a significant impact on the process of standards development.

With these factors as a background, we can now consider how the CE mark has affected US exports to the EU, how US requirements have impeded European exports to the US and what has been done on both sides to address these issues.

REFERENCES

American National Standards Institute (2003a), *A National Standards Strategy for the United States,* Washington: ANSI.
American National Standards Institute (2003b), ANSI membership, at www.ansi.org.
Beck, Paul (1997), *Party Politics in America, 8th ed,* New York: Longman.
Bland, Randell (1993), *Constitutional Law in the United States (re ed.),* San Francisco: Austin and Winfield.
Bridges, Mark and Tiffany Village (1992), *Justice Department Guide to the Freedom of Information Act* Buffalo: Hein.
Dixon, Robert Jr. (1978), *Standards Development in the Private Sector: Thoughts on Interest Representation and Procedural Fairness,* Boston: National Fire Prevention Association.
Hall, Daniel (2002), *Administrative Law in a Bureaucracy, 2nd,* Upper Saddle River, NJ: Prentice Hall.
Hemingway, David (1975), *Industry–wide Voluntary Product Standards,* Cambridge, MA: Ballinger.
Krislov, Samuel (1997), *How Nations Choose Product Standards and Standards Change Nations*, Pittsburgh: University of Pittsburgh Press.

Massey, Calvin (2001), *American Constitutional Law: Powers and Liberties* Gaithersburg, MD: Aspen Law and Business.

National Technology Transfer and Advancement Act, Public Law 104 –113 of 7 March 1996.

Office of Management and Budget (2000), *Fourth Annual Report on Federal Agency Use of Voluntary Consensus Standards: Implementation of Public Law 104–113 and OMB Circular A–119 for the Period of 1 October 1999 through 30 September 2000.*

U.S. Office of Technology Assessment (1992), *Global Standards; Building Blocks for the Future,* Washington: OTA.

Veeck v. Southern Building Code Congress (2002 US App. LEXIS 10963).

Zuckerman, Amy (1997), *International Standards Desk Reference; Your Passport to World Markets ISO 9000, CE Mark, QS—9000, SSM, ISO 1400, Q 9000, American, European and Global Standards Systems,* New York: Amacom, p. 32.

7. Dueling Standards

1. AND THE IMPACT ON TRADE IS. . . ?

In 2002, US merchandise exports to the EU were worth $143.7 billion while US imports from the EU had a value of $226.1 billion. The 2002 trade deficit of $82.4 billion reflected a 34 per cent increase over the 2001 deficit of $61.3 billion.

The Office of the United States Trade Representative is responsible for negotiating international trade agreements on behalf of the president. Every year, the USTR makes a report to Congress on foreign barriers to US exports, including in the European Union. In the *2002 Report on Foreign Trade Barriers. European Union* the USTR's office emphasized the impact of the CE marking system on US exports to the EU.

> As traditional trade barriers . . . have declined in recent years, specific trade obstacles arising from unnecessary divergences of US and EU regulations and the lack of transparency in the EU rulemaking and standardization process have loomed relatively larger in importance . . .

> A number of problems . . . continue to impede US exports. These include: delays in the development of EU standards, delays in drafting harmonized legislation, inconsistent application and interpretation by EU Member States of legislation, overlap among Directives dealing with specific product areas, gray areas between the scope of various directives; and, in some cases, reliance on design–based, rather than performance–based, standards. In addition, there are concerns related to the respective procedures, responsibilities . . . and transparency in both the Commission and the European standards bodies that require careful monitoring and more frequent advocacy efforts. (United States Trade Representative, 2003, p. 111)

We therefore come back to the original question: does CE marking create trade barriers for US exporters interested in European markets?

2. CE MARKING AS A COST OF DOING BUSINESS

The author is affiliated with CITRA, the Center for International Regulatory Assistance at Duquesne University. In our experience, the costs for CE marking relatively simple products can vary from $5000 to over $50 000. The costs of compliance are far lower for manufacturers that have designed to European requirements from the beginning rather than trying to rework a product that has been designed and built to US standards.

Chapter 1 cited the results of a survey on the impact of CE on US exporters that was carried out on smaller Pennsylvania manufacturers. The results of that survey should now be examined in more detail. We asked 1445 Pennsylvania exporters to assess their experiences with CE marking. We received 145 useful responses, mostly from smaller businesses. The impact of CE marking was very real. The average exporting manufacturer reported that problems with CE mark compliance cost them $383 580 in lost sales, an average of 15 per cent of their export markets. The estimated total loss of $241 272 000 for all Pennsylvania exporters paralleled an observed decline of $184 812 000 in Pennsylvania exports to the EU in 1999, at a time when Pennsylvania exports to other major markets were rising. (Hanson and McKinney, n.d.). A senior international trade executive in Pennsylvania state government attributed this drop largely to CE marking problems (Cranville, 1999).

The biggest problem cited by the respondents was a lack of information on CE mark requirements. In the author's experience, this is not just a problem faced by smaller and medium–sized enterprises; project managers from large multinational corporations have also come to CITRA asking for help on CE marking. In part, this unfamiliarity with the CE marking process stems from the differences between the most commonly used conformity assessment processes in the US and EU. Where conformity assessment procedures are required by UL, for example, the assessing agencies tend to take control of the whole process. The CE marking process in Europe, as we discussed in Chapter 3, is characterized by a much stronger reliance on partnerships that give the manufacturer more control, and more responsibility, for the process. American manufacturers, in short, are less likely to have learned how to deal with European style certification requirements from their experiences in producing products for domestic markets.

Another piece of evidence tends to support the conclusion that a lack of information about CE marking is a major problem for US exporters interested in European markets. The responses to the 'magnitude of the problem' and 'lack of information' questions were strongly bimodal. This result is consistent with the explanation that companies tend to have far fewer difficulties with CE marking once they have successfully gone through the process once. However, we are not able to differentiate between the responses of first time European exporters and experienced old hands so this remains an intriguing, but unproven, conclusion.

The importance of this 'lack of information' issue was not the only conclusion to come from the study. Respondents also cited problems with CE mark certification. A path analysis suggested that this was an independent cause of the loss of export revenues. A closer look at the antecedents to the market loss split the cause about evenly between increased costs and declining sales. Either way, conforming to CE marking requirements was costing these exporters significant amounts of money.

To a large extent, CE marking compliance is a capital cost rather than a marginal cost of doing business. The costs of CE marking depend strongly on the complexity or the product and the risks it presents. Unlike, for example, the charges for ocean transportation or border tariffs, these costs are essentially independent of the volume sold. This observation is less valid for the costs of conformity assessment. Developing and certifying an acceptable quality control system is likely to be more expensive for plants with a greater production volume than for smaller factories. However, these are only a part of the total costs of compliance.

The costs of CE marking are likely to have a greater impact on smaller manufacturers than on larger companies. According to the OECD, the average cost of product certification is $39 000. This can be a very significant investment for a company with, for example, gross revenues of $2 000 000 and $100 000 in liquid reserves. On the other hand, Motorola is reported to have gone through CE marking for 135 related products at a total cost of approximately $1 000 000. For a company of this size, this is an inconsequential amount (Zuckerman, 1997a, p. 214). They probably spend more every year on coffee.

The SEMI study on the costs of CE marking in the electronic chip industry is revealing. On average, US manufacturers spend $109 000 to CE mark a new product. Testing costs an average of $46 000, consulting fees average $30 000 and notified body services cost $26 000. Translating the product manual costs a little over $7000 (Haystead, 1998).

3. CE MARKING AS A TRADE BARRIER

There are four probable culprits in these costs. EU program administrators could be implementing the CE mark program in ways that discriminate against US exporters, the New Approach directives may impose product requirements that are not faced by American manufacturers building for domestic markets, the costs could be due to the differences between US and EU standards and/or US companies have difficulty with EU conformity assessment requirements.

The Dormont Manufacturing case is the classic example of reinterpreting the CE marking system to limit imports from the United States. Dormont Manufacturing, a small company in Export, Pennsylvania, makes gas line hose connections that are widely used in the US for commercial ovens, stoves, deep fat fryers and other commercial kitchen equipment.

The traditional method for installing a gas fired appliance is to have a skilled worker braise a permanent black iron or copper connecting pipe to gas piping in the wall and to the connection point on the appliance. The Dormont connector features a threaded collar that attaches to the gas line coming out from the wall and to the appliance. A flexible braided steel hose connects the two collars to supply gas from the wall to the appliance. The hose is attached to the collars with a coupling that can be quickly disconnected with a twist.

The Dormont gas connector has several major advantages over the traditional system. A gas appliance can be installed by simply screwing the two connections to the gas pipe and to the appliance and then connecting them. The Dormont gas connector also makes it far easier to maintain the gas appliance and the surrounding areas. Because of the flexible steel hose, the appliance can simply be pulled away from the wall without having to disconnect it. Finally, it is far easier to disconnect the appliance by twisting the connectors than having to cut a rigid pipe or undo a braised joint. No credible questions have ever been raised about the safety, reliability or durability of the Dormont connector in comparison with the use of rigid piping and braised connections.

Dormont Manufacturing went through the CE mark process for the connector under the Gas Fired Appliance directive and began to ship the connectors to the EU. Euro Disney was being built outside Paris in the late 1980s and Dormont sold hundreds of connectors for use in the restaurants and concession stands. However, the plumbers' unions refused to attach the connectors. The French government looked into the issue.

Their decision was based on an interpretation of the Gas Fired Appliance Directive (European Council, 1990). The surveillance authorities argued that the Gas Fired Appliance Directive only covered the appliance itself. Connectors were not part of the appliance. They were therefore not covered by the directive, and so came under national law. In France, national law required the use of braised black iron pipes for connecting gas appliances to gas sources. The Dormont connectors were not in conformity and therefore could not be used in France.

The CEO of Dormont Manufacturing quickly raised the issue with the head of section in DG Enterprise. He was verbally assured that the directive was intended to cover both the coupling and the appliance, that the French surveillance authorities were wrong and that the use of the Dormont connectors in the EU was perfectly legal. Unfortunately, no one in DG Enterprise would put this opinion in writing. The French interpretation was never reversed despite serious pressure from the US mission to the EU. At one point, the Dormont case was taken up by the US Trade Representative.

Ultimately, the Dormont Manufacturing situation was handled in DG Enterprise as a safeguard clause issue. After the lengthy review, the AdCo concluded that the Dormont connector was potentially unsafe because of the type of threading used at each end of the connector. The Gas Fired Appliance Directive was then amended to explicitly state that connectors are excluded from coverage.

CEN has been developing a design–based harmonized standard for gas connectors that will exclude the Dormont connector. In the words of the United States Trade Representative:

> The U.S. manufacturer has experienced considerable difficulties in gaining access to the standardization process, and has been unsuccessful in countering assertions by the CEN Technical Committee that only fixed/welded connections can be considered safe methods for gas hose connections. (USTR, 2001, p. 111)

Dormont Manufacturing has been able to enter a few national markets in the EU but the promise of the CE marking system for free access to the European integrated market has been denied to them.

The Dormont case has been cited repeatedly as an example of how Europeans can use CE marking issues to protect local markets (Zuckerman, 1997b; Aeppel, 1996). In reality, the outcome of the case probably says more about the strengths of national interest, the politics of standards development and the weaknesses of DG Enterprise than about any hidden motive to use CE marking to block American imports.

For one, the Dormont case started developing over ten years ago. No other horror stories have emerged to equal prominence since then. If this is the only 'worst case', then CE marking is not being widely used as a weapon to keep American exports out of European markets. Instead, the horror stories have generally focused on how the safeguards clause has been used by one European country to slow imports from another European country. Some examples were discussed in Chapter 5. A German government official once expressed surprise that Americans would think that the European governments were targeting them for protectionism. 'Don't flatter yourself' was the breezy comment. 'We are far more worried about being flooded by the French and Italians.'

The Dormont case also occurred in a specific context. There are plausible safety issues with the introduction of this new technology. From the broader perspective of US–EU trade relations, the international market for gas fired appliance connectors is relatively small. This may have contributed to the problem; plumbing connectors generally fall into the category of small, low value, high weight products that are rarely traded internationally. We would not expect to find a strong constituency for promoting international free trade in this industry. The difficulties that have been encountered in extending the CE mark system to cover wall plugs and in developing the building codes and standards needed to implement the Construction Product directive also illustrate this point.

The Dormont case emerged during the same general period that the French surveillance authorities used the safeguard clause to block a number of other products from Italy, Germany and the UK. From the perspective of the French government, the refusal of the union to install the connectors was probably a significant act. Euro Disney was the largest foreign investment in France and the government wanted to ensure that construction would not fall behind schedule. It is also likely that the government did not want to pick a fight with the unions on the eve of a presidential election. The French economy had been in a slump for several years. The socialist president, Francois Mitterrand, was running for re–election against his Gaullist premier, Jacques Chirac (Gordon, 1997).

Finally, the formal tools available to DG Enterprise to force the French government to reverse its position on the Dormont connectors were essentially limited to filing suit in the European Court of Justice. They would probably not file suit except on an important issue and they had strong backing from other Community members. Neither condition was met.

We may never know the details of French and Commission decision–making on the Dormont case. If this analysis is roughly correct though, the Dormont case should be seen as an illustration of the decentralized mode of decision–making in the CE marking system. It does not point to the emergence of any systematic protectionism in the EU. Finally, it suggests that there may be limits to what can be achieved through international negotiations to address trade difficulties posed by the CE marking system.

4. INTERNATIONAL DIFFERENCES IN STANDARDS

The next issue to consider is whether the differences between US and EU product safety requirements are, in general, likely to pose problems for US exporters to the EU. There are basic differences in the strategies for product safety. The New Approach directives require a manufacturer to design out the most serious risks as far as possible, to install safeguards where possible for the more serious residual risks and to use warnings to minimize minor risks. By implication, essential requirements that refer to risks that are not likely to be relevant for the product in question can be ignored.

In order to implement this requirement, companies building products to CE mark requirements have to develop a formal assessment of product safety risks. This is an express requirement in several directives and implied in the rest. In the US, this is a central tenent of good product safety engineering, but it is far from a requirement. In our experience, many project managers are thrown by the need to develop a formal product risk assessment, especially for well–established designs. An assessment may not have been carried out when the product was designed or the original assessment may have been lost in the files. If available, the original risk assessment may not be in a format that would meet the CE marking requirements. This problem of re–formatting the original product design documentation to meet CE marking requirements can be significant.

There are many areas in which the additional costs of meeting CE mark requirements are likely to be minimal because the differences between US and EU regulatory requirements and implementing standards are relatively minor. The differences between the US and EU standards depends significantly on the scope of the industry constituency for international trade.

Some industries, such as commercial shipping, are inherently international. Ship builders, owners and insurers have a strong interest in making sure that vessels that are qualified for service in one country will be able to carry cargoes to all other countries without being turned away as 'unsafe'. Governments also have a strong interest in ensuring that the ships that carry their cargoes and are admitted to their ports are safe, regardless of their flag or registry. Ship design and construction has been subject to government regulation for over a century. Initially, national regulations were generally based on the requirements established by the British marine insurance combine, Lloyd's of London. Since 1959, the safety requirements for international shipping have been coordinated by the International Maritime Organization, a UN affiliated inter–governmental organization. This legacy has an effect on the standards developed for the Recreational Craft Directive. There are few differences between these standards and the US equivalents developed by the American Bureau of Shipping.

Elevators (lifts) are another area in which there has been a general convergence of national standards. There are only a few global corporations manufacturing elevators. Most of the money in the elevator business is in the maintenance of installed elevators. The manufacturers have an interest in the harmonization of international elevator standards so that the same basic products can be used world–wide. Companies in the elevator maintenance business would like to limit their inventory requirements by promoting the global use of the same set of parts. As a result, there are few differences between the US standards governing elevators and the harmonized standards developed for the Lifts Directive.

There are relatively few differences between the European and US standards for medical devices. In fact, the respondents in our study manufacturing medical devices reported lower levels of difficulty than average with the CE marking system. This is an area in which everyone wants to have access to the most modern techniques and technology is developing at a rapid rate on both sides of the Atlantic. Furthermore, administrators in both regions have an interest in lowering medical costs through global buying. As a result, the major regulatory agencies in both regions have become involved in the harmonization of medical standards. This issue will be discussed in greater depth in the next chapter.

The differences between US and EU standards are also relatively minor in the telecommunications area. In Europe, these standards are issued to implement the Radio Telecommunications Terminal Equipment Directive. Again, this is a market that is characterized by a rapid pace of technological development and international sourcing.

However, there are significant differences between the US and EU standards for products covered by several critical directives. These include, for example, the Electromagnetic Compatibility Directive, the Low Voltage Directive, the Machinery Directive, the Pressure Equipment Directive, the Construction Product Directive and the Explosive Atmospheres Directive. With the exception of Construction Products and ATEX, these are the horizontal directives that have the broadest applicability.

Some of the differences between US and EU standards reflect differences in the intellectual frameworks governing standards development. The problems caused by one obvious difference are far from trivial. US products and standards are generally based on the old English imperial (non–metric) system while the rest of the world uses the metric system. These differences can make it difficult for a US manufacturer to restate product measurements in metric terms or to assess the equivalency of a US standard with a harmonized counterpart. A 'soft' conversion, where measurements are generously rounded off, is easy to develop. A 'hard' conversion of US measurements to their exact metric equivalents may involve many decimal places and can be far more difficult to develop and use. US manufacturers are likely to need hard conversions in order to prove the equivalencies of alternative standards or to reference a graph for product classification purposes in, for example, the Pressure Equipment Directive.

There are major differences between the industrial infrastructures used in the US and EU. American products, for example, generally run on 110 volt, 60 cycle line current. European power supplies are generally 50 cycle and between 220 and 240 volts. This difference is more than academic. The probabilities of being killed by an electrical shock at 220 volts are significantly higher than for a 110 volt shock. As a result, Europeans tend to regard electrical shock as a serious risk. Because of this, American manufacturers generally can't just add a step down transformer between the European power line and the American electrical device. To conform to CE marking requirements, American electrical equipment must be designed to handle European voltages and frequencies throughout.

Another difference is the fact that US power cables are more likely to be routed through shielded and grounded conduits than are power cables in Europe. Conduits provide significant protection against ignition in an explosive atmosphere. As a result, US standards governing the design and testing of equipment to be used in explosive atmospheres are significantly different from the standards used to implement the ATEX directive in the EU.

Another example is that American power companies generally put their residential and industrial customers on different lines. This limits the possibility that the industrial equipment will create interference that can affect the use of residential products. In Europe, there is a greater likelihood that both residential and industrial users will be on the same circuits.

Both the FCC and DG Enterprise regulate the level of electronic noise emitted by the types of products covered by the EMC directive (47 *Code of Federal Regulations* section 18.305). However, the Europeans have added the requirement that electronic and electrical products must limit the generation of line harmonics. The intent of this requirement is to limit the possibilities of emissions from industrial products interfering with other units. To comply with this requirement, American manufacturers may have to add an extra filter between the power line and the equipment. The costs of the component and the extra manufacturing steps can be significant; the costs of redesigning the housing to provide room for an extra component can be even more expensive.

Some of the differences between US and EU standards reflect differences in strategies for ensuring product safety. European standards developed for the Pressure Equipment Directive, for example, are based on the use of thin vessel walls, tighter tolerances on materials, highly stressed welds and radiographic testing. In comparison, pressurized bottles for gases and liquids built under the American ASME Pressure Vessel Code are characterized by thick walls, heavy welds, lower stresses and looser tolerances. Although it is generally possible for American manufacturers to comply with the harmonized standards developed for the Pressure Equipment Directive by proofing the quality of the steel used and adding radiographic validation of the welds, these are extra steps that involve extra costs.

There are several areas that pose difficulties for European manufacturers which also tend to be troublesome for US exporters. As discussed in the previous chapter, CEN has had difficulties in developing the standards needed to implement the provisions on European approval of materials in the Pressure Equipment Directive. As shown in Chapter 5, notified bodies tend to rely on national steel standards in reviewing pressure equipment applications. According to the USTR:

> Manufacturers using the ASME Code are now uncertain about continued EU market access, as the European standards incorporate material specifications slightly different from those found in ASME Code. In the absence of a full set of harmonized EU standards (only one has been approved to date), the PED permits manufacturers to file for a . . . European Approval of Materials; however, no requests for an EAM have been approved so far. Another option, the Particular Material Appraisal . . . is not yet a functioning alternative, as the administrative procedure still needs to be established. (USTR, 2001, p. 112)

A decision to use national standards by a French notified body in reviewing equipment made from French steel would not be likely to upset a French manufacturer. An American manufacturer making equipment using American steel could find that the burden of complying with the same decisions would be much greater.

There are other directives in which the Europeans have encountered problems in the development of common internal standards. The Construction Products Directive, to cite one, has been a relative disaster. The wide range of local practices and the tendency for local manufacturers and national governments to protect local building markets and codes has made it very difficult to harmonize European requirements in this area.

Problems caused by differences between US and EU standards could be mitigated in part through a greater willingness to accept foreign standards where they provide equivalent levels of protection. The EU could, for example, implement the promise of accepting diversity in standards that is implicit in the New Approach. CEN, CENELEC and ETSI are private agencies so the use of harmonized standards, as we discussed in Chapter 3, is not mandatory. Notified bodies could recognize that products built to US (and other) standards offer equivalent levels of safety. What is needed is a clear method for proving that foreign standards effectively meet the essential requirements in the New Approach directives and for providing assurances that equivalent standards would be accepted.

European and American standards development organizations could also provide opportunities for the other party to have effective input into the development of standards. Comments could be limited to the general topic of the impact of differences between national standards sets on product safety and free trade.

These difficulties could also be minimized through better international cooperation in the development of product safety standards. For example, European (or American) product safety standards could have been developed by adopting as many elements as possible from the American (or European) equivalents. The requirements that would be unique to each market could have been presented as separate additional standards.

It is in this area of international harmonization in the standards development process that US–EU cooperation is the weakest. In part, this reflects the differences in the organization of the two systems. As we have seen in the last chapter, the US system for developing private standards development is both broader in scope and more decentralized than the European equivalent. Where the Europeans may have only one standard addressing a particular essential requirement in a particular directive, the Americans may have several. If so, then which standards should be harmonized? The answer may not be clear.

There are also significant differences between the US and EU standards development systems in the mechanisms for central coordination. The US system, as we discussed in the last chapter, is highly decentralized and apolitical. The relations between ANSI and the Federal government are relatively weak. The relations between ANSI and the other national standards development organizations are frequently strained.

In comparison, the European system is based on a more centralized public private partnership. In Chapter 3, we pointed out that the Commission pays CEN, CENELEC and ETSI to develop standards implementing the New Approach directives in accordance with specific mandates. The European national standards organizations are the major (and for CEN, only) members of CEN, CENELEC and ETSI. In most cases, there are close working relations between these national standards development organizations and their respective governments. To complete the circle, DG Enterprise works closely with the EU national governments in the development of regulatory policies and implementation of the CE marking system.

These differences limit the possibilities of improving US–EU communications in standards development through direct negotiations between the parties over specific issues in standards development. Who should represent the American side? The government? ANSI? The USTR's office has little interest here. The resources of the organization and its ability to deliver on commitments made on behalf of the American standards community are limited.

However, the Europeans have not promoted international cooperation in the development of standards either. The issue begins with the process of selecting the members of the CEN and CENELEC technical committees and working groups that will develop new standards. The members are chosen by the national standards organizations that are members of CEN or CENELEC. These members are expected to serve as 'national representatives' of their respective countries. In several instances, representatives from the European affiliates of American corporations asked to provide representatives to a working group, only to be turned down on the grounds they were not nationally representative.

ANSI has asked for observer status at CEN and CENELEC. Both agencies refused. However, the chairs of the technical committees have generally been more willing to discuss the work of their units on a more informal basis (Hagigh, 1992).

Under the ISO guidelines for standards development organizations, the sponsoring organization is obligated to make the draft standards available for public comment. Usually, outside groups are asked to provide written comments on a published draft standard during the comment period. At times, public meetings will be held to provide a forum for verbal comments and face to face discussions. At times though, the comments submitted by US interests have been rejected and US representatives at the international meetings have been told they are not welcome to participate. They were told, in effect, that comments were being solicited from European interests and that the US commentators did not represent European interests.

This pattern points to a factor that was first discussed in the last chapter, the subtle politicization of the standards development process by the national governments. There is nothing inherently unreasonable in limiting participation in the development of European standards to European interests. However, this is based on the implicit assumption that the representative unit in the standards development process should be the country or region. An alternative approach would have asked whether a candidate for participation was representative of a particular industry or point of view. It is likely that the restrictions on participation originated in the national mirror committees that nominate the members of the CEN and CENELEC technical committees.

While the Europeans may discourage cooperation between US and EU interests in standards development, they embrace a cooperative relationship with the lead international standards agencies, ISO, the International Standards Organization, and IEC, the International Electrotechnical

Commission. American representation in both organizations is comparatively weak, especially in ISO.

ISO and the IEC function as the peak organizations for the development and coordination of standards, world–wide. ISO and the IEC share a building in Geneva, not far from the UN offices. Although they are chartered under UN mandates, they are not typical intergovernmental organizations. The members of ISO and the IEC are drawn from the lead national standards organizations. Many, but not all, lead national SDOs are loosely chartered by their governments but are organized and funded as private organizations. This list includes, for example, ANSI and BSI.

ISO and IEC develop standards. The quality control system, ISO 9000, and the environmental control system, ISO 14000, are perhaps the best known examples. Perhaps more importantly, ISO develops standards on how to develop standards. In Chapter 4 we discussed a process of developing standards that goes from developing drafts in technical committees, to a comment period and then to final approval. The mechanics of this system are governed by an ISO/IEC Guide 59:1994, *Code of Good Practices for Standardization* (International Standards Organization, 1994). This guide has provided the principal framework for the cooperative development of standards, world–wide. See also British Standards Institution (1997).

There are two routes for the development of ISO/IEC standards. Both agencies can develop standards from the beginning. Alternatively, member organizations can offer national standards for adoption as international standards. The offered standards are then referred to the appropriate technical committees for review as a draft.

The close relation between CEN and ISO in the development of standards is promoted by the rules governing ISO membership. Membership in ISO is based on the principle of one nation, one vote. The European Union is not considered as a 'country'. As a result, the standards development organizations from the member countries in the European Union have 25 votes in ISO while ANSI, the US representative, has one vote.

This pattern gives the European standards development organizations an advantage over the Americans in four ways.

First, as we have already pointed out, American SDOs are often reluctant to submit their standards for adoption at the ISO/IEC level. This desire to keep control over revenues that would be lost if the standards were more widely adopted goes beyond the reluctance of ANSI to contribute standards. As we discussed in Chapter 5, competition over the control of revenues from the sale of standards also limits the willingness of many American SDOs to submit standards for ANSI approval. However, this is a necessary first step in submitting a standard for international acceptance. ANSI is the only US member of ISO and only ANSI standards can be considered for international adoption in ISO.

Second, since the decision on whether or not to accept a CEN request to develop a new standard is by majority vote, this system gives the Europeans a strong voice in the debates over whether or not to accept the CEN mandate.

Third, European representation in ISO technical committees is substantially stronger than US representation. Most ISO TCs are chaired by representatives from European standards organizations. The European representatives collectively have a stronger position in the ISO membership board. As a result, some American observers charge, European interests are more influential than the Americans within ISO. It is as likely, they argue, that ISO will develop standards that reflect European interests as it is that CEN will adopt ISO standards.

Fourth, CEN representatives have a close working relationship with the chairs of the ISO TCs, who are key decision–makers in the standards development process. ANSI officials do not have similar access rights. The relations between ISO and CEN are governed by the Vienna Agreement. Under this agreement, CEN will respond to a mandate from DG Enterprise to develop a new standard by determining whether an ISO standard could be adopted instead. If a new standard has to be adopted, the project is offered first to ISO. CEN will develop a standard only if an appropriate ISO standard is not available and ISO declines to develop one that meets the need of the DG Enterprise mandate. About 30 per cent of the CEN and 60 per cent of the CENELEC standards are derived from international standards.

More relevant for our discussion, CEN and ISO, under the Vienna Agreement, are committed to allow representatives from each organization to consult directly with the technical committees and working groups of the other organization (American National Standards Institute, 1996a, Annex. 3 section 3.2). Under the CEN rules, American companies and standards development organizations can only find out as much about the progress of work on a standard as the chair is willing to divulge.

Under the Dresden Agreement (American National Standards Institute, 1996b), CENELEC is pledged to allow outside groups to sit in on the TC meetings as passive, non–voting observers. The difference is significant. Under the Dresden Agreement, American companies and standard development organizations may have the opportunity to find out for themselves.

ISO and CEN representatives have two responses to these arguments. In the first place, the American National Standards Institute (ANSI) was offered a larger role within ISO and IEC. It would be appropriate for the dominant economies to have a greater level of influence in the development of international standards. This is certainly true for the European Union, which has 25 votes and pays in 25 sets of annual national dues. It would be appropriate for ANSI to be given twice as many votes in ISO deliberations. However, the annual dues that ANSI would pay would also have to double. ANSI, which depends heavily on member dues for funding, declined the offer. Although this decision not to accept the offer may have been fiscally responsible, it undercuts any argument that US interests do not have a representative voice at the international level.

The second argument is somewhat less convincing. EU and ISO advocates often argue that the nationality of the ISO TC participants is less important than their business interests. Taken as a whole, the EU constitutes a very large, diverse and dynamic economy that incorporates a full range of market and technology interests. The European delegates in ISO are far more likely to represent their corporate or national interests than any putative EU interest. The nationality of ISO representation, in short, isn't that important.

This argument runs (or doesn't run) on the rocks of the infamous Japanese letter. According to many American observers, ISO TC 11 had undertaken the task of comparing the major international boiler and pressure vessel codes as a part of their work plan for 2001. There was, by most accounts, a general consensus within the committee on the desirability of this task.

One task in this work plan was to develop a standard that simply listed the standards that would be under review. This would have undoubtedly included the US ASME code, the EU standards for the Pressure Equipment Directive and perhaps Explosive Atmosphere Directive, and the Japanese pressure vessel code. From one perspective, this would be simply a listing, with no comparative evaluations or conclusions about relative worth. As such, this would be an innocuous project.

From a broader perspective, a listing of the major pressure vessel and boiler codes was clearly an invitation for a comparative analysis. For the European Union, so the story goes, this next step would create a great deal of pressure on the EU to accept any standards identified by the ISO as providing appropriate levels of safety as equivalent to the harmonized standards for the purposes of the Pressure Equipment Directive. This, they argued, could bring the essential requirements of the Pressure Equipment and ATEX directives into question. Rather than upset the delicate political balance supporting these directives, they leaned on the member states to direct their ISO TC mirror committees to instruct their national delegates to vote against the proposed standard. As a result, the consensus on the TC and within ISO behind the project collapsed as every European delegate, with the exception of Sweden, suddenly came out against the proposed standard.

The American and Japanese delegates, so the story goes, were furious. The Japanese, with the strong backing of the Americans, wrote a letter demanding that measures be put into place to prevent a recurrence of this political bloc voting. James Rush, the U.S. Assistant Secretary of Commerce, wrote a similar letter to ISO on behalf of the American interests.

Not surprisingly, the incident has been viewed by the Europeans and ISO leadership in very different ways. They argue that there was no bloc voting, that national delegates change their positions all the time. If most of the European delegates reacted negatively to a particular proposal, then the proposal must have been technically flawed. However, it is possible that bloc voting could happen under some future circumstances. It would therefore be appropriate for the ISO leadership to consider measures to prevent this from happening.

Whatever the truth about the Japanese letter, it is apparent that DG Enterprise works closely with the national regulatory bodies, that most European standards development organizations have working relations with their governments, and that the national mirror committees could determine the votes of their delegates within the TCs and on the ISO as a whole. Thus, the organizational potential for bloc voting would seem to be there. The fall-out from the incident is also interesting; as of this writing, no safeguards have been developed at the ISO against bloc voting and TC 11 has not returned to the task of listing the major boiler and pressure code standards.

5. INTERNATIONAL RULES GOVERNING STANDARDS

The relations between the US government and the EU on the impact of CE marking on US businesses are governed in part by the rules of international commerce. It can be more difficult to persuade a country to change a policy or practice affecting international trade unless it can be first shown that they involve some violation of international agreements. We will therefore start with a brief review of the international institutions and practices governing international trade policy.

The foundation for the international trading system is GATT, the General Agreement on Tariffs and Trade. The GATT system was developed in the 1950s when the Western alliance was faced with a major need to promote international trade. Although the GATT agreement was never ratified by the US, the US government has acted as if GATT represented a binding commitment and it has become the major factor in the conduct of international trade negotiations. In 1995, GATT acquired a formal organizational framework with the establishment of the World Trade Organization.

The focus of GATT and the WTO is very much on the traditional tools of international trade policy; tariffs, quotas, export subsidies, domestic content requirements, most favored nation status and similar measures. GATT spurred several revolutions in international trade policy. All GATT signatories must grant most favored nation status to all other GATT members. Quotas and other measures that are intended to directly limit international trade are to be converted to tariffs. Tariffs among GATT signatories are to be negotiated through a series of multilateral 'rounds' involving all GATT members. WTO members can impose punitive tariffs against countries that have violated their GATT obligations once a WTO Dispute Settlement Body has reviewed the complaint and authorized the sanction.

More relevant for our discussion are the GATT rules on the measures a signatory country can take in other areas of public regulation. Contracting parties can take any measure necessary to protect public morals and human, animal or plant life or to meet local economic issues as long as they are not applied in a manner that would constitute arbitrary or unjustifiable discrimination or disguised restrictions on trade between countries (*General Agreement on Tariffs and Trade*, 1947, Article XX). In summary, GATT signatories have authority to take any reasonable measures to protect public security and welfare. The measures adopted must not place an undue burden on international trade. No measure affecting international trade should be adopted without some clear factual justification. Given a choice of several, equally effective regulatory strategies, the alternative that has the least impact on international trade should be adopted.

The Convention on the Technical Barriers to Trade establishes the GATT rules on standards and product requirements. The first version of the TBT was developed during the Tokyo Round. It was subsequently strengthened during the Uruguay Round of trade negotiations.

The TBT distinguishes between voluntary standards and mandatory technical requirements. The rules for technical requirements are simple; they must address a legitimate public purpose, they must be publicly available and they can't be applied in a discriminatory manner. Countries developing new technical requirements must give advanced notice of the requirements, whenever possible. The signatories to GATT are also pledged to use international standards, whenever feasible. The rules for voluntary standards are less restrictive, since they are generally developed by private groups for private use.

Unfortunately, the usefulness of the TBT in addressing US issues with the CE marking system is limited. The Europeans argue that the EN standards are not technical requirements. They are created by private entities, CEN, CENELEC and ETSI. Although their use carries a presumption of conformity with the essential requirements, the use of the harmonized standards is not required. They therefore should be considered under the provisions in the TBT governing voluntary standards, which are far less restrictive.

American manufacturers may argue that the use of the harmonized standards is not really voluntary. DG Enterprise has never discussed what would be required to demonstrate that the essential requirements can be met with the use of other standards. The most common strategy for proving conformity with other standards, the use of a gap analysis, does not really represent an acceptance of other standards. The only use for the gap analysis is to show what additional functions must be carried out so that the alternative standard meets or exceeds the requirements of the harmonized standard in every point.

Unfortunately, this argument is not very persuasive. In fact, the notified bodies have the authority to approve the use of other standards where it is warranted. In fact, it is common practice for the notified bodies to approve the use of draft harmonized standards or European national standards when harmonized standards are either not available or not appropriate. Some notified bodies have suggested that they would consider the use of, for example, the ASME pressure vessel code on products covered by the Pressure Equipment Directive. The United States has therefore not pushed the argument that the EU has created a de facto requirement for the use of harmonized standards so they should be covered by the more stringent provisions of the TBT governing technical requirements.

There is a second problem with the argument that the harmonized standards should be considered as technical requirements. The AdCo for the Pressure Equipment Directive discussed a proposal to consider the ASME pressure vessel code. These discussions were apparently discouraged by ASME, out of concern that this initiative could challenge their control over revenues and updates for the code.

Other provisions of the TBT have a more significant impact on the standards wars. Signatories to the TBT are pledged to use international standards wherever appropriate. This raises the question of how to determine what constitutes an international standard.

The determination of what constitutes an international standard is not a trivial question. Twenty years ago, US manufacturers were exporting more than $900 million per year in industrial equipment to Saudi Arabia. In recent years, US exports have been worth about $200 million. Why the change? It was because the Saudi government began accepting the European definition of an 'international standard'. Several years ago, PEMEX, the Mexican state oil company, published a request for proposals covering about $300 million for refinery upgrades. The specification stated that the equipment must be built to international standards. The Mexican government initially interpreted this clause to mean that the equipment must be built in accordance with ISO standards. Until the American government persuaded the relevant decision–makers to change their mind, equipment built to American standards would not have been accepted.

This issue was raised in the last triannual review of the TBT. The American position was simple; an international standard is one that has been accepted internationally. Since the focus is on the standard, the details of how a standard was developed are not immediately relevant. This definition is consistent with American interests, since many standards developed by American SDOs are widely accepted overseas. Even so, a number of American SDOs have worked to improve foreign participation in standards development.

In contrast, the Europeans argue that an international standard is one that is developed by an international standards development organization. More specifically, the term refers to standards released by ISO, the International Standards Organization or IEC, the International Electrotechnical Commission. The Americans are likely to argue that an international standard is one that is widely recognized and used internationally, regardless of who was involved in the development. A number of US SDOs, under the leadership of ASTM International, have organized the 'Alternative Path Coalition' to promote their position.

To this author, this approach seems to be a defensive strategy that can, at best, limit the inroads of the European argument. Industries in the developed countries have been involved in standards applications and development for years. Because the ASME and ASTM standards were developed and promoted early, many developed countries have built infrastructure using these American standards. The Alternative Path Coalition can provide protective arguments for industries in these countries that want to continue recognizing the relevance of these well–established standards.

Thus, there is an informal international competition between the US SDOs and the Europeans on the interpretation of the TBT. The EU comes down firmly on the side of ISO and the IEC in this argument. They want European standardization to draw heavily on the work of CEN, CENELEC, ETSI, ISO and the IEC. The official EU position includes the following points:

> To have one applied standard and one accepted test for each product, process or service is a trade–facilitating objective. (European Commission, 2001, p. 6)

> To avoid confusion amongst trading partners and to increase transparency, it is necessary to withdraw conflicting national standards . . . as soon as regional or international standards are available, provided legitimate regulatory requirements permit. (European Commission, 2001, p. 5)

In the view of the Europeans only organizations such as ISO and IEC are legitimate sources of 'international standards':

> If regulatory authorities decide to make recourse to international standards, it is important that they make use of standards from standards bodies which can be held accountable for establishing consensus between all national positions and interested parties. (European Commission, 2001, p. 6)

> International standards have a maximum effect on trade facilitation when they are part of a single and coherent set of standards. If international standards are used in relation to technical regulations as promoted by the WTO TBT Agreement, international standards bodies need to have a clearly defined constituency. If standards bodies were to produce simultaneously international and regional or national standards, some partiality, incoherence and conflict in the set of international standards could arise. (European Commission, 2001, p. 7)

The Commission view has been endorsed by the Council (European Council, 2002). If the European argument prevails, then countries can only meet their international obligations by adopting ISO/IEC standards. This will provide a major advantage to the Europeans who have adopted many of these standards and have a stronger voice in these organizations.

However, the action in the international arena is in the development of new standards for new technologies and applications. For the Europeans, encouraging the international acceptance of ISO/IEC standards in these areas can make it easier for European companies to sell in the most dynamic sectors of global markets. The newly industrialized countries are being actively recruited for their participation in the standards development processes. Again, the Europeans will benefit if countries such as Brazil and Argentina choose to participate in the ISO/IEC rather than join the Alternative Path Coalition.

Unfortunately, governments in developing countries may be more interested in sending a senior political associate as their representative in the ISO or the IEC than in trying to find a technical expert who could participate in the American standards development community. The American argument suffers from two other major weaknesses. One is the widespread reluctance of American standards development organizations to make their standards readily available for international use. In the normal course of business, an American SDO would forward a standard to other SDOs for adoption as a national or local standard. This happens all the time. In Europe, CEN standards are all transposed as national standards by the member organizations. Thus, for example, a British medical device manufacturer might acquire the quality control standard EN 13485 as BSI 13485.

Unfortunately, an SDO that adopts a standard from other sources also acquires rights in the proceeds from the sale of that standard and has some control over the frequency of revisions and updates. A number of important American SDOs are dependent on revenues from the sale of their standards. The power to revise standards is also important since the updates have to be purchased as well. Because they are reluctant to lose control over these revenues, many American SDOs are reluctant to offer their standards for international adoption. This undercuts their arguments that these should be regarded as international standards.

The second problem with the American position reflects the differences in representation between ISO/IEC and the American SDOs. The leading national standards organizations are the core members of ISO and IEC, and they often have close ties to their governments. By going with the ISO/IEC alternative, politicians can place governmental representatives in influential positions at the center of international standards development. The members of the organizations belonging to the Alternative Path Coalition are generally technical experts drawn from industry. In many cases, the prospects for effective LDC participation in the American SDOs would seem to be limited and the political advantages would be almost non–existent. In the long term, the advocates of the European view favoring participation in and the adoption for standards from ISO/IEC would seem to have a better position.

The EU system of notified bodies potentially presents a third set of barriers to US companies exporting manufactured products to the EU. The problem can be stated simply; notified bodies are located in the EU, European manufacturers are also located in the EU but American manufacturers are outside the EU. Under the terms of notification, the critical analyses and decisions made by notified bodies must be carried out in Europe where they can come under government supervision. Many notified bodies have affiliates in the US. In some cases, these affiliates can provide useful services in developing product information, helping clients meet the CE mark conformity assessment requirements and coordinating the review process with the European office. For some notified bodies though, US affiliates have the reputation of serving as little more than a marketing and billing arm. If so, relations between a US client and a European notified body could become difficult. Since the American clients are at least three thousand miles further away from the notified bodies than their European counterparts, they are likely to have a harder time straightening out any misunderstandings that may develop during the conformity assessment process.

The United States Trade Representative (USTR) has consistently raised the issue of the notified body system and the promise of the mutual recognition agreement in the annual reports to Congress on trade barriers.

See for example, USTR (1995, p. 17; 1999, p. 94; 2000, pp. 108–9; 2001, p. 110). The complaints about trade barriers were based on the differences in the availability of notified body services to US and EU manufacturers. The report was filed before many notified bodies had developed US affiliates. European manufacturers were naturally favored in a system where the notified bodies could not carry out their functions in the US.

However, it is clear that more notified bodies have begun to market their services in the US and/or develop US affiliates. As we have argued in the last chapter, the relationship between many notified bodies and their clients in the US still tends to be more troubled than the relation with European clients because of differences in access and levels of prior experience. However, the charge that the services are much less available in the US has become much harder to sustain.

REFERENCES

Aeppel, Timothy (1996), 'Europe's "unity" undoes a US exporter' *Wall Street Journal*, p. B1.

American National Standards Institute (1966a), 'Agreement on technical cooperation between ISO and CEN', Annex 3, *American Access to the European Standardization Process,* Washington: American National Standards Institute.

American National Standards Institute (1966b), 'Revised IEC/CENELEC cooperation agreement, Annex 2, *American Access to the European Standardization Proces,* Washington: American National Standards Institute.

British Standards Institution (1997), *A Standard for Standards (BSI 0 –1 –2).*

Cranville, Roger (1999), Associate Secretary, Pennsylvania Department of Community and Economic Development, personal interview, 4 December.

European Commission (2001), *Commission Staff Working Paper: European Policy Principles on International Standardization,* SEC(2001) 1296.

European Council (2002), *Council Conclusions of 1˚ March 2002 on Standardization,*(2002)C 66/01.

European Council (1990), *Council Directive 90/396/EEC of 29 June 1990 on the Approximation of the Laws of Member States Relating to Appliances Burning Gaseous Fuels.*

General Agreement on Tariffs and Trade (1947), at www.ciesin.org TG/PI/TRADE/gaH.html.

Gordon, Colin (1997), 'The business culture in France' in Collin Randlesome (ed.), *Business Cultures in Europe*, Oxford: Butterworth–Heinemann, pp. 87–140.

Hagigh, Sara (1992), 'Hundreds of new product standards will apply to sales in the EC after 1992', *Business America,* 113 (1), p. 6.

Hanson, David P. and Mary C. McKinney (n.d.), 'Is CE marking a barrier for US Exporters?', under review.

Haystead, John (1998), 'Bill Mounts for CE Marking', *Electronic Business*, January 1998, 24 (1), p. 35.

International Standards Organization (1994), *Code of Good Practices for Standardization*, ISO/IEC Guide 59.

United States Trade Representative (1995), *1995 Annual Report on International Trade Barriers, European Union*, Washington: USTR.

United States Trade Representative (1999), *1999 Annual Report on International Trade Barriers, European Union*, Washington: USTR.

United States Trade Representative (2000), *2000 Annual Report on International Trade Barriers, European Union*, Washington: USTR.

United States Trade Representative (2001), *2001 Annual Report on International Trade Barriers, European Union*, Washington: USTR.

United States Trade Representative (2003), *2002 Annual Report on International Trade Barriers, European Union*, Washington: USTR.

Zuckerman, Amy (1997a), *International Standards Desk Reference, Your Passport to World Markets, ISO 9000, CE Mark, QS–9000, SSM ISO 1400, Q 9000, American, European and Global Standards Systems*, New York: AMACOM.

Zuckerman, Amy (1997b), 'CE marking problems on the rise', *Quality Progress*, 30 (9), p. 22.

8. Building Bridges

1. INTRODUCTION

In the last chapter, we discussed some of the issues arising as a result of the differences between the European and American regulatory programs governing product safety. Has anything been done to address these problems?

Both sides have recognized that the issues of standards development and conformity assessment involve interests in both the public and private sector. One approach was to get a private sector assessment of the US EU trade issues in general and of product safety regulation in particular.

2. THE TRANSATLANTIC BUSINESS DIALOG

In 1995, Commerce Secretary Ron Brown suggested the idea for the Trans–alantic Business Dialog to his counterparts in the EU, Martin Bangermann and Sir Leon Brittan. He proposed asking a group of business leaders on both sides of the Atlantic to review trade issues and to develop solutions from an international business perspective. Over 1800 firms were surveyed asking for advice and commitments to the new dialog process. (Trans Atlantic Business Dialog, 2002).

Jurgen Strube, CEO of BASF and Alex Trotman, CEO of Ford agreed to lead the new initiative. The first CEO–level TABD conference was held in Seville, Spain in 1995. Four TABD working groups were organized. They addressed standards and regulatory policy, business facilitation, global issues, small and medium enterprises and e–commerce. In addition, the TABD has organized more than thirty issue groups. They address issues specific to particular product types, such as medical devices and telecom services, and different transactional issues, such as customs procedures and intellectual property.

Technical Committee One addressed the issue closest to the theme of this book; the impact of international differences in standards and conformity assessment on US–EU trade. The preliminary report of the Committee concluded that incompatible product standards and conformity assessment requirements represented a serious trade barrier to exporters on both sides. Both sides were exhorted to reduce these barriers. However, the TABD participants did not have any clear suggestions as to how this issue could be addressed.

The TABD participants also concluded that trade issues affected different companies in different ways. In particular, the TABD could not effectively represent the interests of smaller exporters and other constituents. As a result of a TABD recommendation, the US and EU promoted the organization of TASBI, the Transatlantic Small Business Initiative and TACI, the Trans–atlantic Consumer Initiative. The TABD is now being managed at the American side by the National Chamber of Commerce, TASBI is now a project of the International Trade Administration in the Department of Commerce and TACI is housed in the US Department of Labor. All three of these initiatives have become relatively inactive.

The issue of international differences in standards and certification requirements was assigned to Working Group One (Transatlantic Business Dialog, 2003a). The first working group report recommended that the US and EU should negotiate a mutual recognition agreement covering medical devices, telecommunications terminal equipment, information technology products and electrical equipment. The two regions should also develop a common process for drug registration. Under a mutual recognition agreement, Conformity Assessment Bodies (CABs) in the US would be able to perform conformity assessments to meet European CE mark requirements, and EU CABs would be able to certify that European products meet US regulatory standards. This has been an important recommendation that will be discussed below. Working Group One also recommended that:

> The EU and US should aim to develop and adopt common and open standards wherever possible based on international product standards such as those of the ISO and IEC, where appropriate and supported by industry. (Transatlantic Business Dialog, 2003a, p. 1)

This is, the reader may note, a European perspective. If fully implemented, this recommendation would exclude US voluntary standards from the international marketplace. The subsequent analysis emphasized the need for a better coordination of technical requirements for automobile design and performance. This discussion points up the extent to which multinational enterprises have an interest in conforming all national standards to the international/EU model.

The TABD also recommended that the lead standards development organizations should recognize the international impact of national decisions. The major American SDOs should invite European participation at the membership and technical committee levels. The TABD recommended that CEN, CENELEC and ETSI should extend membership to US SDOs on the basis of reciprocity. Furthermore, the results of the 1995 US–EU summit at Madrid should include a joint commitment to:

> concrete reforms of standards, certification and regulatory policy aimed to reducing or eliminating the impact of these policies as barriers to trade and commerce. (Transatlantic Business Dialog, 1997, recommendation 1.10)

The implementation of this recommendation should be backed up by the organization of a Transatlantic Advisory Committee on Standards, Certification and Regulatory Policy that would provide guidance and monitor progress in the implementation of these recommendations (recommendation 1.11).

These recommendations recognize that the issue is fundamentally political. Concrete progress towards US–EU convergence in standards and conformity assessment requirements will require a willingness to change the political context in which the standards are developed and enforced.

The 1995 summit resulted in the New Transatlantic Agenda for giving new focus and direction to US–EU cooperation on the topic of standards, certification and regulatory policy. The Agenda pledged both parties to:

> follow up on the recommendations in the TABD Chicago Declaration . . . consider inclusion of new product sectors for mutual recognition, expand regulatory cooperation on regulatory issues, with special attention to biotechnology, [and] international harmonization in the automobile sector. (Directorate General Trade, 2003)

Note that the TABD recommendation for concrete reforms in standards and conformity assessment policies did not make it into the New Transatlantic Agenda.

The priorities in the European position on the New Transatlantic Marketplace (an offshoot of the New Transatlantic Agenda) strongly stress the need for regulatory autonomy to ensure product safety.

> The key to barrier–free trade is to achieve a climate of public confidence in the safety and security of products placed on the market, on either side of the Atlantic . . . [A]ll measures . . . aimed at removing technical barriers to trade . . . should at least maintain our existing high levels of protection . . . The EU should also be able to develop further its levels of protection in these areas, while taking into account the differences that may exist in regulatory approaches and traditions . . . To the extent that those public policy concerns are already being pursued through different means on the two sides of the Atlantic, there is room for acceptance of such alternative means to achieve them, insofar as the levels of protection to be achieved are equivalent. (Directorate General Trade, 2003)

The 1995 meeting authorized the organization of the Transatlantic Advisory Committee on Standards, Certification and Regulatory Policy (TACS). Since then, the political commitment to achieve international harmonization in technical requirements, product standards and conformity assessment has been weak. According to the *TABD* (1997, p. 6);

> The TACS agrees with the . . . EU White Paper of November 1996 that there is no single solution and that the choice between mutual recognition agreements, regulatory harmonization or the exclusive use of international standards for regulation must be made on a case by case basis.

A Joint Statement on Regulatory Cooperation was issued in December 1997 which called for enhanced cooperation, whenever possible, in consultations during the early stages of drafting regulations, a greater reliance on each other's technical resources and expertise, together with better harmonization of regulatory requirements or mutual recognition. The Bonn Summit in June 1999 resulted in the approval of a *Joint US–EU Statement on Early Warning and Problem Prevention:Principle and Mechanisms*. By 2002, both parties had approved the *Guidelines on Regulatory Cooperation and Transparency*. The guidelines apply to the development of new regulations and to amendments to existing ones. Seven objectives are listed in the Guidelines:

a. To improve the planning for regulatory proposals
b. To improve the predictability of regulations
c. To grant regulators an opportunity to provide meaningful input to the other side
d. To promote public participation through increased transparency
e. To allow each side to gain access to the expertise of the other side
f. To provide public explanations for technical regulations, and
g. To promote public understanding of the purpose and effect of regulatory proposals

The authors' expected that 'these steps will help minimize and resolve trade frictions and facilitate trade in goods' (Transatlantic Business Dialog, 2002). This is a long way from the original TABD call for work on the international harmonization of existing product requirements.

The report on the 2002 TABD Conference in Chicago, 7 and 8 November 2002, included a call to:

> see more progress . . . ensuring that products can be placed on the market without multiple approvals and product variations. Domestic legislation that does not take

into consideration the global nature of today's marketplace . . . can have far reaching consequences . . . reducing opportunities for economic development around the world. (TABD, 2002)

The report goes on to state that these barriers will not be reduced on a broad scale unless there is a 'strong political will at the highest level'.

So far, governments have not made the commitment to apply the principles to the implementation of the TEP Action Plan from 1999, and the specific target actions in the technical barriers to trade were never followed through by governments. (TABD, 2002)

The TABD report goes on to recommend specific harmonization measures in three areas; dietary supplements, cosmetics and chemicals.

A number of observers have concluded that the efforts of the TABD have largely led to a recognition of the obvious; that national differences in standards and certification requirements impede international trade. The TABD has been effective on specific issues that involved the business interests of the principal involved in the process. However, this effort has not led to any effective, systematic program to promote transatlantic convergence. The effort has lacked the backing of a 'strong political will at the highest level'.

The outcomes might have been different had this not been structured as a formal exercise. The principals on both sides tended to delegate the work on general issues to staff specialists. The reports, as a result, were excellent, but there was no commitment by senior management to implementing the recommendations. Outcomes might have been different had the principals been more willing and/or able to push for systematic changes.

However, this has not been a useless exercise. The TABD is a creation of the EU and the US, and the parties have felt some obligation to take the advocacy of broader avenues for international consultations seriously. This led to the organization of a Transatlantic Small Business Initiative, the Transatlantic Consumer Initiative and the Transatlantic Labor Initiative. Unfortunately, these incarnations of trans Atlantic consultations through the private sector have not been as effective as the original.

3. THE MUTUAL RECOGNITION AGREEMENT

The USTR has included a discussion of the notified body system in most of the annual reports to Congress on trade barriers since 1995. The trade barrier was based on the differences in the availability of notified body services to US and EU manufacturers. The report was filed before many notified bodies had developed US affiliates. European manufacturers were naturally favored in a system where the notified bodies could not carry out their functions in the US.

The Europeans had several responses to this position. More notified bodies began to market their services in the US and/or develop US affiliates. As we have argued in the last chapter, the relationship between many European notified bodies and their clients in the US still tends to be more troubled than their relationship with European clients because of differences in access and levels of prior experience. However, the charge that the services are less available in the US is becoming harder to sustain.

The TABD followed through on this issue by recommending that the EU and US enter into a formal 'mutual recognition agreement' that would allow each side to accept evaluations by parties in the other side for the purposes of domestic conformity assessment. Both the EU and the USTR strongly supported the proposal. Given the decentralized nature of the US regulatory system, only a sector by sector approach would have a chance for success (US Mission to the EU, 1998). This led to the negotiation of a Mutual Recognition Agreement between the US and the EU.

The specific applications of the MRA to the notified body issue are developed in a series of annexes to this framework agreement. Under the MRA and annexes, Europeans would recognize certifications provided by the American 'competent bodies' for CE marking purposes on the basis of reciprocity. American regulatory agencies would also have to recognize certifications made by European competent bodies for US regulatory purposes. This reciprocity limits the potential scope of the MRA. The agreement can only be applied to areas in which the US and EU authorities have established equivalent levels of product regulation and equivalent levels of competent body supervision. Eventually, annex agreements were reached for the telecommunications equipment, low voltage, electromagnetic compatibility, recreational craft and medical device directives. There was also an agreement promoting transatlantic convergence on good manufacturing practices for pharmaceuticals. Most of the attention has been centered on the medical device MRA since this is the only directive on the list that generally requires notified body services and is a covers a major area of US–EU trade (National Institute for Science and Technology, 2004).

The development of competent bodies for the medical device directives has been a major goal for many supporters of the EU–US MRA. On the American side, the regulatory agency involved in the process has been the FDA, the Federal Drug Administration. The process has gone in stages. First, the regulatory authorities on each side develop written guidance documents for the evaluation of potential CABs, the conformity assessment bodies that will be responsible for conducting the conformity evaluations on the other side.

There is then a period of mutual training and reviews of the qualifications and performance of the CAB nominees. This 'confidence building' period can be extended by either side for as long as needed. Finally, when each side is confident that CABs on the other side will exercise sound judgments in conformity assessment, the system can go into operation.

The US–EU medical MRA has been, at best, a mixed success. For the FDA, participation in the MRA process has required a significant change in policy. Medical regulation in the US has historically been more rigorous than in Europe and the process of product review and acceptance has been more difficult. The horrors of the thalidomide scare have left organizational scars in the FDA and a commitment to regulatory rigor. As a result, the FDA has been reluctant to trust steps in the approval decision to outside bodies and has been a relatively unwilling partner to the MRA process. The FDA has historically relied on an in–house inspection process rather than delegating regulatory approval decisions to outside groups in the private sector.

These differences in US and European regulatory experiences have an effect on the potential competent bodies on both sides. The Europeans complain that the FDA has an adversarial attitude towards client companies. The FDA complains that the European competent bodies are more like consultants than watchdogs. As a result, American medical device manufacturers would often prefer to use the EU notified body system for access to European markets than to work through a more troublesome relation with American competent bodies. As a result, the demand for American competent body services is likely to be limited and the Europeans have not named any competent body candidates in the US.

A common pattern has been for manufacturers to use the experience gained through their relatively easier access to European markets as the basis for their FDA clinical applications. Companies ask for the FDA after they have resolved any problems that have emerged from their European experience.

The FDA has identified a number of competent body candidates in the EU. However, the management of the FDA has resisted the prospects of delegating product review authority. In fact, the FDA is reluctant to recognize European competent body nominations for the medical devices that present the greatest potential risks unless Congress enacts an explicit statutory authorization. The confidence–building process for the recognized European competent bodies has been extended for two additional years with no real end in sight. The US–EU MRA for medical devices is not likely to generate any significant increases in transatlantic trade for several years.

On the other hand, the process of negotiating and trying to implement the MRA has given a significant impetus to regulatory convergence and reform. Senior managers with the FDA medical equipment office and their British counterparts, the Medical Device Authority, communicate at least on a weekly basis. The FDA has come to recognize the virtues of third–party certification systems. Both the FDA and their British counterparts have become far more committed to the goal of regulatory convergence. Given the importance of the British medical device regulatory system in the EU, this is also promoting a broader, but slower process of EU–US convergence.

In all likelihood, the gaps left by the failure of the MRA process will be addressed by other commercial initiatives. The problem of improving the access by US manufacturers to European notified bodies could be met by expanding the network of US subsidiaries of EU notified bodies and by authorizing them to carry out a greater range of conformity assessment functions within the US.

Part of the problem for American manufacturers has been the scarcity of US affiliates of EU notified bodies that can offer effective services. A major continental notified body, which shall remain nameless, has developed a reputation for offering poor service to American clients because of the limited range of functions that could be carried out by their American offices and because of the poor coordination between their American offices and the European headquarters. Nothing could be done until the European inspectors came. The American offices could not offer a US client much advance warning as to who was coming, when they were coming and what they would be looking for.

The legal issue here is the scope of functions that can be done by the US office under the terms of notification. Under EU law, the review and decision–making on an application for notified body services must be done where it can be supervised by EU authorities, that is, in the EU. However, the collection of the data and the organization of the file can be carried out by notified body employees in the US, as long as they are trained and supervised by the European organization. The US organization should also be able to carry out a wide range of liaison functions, such as scheduling, pre–audit guidance and helping to manage the process of correcting discrepancies. The development of a network of US affiliates to EU notified bodies that could carry out these functions would go a long way towards addressing American concerns about access to notified body services.

Commercial pressures are driving the European market for notified bodies towards better service in this direction. Manufacturers are likely to select notified bodies that can provide and develop stable, long–term relationships. Manufacturers of higher risk products will need either an on–going system for product evaluation or periodic audits of their quality assurance systems. Even for a type assessment certificate, a manufacturer will have to go back to a notified body for a review of any changes in product design, manufacturing process and/or component sourcing. It would be easier to go to a notified body that is already familiar with the product.

These market incentives in favor of stable relations between manufacturers and notified bodies will favor the larger notified bodies that are more likely to provide assurances of long–term stability and the technical capabilities to handle a wider range of future projects. Manufacturers selling throughout the EU have an incentive to use notified bodies that are likely to be credible with a wide range of surveillance authorities.

This process of consolidation in the market for notified body services may be underway. In the US, Underwriters Laboratory is a market leader in this process. The domestic market for UL services is not likely to grow substantially. The long–term strategy of UL is based heavily on expanding into, among other areas, the European market for notified body services. UL bought DEMKO, a small Danish notified body specializing in the medical device directives. They also have affiliates under the UL name in the UK, Netherlands and Italy. Each office specializes in providing notified body services for a different set of New Approach directives. Every UL office can serve the full range of clients. Files on products that fall out of the range of local office competencies are forwarded to other offices in the network. This network includes the UL offices in the US. A market for notified body services that is dominated by a smaller number of larger notified bodies is more likely to offer effective services to American manufacturers through a network of US subsidiaries. Given the direction in which the EU market for notified body services seems to be moving, the future need for the implementation of the MRAs would seem to be decreasing.

4. THE GLOBAL HARMONIZATION TASK FORCE

The medical device industry is characterized by rapid innovation in the context of a global market. Medical service providers have a strong incentive to take advantages of the latest innovations for lowering cost and improving medical effectiveness. National differences in the regulation of medical devices are a major barrier to the development of a true global marketplace.

In 1992, industry representatives and senior regulatory officers from the US, EU, Canada and Japan met in Nice, France to discuss the formation of a global partnership with the goal of lobbying for the harmonization of regulatory practices governing medical devices (Global Harmonization Task Force, 2003a). The Global Harmonization Task Force was organized in January 1993. The steering committee has grown to 25 members, drawn from both regulatory agencies and industry groups in the US, Canada, Australia, Japan and the European Union. The EU delegation includes representatives from DG Enterprise as well as regulatory and industry representatives from the UK, Switzerland, Germany, France and Belgium. Representatives from the two major medical device trade associations, Advamed and Eucomed, have also been involved in the project.

The goal of the GHTF has been to develop regulatory guidelines on critical topics that, if adopted, would promote the development of mutually consistent regulatory policies on a global basis. Under this approach, there would be no need for any formal agreements among different national regulatory agencies. The goal of harmonization would be achieved if the national authorities individually implemented the GHTF recommendations in their regulatory programs.

The GHTF has also signed a Memorandum of Understanding with ISO/TC 210, which is charged with developing standards for quality management in the medical device area. The purpose of the memorandum is to promote communication and a coordination of the efforts of the two groups (Global Harmonization Task Force, 2003).

The work of the GHTF has largely been carried out through a series of working groups. The topics assigned to these groups have changed over time. In general, they have focused on four general topics:

- Essential principles of safety and performance assessment
- Adverse event reporting systems
- Design control guidance for medical devices
- Guidelines for auditing manufacturing quality control systems

The GHTF is clearly having an impact on national policy. As the Commission has pointed out, 'it has become impossible to ignore the work of the Global Harmonization Task Force . . . on medical devices.' (European Commission, 2003). However, protectionist interests are never far from sight. The authors also said that they were interested in assessing

> the strengths, weaknesses, opportunities and threats to the medical devices sector in Europe, its competitiveness and potential to innovate, in particular in comparison with its current main competing regions, US and Japan. The study should in this way allow national and Community authorities to determine framework conditions allowing companies . . . to increase competitiveness and innovation. (European Commission, p. 8)

The GHTF has been taking small, but very useful steps. The first project, for example, is to promote the development of a common application form for new medical products by the national regulatory agencies of the GHTF members. These efforts may succeed. Although the US–EU MRA for medical devices has not yet led to an upswing in international trade, it has led to closer international contacts among medical device regulatory agencies that generally support the efforts of the GHTF.

Overall, the GHTF will probably have a more significant impact on international convergence in standards and conformity assessment than the TABD. The political lessons seem to be clear. The efforts of the GHTF are focused on specific markets in which there is a strong constituency for international free trade. The corporate participants are involved in the advocacy of policies that can have a direct impact on their corporate fortunes. The regulatory authorities they are trying to lobby are directly involved in the advocacy process. The public sector participants in the GHTF come from senior positions.

5. THE IEC AND THE CB SCHEME

IEC, the International Electrotechnical Commission, has been promoting a series of programs to reduce the costs and confusion of cross–national conformity assessment to IEC standards. Perhaps the best known program is the CB scheme, which focuses on electrical devices.

Laboratories and test houses participating in the CB scheme are pledged to recognize the results of testing a particular product to specific IEC standards that have been issued by other CB scheme participants. Many of the harmonized (EN) standards which have been developed by CENELEC to implement electrotechnical aspects of the CE marking system are based on IEC standards.

This can be helpful for CE mark conformity assessment purposes. For example, an American company that needed to have a product tested to a particular IEC/EN standard for conformity assessment purposes could have the testing done by an American test house that was a member of the CB scheme. They would then apply for a test certification from an EU test house that was also a CB scheme member. No retesting would be required. The EU test house would be able to issue the test certificate on the basis of the American work. Participating in the CB scheme would also make it more likely that the European notified body would simply accept the American test results directly.

The CB scheme has been quite successful. The number of certificates issued per year has risen from less that 5000 in 1994 to 27 000 in 2002 (International Electrotechnical Commission, 2003a).

There are, of course, limitations to the CB scheme. The standards governing the testing must be covered by the scheme. Participation in the scheme does not guarantee that the test results from a particular laboratory will be accepted by anyone other than another CB scheme participant. The product, standards and test conditions on which the results from the testing laboratory are based must exactly match the conditions on which the accepting test house is expected to issue its report. Finally, not all test houses are eligible to be CB scheme participants. To be eligible for participation in the CB scheme, test houses must be certified under the IEC/EN 17 000 series of standards. Not only do the test houses have to meet these requirements, they must also be certified as in compliance by a recognized registration agency.

There are drawbacks to using laboratories that are CB scheme participants. Because of the certification requirement, the cost could clearly be higher and the availability might be reduced. Furthermore, laboratories (and notified bodies) certified under the ISO/EN 17 000 series are barred from providing consulting services. A test house participating in the CB scheme could tell you how and why your product failed a particular test. However, they would be prohibited from telling you how to fix it. Some manufacturers who feel they need this type of consulting service have taken to testing their products at non–accredited test houses and then using a CB participating test house only when they are sure their products will pass.

The CB scheme only covers a narrow range of standards and products that apply in the electrotechnical area. Under a related program, conformity certification for electrical components would be carried out under the auspices of an international body, the IECQ, and the certificate would be recognized world–wide (International Electrotechnical Commission, 2003c). A related program, which is called the IECEx scheme, covers testing for electrical equipment intended for use in explosive atmospheres (International Electrotechnical Commission, 2003b).

6. CERTIFICATION AND ACCREDITATION SYSTEMS

A common issue facing US companies interested in exporting to the EU has been an uncertainty about the acceptability of US test laboratory results. Many times, it is far easier to have US laboratories test products that are manufactured in the US than it is to send them to the EU for testing. However, the potential advantages of local testing would be rendered void if the US test results were not accepted by EU notified bodies and surveillance authorities. The approval of US laboratories by accreditation and/or certification bodies recognized in the EU for the performance of testing to EU standards would go a long way to achieving that result.

There is an international hierarchy in accreditation and certification systems for testing and conformity assessment. 'Certification' provided assurances that a particular requirement has been met or that a specific procedure has been carried out in a specific way. The purpose of 'accreditation' is to provide assurances that the administering entity is competent. Accreditation covers such issues as technical competency, the scope, accuracy and security of data handling systems and organizational resources.

International convergence in accreditation and certification is more likely to expand market opportunities for test houses and certification bodies than to create unwanted competition. Clients are more likely to use agencies that can provide testing and/or certification services for all major markets in which they have an interest.

As a result, there has been a high degree of cooperation among national certification and accreditation bodies. This has been promoted by several factors. There has been strong international acceptance for using ISO 17025 and/or IEC Guide 58 or related standards as the basis for accreditation. These are the successor standards to the EN 45000 series that were initially used in the EU for the approval of notified bodies.

The peak organization is ILAC, the International Laboratory Accreditation Cooperation. The purpose of ILAC is to promote international convergence among the regional and national organizations that, in turn, will review, certify and/or accredit the groups that are actually providing these services. ILAC has entered into a series of mutual recognition agreements with the regional and national bodies (International Laboratory Accreditation Cooperation, 2003a).

Two European associations, the European Accreditation of Certification and the European Co–operation for Accreditation of Laboratories, joined together in 2000 to form the European Cooperation for Accreditation (EA). The EA members include the nationally recognized accreditation and certification bodies in the EU, EFTA and accession countries. The goal is to improve the coordination of accreditation and certification activities in accordance with ISO/IEC 17025, Guide 58.

The American system is characterized by a proliferation of private sector laboratory accreditation and certification systems. A number of private sector, non–profit organizations have emerged to provide accreditation and/or certification services for particular types of laboratories. Partly as a result of this proliferation of systems, there was no organization in the US that was comparable to either ILAC or EA. To meet this need, NIST (the National Institute for Science and Technology, a part of the US Department of Commerce) sponsored the organization of two umbrella programs, the National Cooperation for Laboratory Accreditation (2003) and the National

Voluntary Conformity Assessment System Evaluation (National Institute for Science and Technology, 2003).

Despite the scope of private sector laboratory accreditation systems, the participation of US laboratories in the CB scheme in the early years was held up by the lack of access to a recognized registrar. NVLAP was initiated by NIST in order to provide US test laboratories with the necessary accreditations.

In the private sector, A2LA, the American Association for Laboratory Accreditation, was organized in 1978 as a public service, non–profit organization to provide accreditation for test houses, calibration houses, inspection bodies, proficiency testing services and providers of reference materials. More importantly for CE mark certification, A2LA has signed a bilateral mutual recognition agreement with the European Cooperation for Accreditation. This relationship is intended in part to improve the likelihood that European notified bodies will accept test results from A2LA accredited laboratories. With the emergence of A2LA, the commercial importance of NVLAP has been partly eclipsed.

A2LA, NVLAP and NACLA are all members of the International Laboratory Accreditation Cooperation. All of these arrangements increase the probability that laboratory accreditation by A2LA or NVLAP will improve the prospects that test results from American test laboratories will be accepted by European notified bodies and surveillance authorities.

It is important to note what these systems can and cannot do and to point out the differences between the CB scheme and the other two ventures. Laboratories and test houses participating in the CB scheme are under an obligation to recognize the validity of test results from another CB scheme participant as long as all of the mutual recognition requirements have been met. If the other CB scheme participant is a European laboratory that has a close working relationship with the notified body or surveillance authority, then the probability that the test results will be accepted will be much higher.

In contrast, the decision on whether or not to accept test results from an American testing laboratory is in the hands of the European notified body or surveillance authority. There is no contractual obligation for any test house subject to ILAC or EA requirements or for any notified body or surveillance authority to recognize test results from an A2LA or NVLAP accredited laboratory. However, accreditation under the same set of standards used for European laboratory accreditation is expected to increase confidence in the validity of the results.

The reader may note that the affiliates with ILAC and EA both include conformity assessment functions as well as testing. The purpose of NVCASE, the National Voluntary Conformity Assessment System Evaluation, is to promote the international acceptance of conformity assessments carried out by US bodies. This would seem to raise the possibility that an American conformity assessment body could be approved to carry out notified body functions through accreditation under the auspices of ILAC and/or EA. Unfortunately, the EU has kept control over the notified body process through the requirements that a) only EU member governments can carry out the notification process, b) the Commission must assign a serial number to a nominee and the name must be published before the notification is official, and c) the conformity review process must be carried out within the EU. Under these rules, there is no possibility that a US organization could gain recognition as a conformity assessment body through the private accreditation or certification route.

7. ANSI AND EUROPEAN STANDARDS DEVELOPMENT

These bridges do not address the other half of the issue; the development of standards. However, ANSI may be able to provide assistance for US companies that are potentially faced with the development of protectionist standards by CEN, CENELEC and ETSI.

The framework for ANSI's involvement is set by the Vienna Agreement between CEN and ISO and the Dresden Agreement between CENELEC and IEC (American National Standards Institute, 1996). Under the Vienna Agreement, CEN and ISO agree to share work information on a technical committee by technical committee basis, including the exchange of observers. CEN can propose to transfer the development of a particular standard to the relevant ISO technical committee. Alternatively, ISO propose shifting responsibility for the development of a draft ISO standard to CEN. For a third option, work can be shifted to ISO. Both the CEN and the ISO technical committees can engage in parallel voting. If approved, the ISO draft would also be adopted as a CEN draft standard. To invoke the provisions of the Vienna Agreement, both the ISO technical committee and the CEN technical committee must agree.

Under the Dresden Agreement, the IEC has rights of first refusal on projects assigned to CENELEC. CENELEC will work on the project only if the IEC refuses to work on it. Final drafts of CENELEC standards are also to be offered to the IEC technical committee for comment and voting. In general, CENELEC technical committees are not open to representatives from non–European organizations.

There is less of a need for the equivalent of a Vienna or Dresden Agreement to govern the relations between ETSI and the IEC or the International Telecommunications Union. There is a strong constituency for the globalization of telecommunications standards. Most of the leading US telecommunications companies have an international presence. ETSI has granted ANSI guest observer status. ETSI also provides for corporate membership. As a result, American interests are usually considered in ETSI TCs.

As of 1 July 1998, CEN had shifted responsibility for standards development to CEN on 298 projects and CEN had delegated responsibility to ISO on 756 items. At that time, ISO technical committees were actively engaged in 6431 projects (American National Standards Institute, 1998).

ANSI and US manufacturers generally have more access to the ISO and IEC process than to CEN. This access can be used as a basis for influencing the development of a CEN standard. ANSI has provided several case studies of this process (American National Standards Institute, 1998, pp. 18–23).

For example, the US–based Rieke Corporation makes an innovative device that seals the lids on steel drums. Although it doesn't export directly to Europe, many of the closures manufactured by Reike are bought by companies that export the drums after they have been filled and sealed. Initially, there were no standards at the international level or in use in the US governing steel drum closures.

CEN TC 261 on packaging was organized in 1990. Around 30 working groups were formed, including one that was responsible for developing standards for drum closures. Rieke found out about the TC's work in 1994, when a draft standard on drum closures was almost ready for public comment. The draft standard was designed based. Adoption would have barred steel drums using the Rieke closure from use in the EU.

ANSI, with the strong backing of the US Department of Commerce and the US mission to the EU, strongly objected to the approval of the draft standard. As a result of these efforts, a representative from Rieke was invited to the CEN TC 261 working group to discuss the development of a broader standard that would cover the Rieke closure. As a result, Rieke has been able to continue selling the closure to companies that export to the EU.

For example, standards developed by the US–based Association for the Advancement of Medical Instrumentation for sterilization equipment and procedures had traditionally been used world–wide. CEN then created TC 102 (sterilizers for medical purposes) and TC 204 on the Sterilization Process. If the CEN standards had been different from the AAMI standards, American access to the European market for sterilization equipment could have been impeded.

ANSI led the fight at ISO to create TC 198 that would also produce sterilization standards. The secretariat for TC 198 was assigned to ANSI, which then delegated it to AAMI. Although the organization of TC 198 was opposed by many European interests, it has been effective in developing standards for sterilization equipment and procedures at the international level in which American interests are well represented. This has limited the development of European standards through CEN TC 102 and 204 (pp. 20–21).

Another example, the Toy Directive, came into effect on 1 January 1990. CEN TC 52 began work on toy safety standards. ISO TC 181 had jurisdiction over toy standards at the international level. Denmark had the chair of both the CEN and ISO committees. Initially, ISO TC 181 was largely inactive.

US manufacturers became worried about the work of CEN TC 52. The committee was closed to outside observers. The first standard, EN 71, was sufficiently different from the corresponding ASTM standard to bar many US manufacturers from European markets. For example, the European tension test was set for a pull strength at 20 pounds while the US norm has always been 15 pounds. In the opinion of US toy manufacturers, these differences were not backed up by any technical justifications (Hagigh, 1992).

US industry initially opposed assigning new work to ISO TC 181 on the grounds that new standards were not required. The committee was dominated by countries without significant toy manufacturing industries that were politicizing the process. ANSI became involved when it was clear that CEN was taking the lead in what would probably become an ISO standard. ANSI also encouraged US toy manufacturers to become more involved in CEN through their European subsidiaries. Non–European countries with significant toy manufacturing industries were also urged to become more involved.

Two toy standards were developed by CEN. A third draft standard was rejected by CEN. However, the corresponding ISO standard was narrowly approved. The US and allied countries prompted ISO to reactivate IC 181. The Danish secretariat for the committee was invited to hold a meeting in the US. In this meeting, the CEN draft was rejected by ISO TC 181 and the linkage between ISO and CEN on the development of toy safety standards was broken.

Note that not all of these cases have equally happy endings. In the steel closure case, ANSI was able to influence the development of the European standard. In the sterilization case, ANSI was able to encourage the development of ISO standards that CEN could use at the European level. In the toy safety case, ANSI was able to prevent the CEN standards from being adopted at the ISO level. However, toys sold on the European market would still have to meet the first two TC 52 standards.

8. CONCLUSIONS

These data fall into a familiar pattern. Commercial solutions are being found for problems of international conformity assessment in industries where there is a strong constituency for free trade and global markets. Missing from the discussion in this chapter is any extended mention of initiatives to harmonize either standards or conformity assessment procedures in industries such as metals in which free trade is not greeted with cheers. Thus, one of the core problems discussed in the last chapter is not likely to go away. Restrictions on trade in materials and components that are used in finished products also act as restrictions on the products themselves.

Another familiar theme emerges from the discussions in this chapter; government to government discussions have relatively little relevance for addressing the problems of international harmonization. The major public initiative, the MRA, has had, at best, limited success. Market pressures are likely to push notified bodies to achieve substantially the same goals through commercial means. However, this is an area that calls for public – private partnerships. The TABD, a private sector venture, is one example. However, the success of the TABD has been limited. The success of the GHTF, another private sector venture, will require the active cooperation of the national regulatory agencies for medical devices in the participating countries.

In the first chapter, we pledged to evaluate the issues posed by US – EU differences in product safety regulation systems in the context of evolving systems. How then are these systems changing? Is there any reason to believe that the prospects for addressing these issues will improve in the near future? These topics will be discussed in the next chapter.

REFERENCES

American National Standards Institute (1998), *American Access to the European Standardization Process: Supplement, August 1998,* Washington: ANSI.

American National Standards Institute (1996), 'The Dresden Agreement', Annex 2 in *American Access to the European Standardization Process,* New York: ANSI.

Directorate General Trade (2003), 'New transatlantic agenda; senior level group report to the US EU summit', at www.useu.be/TransAtlantic/ ntahtml.

European Commission (2003), *Communication from the Commission to the Council and the European Parliament on Medical Devices*, COM(2003) yyyy final.

Global Harmonization Task Force (2003a), 'History of the GHTF' at www.ghtf.org/ information/history.html.

Global Harmonization Task Force (2003b), 'Memorandum of Understanding between ISO/TC 210 and the Global Harmonization Task Force' at www.ghtf.org/information.html.

Hagigh, Sara (1992), 'Hundreds of new product standards will apply to sales in the EC after 1992', *Business America* 113 (1), p. 16.

International Electrotechnical Commission (2003a), 'IEC–IECEE home page', at www.iecee.org/cbscheme/html/cbstand.html.

International Electrotechnical Commission (2003b), 'About the IECEx', at www.iecex.com/about.html.

International Electrotechnical Commission, (2003c), 'The world wide approval and certification program for electronic components, IECQ home page', at www.iecq–cecc.org.

International Laboratory Accreditation Cooperation (2003a), 'The ILAC mutual recognition arrangement', at www.compad.com.au/cms/ilac /siteArticleDisplay.php?artLd=53.

National Institute for Science and Technology (2003) 'National Voluntary Conformity Assessment System Evaluation (NVCASE) program' at www.nist.gov/tys/htdocs/210/gsig/nvcase.html.

National Institute for Science and Technology (2004), *Agreement on Mutual Recognition between the European Community and the United states of America.*

National Laboratory Accreditation Cooperation (2003b), 'NACLA' at www.nacla.net/default.html.

Transatlantic Business Dialog (2003a), 'TABD History: 1995 – 2002', at www.tabd.org/history.html.

Transatlantic Business Dialog (2003b), 'Working Group I; standards, certification and regulatory policy: final recommendations' at europa.eu.int/eu–us/pub/tabd/wg1.htm.

Transatlantic Business Dialog (1997), *Priorities for the Mid--Year Summit, 13 May 1997: Guidelines on Regulatory Cooperation and Transparency; Joint US–EU Statement on Early Warning and Problem Prevention Principle and Mechanisms.*

Transatlantic Business Dialog (1999), *TABD Mid–Year Report*, at http://www.tabd.com/about/MYMExecSummary 1.html.

Transatlantic Business Dialog (2002), *2002 TABD Chicago Conference Report, Executive Summary.*

United States Mission to the European Union (1998), 'America's trade agenda in Europe; remarks by USTR Charlene Barshefsky to the EU Committee of AmCham', Press Release 10/19/98, Code ETR–05, at www.useu.be/issues/barsh1019.html. .

9. New Directions

1. INTRODUCTION

In Chapter 1, we defined the central theme of this book; how the CE mark system affects international trade. The analysis was conducted in an international context that highlights the substantial differences between the EU and US systems of standardization and conformity assessment. It was noted that that the politics, policies and institutions of the European Union are changing rapidly. The impact of CE marking should therefore be assessed in light of what it may become, rather than what it is now. We can now revisit this thesis in light of the materials discussed in the previous eight chapters.

Our thesis can be stated simply; the regulatory systems in the European Union are evolving rapidly. Many of the administrative and political problems with the CE marking system are being addressed. The international importance of the CE marking system is increasing with the expansion of the EU and with the growing acceptance of the New Approach outside the EU.

The expansion of the European Union will force institutional changes that may facilitate this reform process. However, the EU is also expanding the scope of environmental regulations that will affect product design and packaging, use and disposal. For the moment, these new sets of product regulations seem to be outside the scope of the CE marking system and potentially inconsistent with it. The net effect of these changes on manufacturers, markets and international trade is not clear.

The overall impact though is apparent; the EU is likely to pose significant challenges to the US in the search for new markets, and the international promotion of the CE marking system is a key component of their strategy. One searches for evidence that the public or private sectors in the US are responding to these challenges in a vigorous and systematic way.

2. THE EVOLUTION OF CE MARKING

We can begin by considering the recent evolution of the CE marking system.

CEN has been addressing some of the problems inherent in the earlier standards. Four years ago, the EMC directive was widely regarded as a problem child for testing new equipment. It was relatively easy to test for electromagnetic emissions under the published standards. However, the test for electromagnetic immunity was regarded as very difficult. In effect, the manufacturer had to prove a negative, that the product would not fail or dangerously malfunction under the test conditions. The test conditions were not well specified, so the prospect of a failure under some variant condition was always present. It was frequently assumed that most products would fail the tests for the EMC susceptibility requirement, if tested for enough time and with sufficient imagination.

On the other hand, the consequences of a failure were rarely dangerous for most products. As a result, sophisticated manufacturers would negotiate with their notified bodies and test houses over pass/fail criteria for the EMC susceptibility requirement before signing contracts.

Since then, the Electromagnetic Compatibility Directive has gone through the SLIM review (which will be discussed below) and the standards have been tightened up. The basic standards have been reissued in 2001 as EN 6100–06–2: 2001 and EN 6100–06–4: 2100. The changes in these standards have essentially taken care of the problem.

The widespread lack of harmonized standards, coupled with the comparative lack of effective coordination among the notified bodies, created problems for manufacturers in Europe and the US in the past. Four years ago, manufacturers would be likely to find that CEN had not developed all of the standards that were needed to implement the essential requirements of the Machinery Directive. Now, most of them are in place. The work of developing the standards needed to implement the directives has continued and the process for standards development has been tightened up.

In 1998, the Commission issued a white paper analyzing the problem of the missing standards (European Commission, 1998). CEN came in for some fairly harsh criticism for the slow pace of standards development. CENELEC and ETSI were not seen as contributing to the problem. In the electrotechnical and telecommunications fields, there was a greater tendency to adopt standards that have already been developed in IEC and ISO. Because there were fewer entrenched commercial interests in these areas in the EU, the time required for CENELEC and ETSI to develop standards was considerably shorter.

Since then, the problem of the non–existent standards has been effectively addressed. The passage of time has made it possible for CEN to substantially reduce the backlog of standard development projects. The Commission has started placing developmental due dates and late penalties in the mandate and financing for new standards development projects. The pace for drafting and implementing directives that are needed to complete the New Approach has dropped off significantly. As a result, the need to develop new standards has also dropped off. With the decline in funding from the Commission for new standards development, CEN has become a much leaner organization. Recent data on the rate of standards development are presented in Table 9.1.

Table 9.1. The development of the harmonized standards

Year	Number of harmonized standards	
	1999	2001
CEN	717	1029
CENELEC	754	790
ETSI	114	203

Source: European Commission (2001c).

The process of coordinating the interpretations of the directives by the notified bodies has improved substantially. As we discussed in Chapter 6, the efforts of EOTC to provide authoritative coordination of the notified bodies through the AdCos have largely failed. However, the leading notified bodies have a strong interest to coordinate their interpretations of ambiguous issues in order to forestall conflicts with notified bodies and surveillance authorities in other EU countries. General Enterprise has been able to coordinate these consultations and to publish the conclusions as a series of 'guidance documents' that provide analyses and conclusions to questions about the interpretation of the directives. These advisory bulletins are available for most of the directives. Although they carry no legal authority, they have become quite influential. They have therefore provided a new tool for coordinating the interpretations of the New Approach directives.

The impact of these measures is shown in the changing pattern of safeguard clause exercises. Recent data are presented in Table 9.2. The number of exercises per year has dropped significantly. Instead of covering virtually all directives, the exercise of the safeguards clause is now almost exclusively restricted to the Low Voltage Directive (LVD). This change suggests that a substantial consensus has been reached on the interpretation of the other directives.

Table 9.2. Safeguard clause actions: Low Voltage and Gas Fired Appliance directives

Year	Number of safeguard clause invocations	
	LVD	GFAD
1997	25	10
1998	135	9
1999	200	4
2000	345	17
2001	425	7

Source: European Commission (2003c).

The Commission launched the SLIM initiative (Simpler Legislation for the Internal Market) in May 1996. The goal is to identify ways in which the legislation governing the internal market could be simplified. Each round of the SLIM review focuses on legislation in specific areas. Each area is reviewed by a small group of experts who are named by the member states and by groups directly affected by the legislation under review (DG Internal Market, 2003). Each SLIM team is chaired by a representative from the responsible Directorate and works under a mandate from the Commission. The SLIM process has covered a wide range of topics. The construction product directive was considered in Phase I and the EMC directive was reviewed in Phase III. The report and recommendations from the SLIM teams are reviewed by the Commission (European Commission, 2001d; European Parliament, 2000).

The SLIM team reviewing the EMC directive suggested amending the directive to:

- Provide a more coherent definition of the scope,
- Simplify the conformity assessment procedures
- Provide a regime for fixed installations
- Define the essential requirements more clearly and
- To clarify the use of the harmonized standards

The SLIM process will probably cover most of the New Approach directives. However, the process focuses on the specific elements of the legislation under review, and not on the process through which the directives are being developed.

The process for legislative development is also being reformed. The tradition in the EU, as we discussed in Chapter 2, is for the political leadership to control interest group access to the policy process. Policies are set, to a significant extent, by specialized bodies operating outside the public view. In effect, only the business interests that have been invited in get a chance to have an influence on policy. Virtually all of the access points to the development of the New Approach directives have been controlled by DG Enterprise. Most of the favored corporations gained access through their close ties to their national governments. Few companies have tried to lobby Parliament.

Political pressures have pushed the Commission and Council towards a much greater emphasis on transparency and responsiveness. The narrow victories and occasional defeats for the EU in national referenda on EU expansion have demonstrated the extent to which many Europeans are still suspicious of the EU bureaucrats in Belgium. The 'Eurobarometer' program was developed by the EU to assess public attitudes towards the Union. Unfortunately, the results of the polling have not been especially comforting for the proponents of a closer union. In 1991, 69 per cent of those polled said that their country's membership in the EU was a 'good thing'. This had dropped to 53 per cent by 1995 and 49 per cent by 2003. The percentage of respondents expressing "trust" in the EU fell to 42 per cent in 2003. (Directorate General Press and Communication, 2003, 1995, 1991).

The strategy adopted for improving European support for the European Union is to promote opportunities for local interests to contribute to EU decision–making and to make the activities of the Union more visible to the public. In 2001, the Commission issued a white paper on European governance (European Commission, 2001a). The reforms outlined in the white paper focus on four areas;

- Developing minimum standards for consultations by the
- Commission with interested outside parties
- The use of experts in all stages of Community policy-making.
- Improving the use of advisory committees by the Commission
- Improving the effectiveness of the impact statements that are
- developed for major legislative initiatives

The easy reliance of the Commission on in–house experts and advisory committees is also under review (European Commission, 2002a: European Commission, 2002b). Some necessary attention is being paid to the development and use of the impact statements that are routinely prepared for all major legislative initiatives (Directorate General Governance, 2003). The leadership of European Parliament is also showing signs of a greater receptivity to the views of business on regulatory issues. The intellectual framework for parliamentary discussions is usually set out in the committee reports on a particular topic. The committee rapporteurs are responsible for developing the draft committee reports. Few resources are available to the rapporteurs through Parliament for the development of these drafts. Business experts that can provide the rapporteurs with comprehensive, accurate and balanced analyses of their issues will often receive a friendly hearing. However, this invitation applies only to European business, no American interests need apply. These developments are providing the basis for the 'better regulation' initiative (Directorate General Enterprise, 2003a).

To the author, who was a federal bureaucrat in a previous life, these proposals still reflect the assumption that input from outside groups into the political process is a privilege that should be controlled by government bureaucrats. However, the assertion that this privilege should be widely extended and that the results should be considered seriously represents a major change in the administrative philosophy of the European Union. This change in emphasis is being resisted and the development of a culture of consultation will take years (European Commission, 2002a).

3. ENVIRONMENTAL REGULATIONS

European interests are likely to applaud these movements towards a more effective administration and a more open and efficient CE marking system. However, they may question the increasing scope and rigor of European product regulation from an environmental perspective. The power of the European Parliament has been increasing and the influence of the Greens in parliament has been growing. The Greens are also a member of the ruling coalition in Germany. The fact that DG Environment has significant control over the Packaging and Packaging Waste Directive, the Waste from Electronic and Electrical Equipment Directive, the Removal of Hazardous Substances Directive and the proposed Energy–Using Products Directive is an indicator of how the relative influence of DG Environment has grown.

Together with the European traditions of an activist government, the nature of the environmental coalition has led to a broad vision for environmental management. The Commission issued a 'green paper' on a new concept, the Integrated Product Policy, in February 2001 (European Commission, 2001b). (A green paper covers policy initiatives that are still under discussion. A white paper discusses policies that have been approved but not implemented.) The paper was based on a 1998 report from Ernst & Young (Directorate General Environment, 1998), a series of public consultations (European Commission, 2003) and a follow–up study issued in 2000 (Ernst & Young, 2000). The IPP is a major innovative element in the 6th Environmental Action Programme. The Commission held a workshop on 18 June 2001 on the relations among the IPP, standardization and the New Approach (European Commission, 2001f). The Council discussed and approved the 6th Environmental Action Programme (European Council: Environment, n.d.) The IPP has become a component of the EU strategy for the Gothenburg Summit on sustainable development.

Rather than addressing each environmental situation as a separate issue, the IPP calls for a greater emphasis on controlling product life cycle pollution load (European Commission, 2001d). The program would be implemented through a framework directive and a series of implementing regulations (European Commission, 2001b).

The 'precautionary principle' is becoming a key element in the development of the IPP. Under the precautionary principle, the burden of proof on environmental regulation is essentially reversed. It might be assumed that governments should not regulate unless an activity has been shown to be harmful. Under the precautionary principle, governments should regulate unless an activity has been shown to be safe.

> When an activity raises threats of harm to human health or the environment, precautionary measures should be taken even if some cause–and–effect relationships are not fully established scientifically. (Science and Environment Health Network, 1998)

The precautionary principle has received qualified support from the Council as a basis for environmental regulation (European Commission, 2000). Under the Commission guidelines, the precautionary principle can be used as a basis for setting policy when potential dangerous effects from a phenomenon, product or process has been identified but no scientific basis have been established for evaluating the nature or magnitude of the risk with any degree of certainty. Any measures taken under the precautionary principle must be:

- Proportional to the chosen level of protection
- Non-discriminatory
- Consistent with other measures taken
- Based on a cost/benefit analysis
- Subject to review in the light of new scientific data, and
    capable of assigning responsibility for developing the scientific
    data

The enthusiasm in the EU for the precautionary principle has become another element in the on–going discussions over international regulatory convergence. The US has never formally accepted the precautionary principle as an element of domestic regulatory policy. *Executive Order 12866* of 30 September 1993 states that:

1. a). Federal agencies should promulgate only such regulations as are required by law, are necessary to interpret the law, or are made necessary by compelling public need, such as materials failures of private markets, to protect or improve the health and safety of the public, the environment or the well–being of the American people.

7. Each agency shall base its decisions on the best reasonably available scientific, technical, economic or other information concerning the need for, and consequences of, the intended regulation.

In reality though, the US has pursued a policy of strong regulation in such areas as nuclear power and pharmaceuticals. However, the combination of international differences in the acceptance of the precautionary principle and the areas and ways in which it is used in reality has complicated the process of international negotiation in areas in which either side has adopted more cautious regulatory strategies (European Commission, 2002b).

The implementation of the IPP will lead to the development of an integrated system for pollution control, focusing on a product life cycle pollution impact and utilizing a market–based approach whenever possible. The Commission has suggested several measures for improving the market for green products. These include promoting public awareness of green issues, lowering the VAT on eco–labeled products and encouraging member governments to limit procurement to eco–labeled products. On the supply side, the Commission has suggested the development of guidelines on green design.

The development of the 'eco–labeling' program in 1993 was a major step in the development and promotion of environmental product standards in the European Union. Eco–labeling is a voluntary program that offers commercial distinction to consumer products that meet rigorous environmental standards. The eco–labeling criteria for different categories of products are developed by the EUEB, the European Union Eco–labeling Board. The manufacturers of products that meet the EUEB criteria can use the eco–labeling flower logo on their product packaging and promotion materials. The eco–labeling program goal is intended:

To achieve significant environmental improvements – by developing, publishing and promoting criteria that push the market forward, in order to minimize the environmental impacts of a wide range of products over their whole life cycle. (European Union Eco–labeling Board, 2004)

This goal is to be achieved by working:

> For the Flower to be recognized as Europe's premier award for products which are a genuinely better choice for the environment, helping manufacturers, retailers and service providers to get recognition for good standards, and purchasers to make reliable choices. (European Union Eco–labeling Board, 2004)

Directorate General Environment has organized an administrative framework to promote the development and adoption of the eco–labeling system. The eco–labeling criteria are to be developed by the European Union Eco–labeling Board, after consultations with governmental experts from the Member States and with stakeholders in industry and the public sector. At the national level, a series of 'competent bodies' are charged with accessing applications and awarding eco–labels for products and companies that meet the criteria developed by the EUEB. Most of the competent bodies are government ministries or non–profit environmental associations (Directorate General Environment, 2004).

Eco–labeling criteria have been established for household cleaners, mattresses, detergents, dishwashers, washing machines, vacuum cleaners, shoes, light bulbs, personal computers, TVs, soil improvers, paints, textiles and tissues.

The eco–labeling system has faced several challenges. Businesses have generally fought proposals to make the voluntary eco–labeling system somewhat less voluntary by requiring that government procurement favor eco–labeled products. The European system also faces challenges from similar systems in other countries where the labeling standards may not be as rigorous.

The environmental product initiatives are also being implemented through several directives in the area of product regulation. One of them was the *Packaging and Packaging Waste Directive* (European Council, 1994). The directive was originally developed by DG Enterprise as a New Approach directive in order to stake a claim over environmental aspects of product regulation. This effort ultimately failed. CEN was asked to include environmental interests in the standards development process (European Commission, 1998). The European Environmental Bureau was invited to participate in the TC developing the standards needed to implement the directive. They walked out in a noisy divorce when they found that the standards development process was dominated by business interests.

The Packaging Directive directs the member states to develop of a nomenclature for classifying packaging. Targets are set for the per centage of weight that can be devoted to packaging and what fraction of that should be recyclable. National governments are then invited to set goals and administrative systems for limiting and collecting packaging waste.

WEEED, the *Waste Electrical and Electronic Equipment Directive* (European Council, 2003), directs national governments to develop and enforce systems for collecting, reusing, recycling and disposing of used electronic products. Manufacturers are to pay for the costs of handling their used equipment. The costs of handling 'orphan' equipment, where the manufacturer is either unknown or unavailable, are to be assessed among the responsible manufacturers on a pro rata basis.

WEEED has generated a lot of comment. It is expected that implementation of the directive will generate a waste stream that is sufficiently large to support private initiatives (*Economist*, 2003b). A few multi-national corporations are exploring the possibility of jointly developing a private collection and disposal network (*Country Monito,r* 2003). On the other hand, many companies may not appreciate the scope of their new responsibilities (*EE Times*, 2002) This made lead to a pattern of dumping end of life products in third world countries to avoid problems with domestic disposal (*EE Times,* 2002b; *Knight Ridder Tribune Business News*, 2002).

The WEEE Directive came into force on publication. The passage of the WEEE Directive was triggered by the development of a similar law in the Netherlands. The Dutch national law seems to work well. However, a number of the EU member states have not yet developed the national legislation and institutions needed to implement WEEED. It is not clear how long it will be until an effective system is developed in countries such as Italy. Many of the lower income countries seem to have little interest in developing the programs necessary to implement WEEED.

RoHS is the *Removal of Hazardous Substances Directive* (European Council, 2003). This is the environmental directive that is potentially the most troubling for manufacturers. The directive has been adopted and is scheduled to come into force on 1 July 2006. The directive requires EU member states to develop and enforce programs for eliminating the use of lead, cadmium, hexavalent chromium, and mercury in equipment sold or placed into service in the EEA. The use of lead will still be allowed for high temperature soldering purposes.

There are several difficulties with the RoHS directive. First, it will have little effect on the industrial use of, for example, lead. The US Geological Survey estimated that 426 tons of lead were used for solder in the first two months of 2001. In contrast, 231 000 tons of lead were used for storage batteries during the same period. However, this inconsistency may be addressed through a proposal to ban the use of lead in car batteries as well.

Second, the capital cost of converting to lead–free production can be substantial and processing temperatures can affect sensitive components. (*EBN*, 2001). It is not certain that there is a reliable substitute for lead in soldering electric and electronic circuits. Sony has been promoting the use of bismuth, but it may lead to reliability problems.

Third, American manufacturers may have difficulties finding components that meet the RoHS standards. Since compliance with the RoHS directive will be required for most equipment sold in the EU, European component manufacturers will have a strong incentive to come into compliance at an early date. However, American component manufacturers will not have the same incentive, since only a small fraction of their products are likely to be incorporated in products going into European markets.

Fourth, how these additional product design requirements will be coordinated with the CE marking system is not clear. Program managers in DG Environment tend to see themselves as defending the environment against the ravages of business. DG Enterprise is generally regarded within the Commission as the handmaiden for business. Communication channels between the two directorates are not always clear. After the noisy resignation of the European Environmental Bureau, CEN is certainly seen as a conscious, card–carrying agent of European business. As a result, the directives drafted and managed by DG Environment generally incorporate the detailed product requirements rather than relying on standards developed by outside agencies for implementation. However, this issue is addressed in part by the 'green standards initiative' that is discussed below.

Fifth, the implementation of the RoHS directive could have an impact on the internal free market. The RoHS directive comes under a different provision of the Treaty of Rome and the member states are free to impose more stringent requirements on products sold and used in their national territories. The New Approach directives are an integral part of the internal free market program. They come under Article 95 of the Treaty, which requires the member states to conform exactly to EU legislation. The RoHS directive comes under the environmental program and is governed by Article 125 of the Treaty. According to this article, Commission legislation sets the minimum required level of environmental protection. The member states are free to set more stringent requirements, as long as they are not inconsistent with EU policies and programs.

A fourth directive, *Energy Using Products,* is still in the draft stage (European Commission, 2003a). The goal of the proposed EUP is to reduce the environmental impact of products sold or placed into service in the European Economic Area by requiring manufacturers to implement green design criteria in product development. The EUP is expected to cover all products that use electricity or solid, liquid or gaseous fuels. Components as well as completed products would be covered. Cars, trucks and other types of transportation would probably be exempt since they are already covered by other types of environmental regulations.

The proposed EUP would be a framework directive that would have no legal effect until implementing measures were subsequently developed. These measures would be developed by the Commission after consultations with an as yet undefined regulatory committee. The implementing measures would be developed for specific categories of products. The products to be covered by EUP would be selected on the basis of the volume of trade, the environmental impact, the potential costs and benefits of green design and the environmental priorities of the Community. The implementing measures would have to consider the pollution impact during the entire product life cycle. Implementation of these measures should not have a significant impact on product cost, performance or safety, nor should they have a significant impact on the competitive position of the manufacturers. The implementing measures could also incorporate specific eco–design requirements. EUP is viewed, for example, as one of the tools for implementing the Kyoto energy consumption and greenhouse gas emission targets on the basis of studies developed by the European Climate Change Programme (Directorate General Environment, 2003b).

Even though the development of the draft directive has been controlled by DG Environment, the proposed EUP would be considered as a New Approach directive requiring the use of the CE mark symbol. There would be three routes to conformity assessment: internal design control, participation in an approved design group or product testing. The assessment of internal design controls would be based on the company's technical file. Companies that have a valid EMAS (Environmental Management Assessment System) certificate would be presumed to comply with the environmental management system requirement (Directorate General Environment, 2003c). To get EMAS certification, companies would have to show that they have effectively implemented ISO 14001 in their company control and documentation systems. The "design group" option would exempt manufacturers from conformity assessment if they could show that the design of their product was developed by an organization with a valid EMAS certificate. Notified bodies could also use ISO 14001 as the basis for conformity assessment.

The implementation of the product testing alternative to conformity assessment would require the development of the appropriate harmonized standards. The draft directive assumes that standards would be developed by the member states to implement specific EUP requirements. As we discussed in Chapter 2, Community legislation sets the minimum requirements for environmental legislation. The member states are free to develop more stringent environmental regulations as long as they are 'consistent with' the Treaty of Rome. However, participation in the process of developing these environmental standards would be opened up.

> Member states shall ensure that appropriate measures are taken to enable interested parties to be consulted . . . on the process of preparing and monitoring the harmonized standards. (European Parliament and Council, 2003)

The implementation of these requirements would significantly change the process for developing harmonized standards in the EU. These developments could lead to a further politicization of the standards development process. The draft EUP Directive also includes a safeguard clause that authorizes member states to protest against standards that do not meet the essential requirements of the EUP. The Commission decision on the protest is to be published in the Official Journal. Approval for the standard can be withdrawn and a new mandate can be issued to the relevant standards development organization (we assume it will still be CEN, CENELEC or ETSI) for the development of a revised or new standard.

The terms of article 9 potentially give the member states the last voice on what interests are represented in the technical committees that are charged with developing the standards that will be used to implement the EUP. Since the purpose of many EUP standards is likely to be to force design changes, the experiences of industry representatives who are members of the TCs with existing designs would be far less relevant. Tensions will probably arise between industry representatives defending existing design requirements and environmental representatives pushing for more radical design changes. This would probably complicate efforts to achieve consensus decision–making at the TC level. The messy relations between CEN and the BEE in the development of standards for the Packaging and Packaging Waste Directive that we discussed in Chapter 6 might be an example of this process.

Under the terms of the draft EUP, the member states could have an important role in approving (or not protesting against) harmonized standards. An informal review and approval of a draft standard by national regulatory authorities could become as important as the present process where standards are accepted by a vote of the CEN, CENELEC or ETSI members. The protest review process would give DG Environment an important role in reconsidering the terms of a challenged standard through the process of developing a new mandate.

However, we assume that the development of the standards implementing the EUP would still be subject to the controls that are already in place. As we discussed in Chapter 2, member states are required to notify Brussels under the Mutual Information Directive (European Council, 1983) before adopting any requirement that could interfere with the internal free market. The Commission can impose a standstill period to allow for a free market solution to be developed. We assume that the Mutual Information Directive would apply.

The impact of the EUP on US exporters to the EU could be substantial, depending on if or how it is implemented. In the explanatory memorandum for the proposed EUP, the Commission discusses several arguments as to why the economic impact of implementation on European manufacturers might be relatively modest. In addition to the safeguards built into the implementation process, the Commission assumes that costs will come down as energy costs are reduced, manufacturers become more familiar with green design requirements and component manufacturers offer a larger range of conforming products.

US manufacturers trying to adopt products built for domestic markets to meet European requirements may have to redesign and re–document the process of product development. This can be very expensive. In order to benefit from the learning curve, it would be helpful for a manufacturer to be working in a market in which these requirements are generally applied. This condition would not apply to most American manufacturers.

The EU is also considering new regulations in the chemicals sector that would have a significant impact on manufacturers. The proposed regulations could have a significant impact on companies using specialty chemicals in their manufacturing processes as well as on the chemical companies that produce them.

Under the current system, companies introducing 'new chemicals' to the European marketplace after September 1981 in quantities greater than 10 kilos must first assess the risks to human health and the environment. 'New chemicals' sold in larger volumes must first undergo more rigorous testing on the effects of long–term exposure (Directive 67/548). An estimated 99 per cent of all chemicals in general use are not covered by the directive and are not subject to the same testing requirements.

The Commission therefore proposed a new chemicals policy. Under the proposed REACH (Registration, Evaluation and Authorization of Chemicals) program, all chemicals produced or sold in volumes greater than one metric ton would have to be assessed for toxicity. The results would have to be filed in a central database. Chemicals produced or sold in volumes greater than 100 metric tons per year would have to be evaluated by the Community authorities. The production or use of chemicals that meet guidelines defining potential high toxicity would require prior authorization by the Commission (European Commission, 2001c). The business impact assessment on the proposal estimated that the costs of testing would range from 1.91 billion euros to 5.01 billion euros, depending on the estimated number of chemicals in each category (Risk and Policy Analysts Ltd, 2002).

The Community is not likely to allow the CE marking system to be seriously jeopardized by a lack of communication among different directorates or that the member states would be allowed to clog up the internal free market through inconsistent applications of RoHS and other directives. However an institutional resolution of these issues will probably require strengthening organizational leadership of the Community, both within the Commission and between the Commission and the member states.

Change in the EU tends to come during periods of crisis. Fortunately, the upcoming expansion to 25 member states may provide the occasion.

4. COMMUNITY EXPANSION: THE PECA AGREEMENTS

More changes in the administration of the CE marking system will probably be implemented as a result of the accession of ten more countries into the European Union on 1 May 2004. The expansion has brought the Czech Republic, Estonia, Cyprus, Latvia, Lithuania, Hungary, Malta, Poland, Slovakia and Slovenia into the European Union (European Commission, 2003b). Accession is a political rather than administrative decision. Once they have formally joined the EU, the new members will have full authority to notify national bodies and to appoint and supervise the surveillance authorities.

The negotiations over accession have led to a new development in the appointment of notified bodies, the Protocols for the Evaluation of Conformity Assessment (PECA) Agreements. As a practical matter, the candidate notified bodies in the new member states were facing a 'black hole' of up to six months after accession. The new member states could not complete the formalities of 'notifying' local organizations to Brussels until they joined the Community. After accession, companies located in the new accession countries had a strong interest in CE marking their products as soon as possible so they can stay on the market. The expected result was a rush by countries in the new member states to do business with established notified bodies in other member countries of the EU. This tendency to divert business to notified bodies outside the accession countries would also be supported by the potential lack of credibility of the accession country notified bodies. Manufacturers have a strong interest in using notified bodies that have credibility, whose judgments would be upheld by the surveillance authorities if their products were ever challenged. It has been difficult for notified bodies in new member states to develop a Community-wide reputation for technical expertise, rigor and integrity in a short period of time. Thus, the accession states and the candidate notified bodies had a strong interest in a program for 'pre–approving' their status.

The European Union also has a strong interest in ensuring the competence and integrity of the notified bodies in the new member states. The Commission wants to ensure the integrity of the conformity assessment process. The notified bodies in the established member states have an interest in limiting competition from new, permissive, low–cost rivals.

The PECA process was developed to address this convergence of interests. The EU signed a PECA Agreement with an accession country after the Commission has reviewed and approved the legal and administrative frameworks for administering and enforcing the CE mark requirements, the process of notifying new bodies and for transcribing the harmonized standards for local use. Although a PECA agreement could have been concluded for Any New Approach directive, the agreements tended to be limited to specific directives selected by the accession country.

The PECA process provided the accession countries with an opportunity to submit the names of 'conformity assessment bodies', their future notified bodies, before accession. For the accession countries, concluding a PECA agreement with the EU meant that the designated conformity assessment bodies were recognized as notified bodies as soon as the host country formally joined the EU. For the Commission, the PECA process provided a stronger basis for ensuring that the accession process would not lead to the proliferation of inexperienced notified bodies that lacked both expertise and integrity. For the notified bodies in the established EU member states, the PECA process provided assurances that enlargement did not lead to new competitive pressures for lower costs and lower standards. It also provided the candidate notified bodies with a chance to be evaluated and ultimately approved by a well–established notified body before accession. The PECA agreements concluded with the accession countries are listed below in Table 9.3.

Table 9.3. PECA Agreements signed with Accession Countries

Country	Directives covered by completed PECA agreements
Czech Republic	Machinery, Lifts, Personal Protective Equipment, EMC, ATEX, Hot –water boilers, Gas Fired Appliances, Pressure Equipment, Medical Devices (quality control)
Estonia	EMC, LVD, Lifts, Toys
	Hungary Machinery, LVD, EMC, Hot Water Boilers, Gas Fired Appliances, Medical Devices
Latvia	LVD, EMC, Toys, Construction Products
Lithuania	Machinery, Lifts, PPE, LVD, EMC, Simple Pressure Vessels
Slovakia	Machinery, PPE, LVD, EMC, ATEX

Source: Directorate General Enterprise (2003b).

The PECA process began when an accession country asked for a PECA Agreement. The request specified the New Approach directives that the PECA would cover. Before signing an agreement, the Commission required the candidate country to undergo reviews in two areas. One was to assess the legal bases and administrative procedures that the accession country was going to use for notifying a body. A lot of this work is done under contract with groups such as the EOTC. The second review evaluateed the technical and administrative competencies of the proposed notified bodies. This process was generally carried out by highly respected notified bodies, such as one of the TUVs, working under contract with the Commission. The Commission also provided technical assistance and funded a substantial portion of the costs incurred by the government of the accession country and the candidate notified bodies to come into conformity with the PECA requirements.

The PECA agreements were signed when the Commission was convinced that the accession country and candidate notified bodies were in compliance with the CE mark requirements. As soon as it was signed, the candidate notified bodies were designated as 'conformity assessment bodies'. They become recognized as notified bodies at the moment of accession.

The process of negotiating a PECA Agreement was often difficult for the accession states. Fundamental legal issues have arisen in several accession states. The differences between the Hungarian legal system, for example, and the West European norms, made it difficult to incorporate the required framework legislation governing notified bodies within the general Hungarian legal order. Translation issues have been likely to arise since the accession states are less likely to be familiar with the details of CE mark administration in Western Europe. Local administration of the CE marking system will be governed by Community law, as it has been implemented in the accession country. It may take a while to determine whether and to what extent the local law has deviated from what was intended in the *acquis communitaire* which was developed in different countries in different languages.

A number of the accession states have encountered political difficulties with the notification process. In some of the accession countries, the old Russian habits of hierarchy and politics in an all–powerful government have not yet dissipated. In most of the accession countries, the leading candidates for notification and for the role of the national standards organization tended to be recently privatized government ministries. These candidates may not yet have acquired the technical and marketing competencies needed to survive in the competitive world of European notified bodies.

On the other hand, the EU internal review process is inherently rigorous. A PECA Agreement is a formal agreement among governments. The review process within the EU bureaucracy therefore includes DG Enterprise, DG External Relations and the Council of Foreign Ministers. The rigor of the process reflects the extent to which the participants in the process take their interests seriously.

The completion of the accession process on 1 May 2004 ended a further problem that American manufacturers are encountering with the PECA process. The PECA agreements included free trade rights for CE marked goods before accession. This involved the elimination of duties and the customary requirement for product certification under the pre–existing national system. Since these were agreements between the EU and the accession countries, these rights were often limited to CE marked goods originating in the EU. In some cases, CE marked goods manufactured in the US were not eligible for free trade status.

The European Union has argued that they never intended the PECA agreements to discriminate against foreign manufacturers. In negotiations with the Americans, they reportedly took the position that they would have no objection to amending the agreements to make them generally applicable. However, the treaty review process on both sides was so lengthy that few agreements were amended before accession.

The recent expansion of the EU to include 10 more countries does not end the planned extension of the CE marking system to new markets and countries. There is another set of countries that are scheduled to be considered for accession to the European Union: Bulgaria, Romania and possibly Turkey (Directorate General Enterprise, 2003c).

The terms of accession will change somewhat from the present rules. The Commission will be pushing for the acceptance of regional notified bodies. Malta has already signaled a willingness to act as a 'flag of convenience' for European notified bodies. Rather than trying to notify Maltese organizations, the government will notify the most qualified applicants from other European member countries.

The second change is the addition of a 'super safeguard' clause in the next set of accession agreements. To be eligible for membership, a candidate country should have incorporated the *acquis communuatarie*, the core body of EU law, into national law. However, extending membership to a new country is a political and not an administrative decision that is not likely to be withdrawn if the transposition of EU rules into national law is not complete. Under the present rules, the Commission has to file a lawsuit with the European Court of Justice to force national compliance with the rules of the European Union. Under the new rules, the Commission will be able to suspend national participation in specific EU programs if national participation does not follow the proscribed rules. This will provide a stronger incentive for all countries to go through the PECA process. It may also signal a push for developing more stringent rules governing the notification process and the supervision of notified bodies within the present member states. However, this would probably require a change in the political ground rules of the EU.

5. EXPANSION AND ADMINISTRATIVE CHANGE

The expansion of the EU will bring in a new set of political issues. There are problems as present, as we have noted, with the effective coordination within the Commission among the directorates. They are likely to become worse with expansion. Before the recent expansion, all member states had the right to name at least one commissioner. After expansion, the smaller countries will have to share naming rights. Without other changes, this will be likely to increase the prospects for confusion as a potential lack of continuity will be added to the present problems with the coordination of CE marking policies.

During their meeting on 14 and 15 December 2001, the Council of Europe issued a mandate for a Convention to review the basic constitutional framework of the European Union (European Convention, 2003a). The Convention was chaired by Valerey Giscard d'Estaing. The report of the Convention and a new draft treaty was released to the public on 18 July 2003 (The European Convention, 2003b). A number of the issues we have discussed on the implementation of CE marking would be affected by the implementation of the draft treaty.

The role of the European Union would be enhanced. The European Union would become a legal personality, competent to enter into international treaties that would be binding on the member states. The Union would be given new administrative tools for the coordination of foreign policy (Sciolino, 2003).

The basic framework of a council, commission, parliament and court of justice would be retained. However, the administrative competencies and political roles of these institutions would be increased. The role of the Council would be strengthened. The president of the Council of Europe would be elected by the council members to a two and a half–year term, with a possibility for re–election for an additional term. The Council would assume responsibility for conducting the foreign policy of the Community. The Union Minister for Foreign Affairs would be elected by the Council and would work as a member of the Council. The Council of Ministers would be responsible for conducting the foreign policy of the EU. The roles of the member states in international relations would be cut back substantially.

The Commission would consist of 13 commissioners, named by the member states on a rotating basis The Commission would be headed by a president, who would be nominated by the Council and elected by Parliament. The Union Minister for Foreign Affairs would serve as a vice president of the Commission. The European Parliament would be expanded to 736 members, who would continue to be elected directly for five year terms. The co–decision process, which grants the European Parliament the broadest participation, would become the norm for Community decision–making.

Critics of the draft convention have already emerged. A minority report was filed to the final report that questioned whether the proposal did much to address the democratic deficit issue. The wisdom of electing two presidents, one for the Council and one for the Commission, has been questioned. Many eurosceptics have challenged the expansion of Community competencies and administrative capabilities (*The Economist*, 2003). Nevertheless, any move to expand and rationalize the Commission's administrative capabilities and internal coordination processes would help address some of the problems that were discussed in chapters 5 and 6.

6. PROMOTING CE MARKING OUTSIDE OF THE EU

The European Union is also promoting the adoption of the CE marking system outside the member states. Australia and New Zealand have adopted the medical device directives and the associated harmonized standards in their entirety. These programs provide support for the free trade agreements with the EU. CEN, CENELEC and ETSI have also accepted membership from countries that have free trade agreements with the EU, even if they are not formally EU members.

The Chinese CCC system for regulating higher risk products is remarkably similar to the CE mark system. The system came into force on 1 July 2003 as a replacement for the CCEE and Great Wall systems, which were inconsistent with WTO obligations. The purpose of the CCC system is to provide conformity assessment requirements and procedures for hazardous products. CCC is not a stand–alone system; it should be regarded as an integral part of a program for product regulation that also includes the mandatory system of GB standards.

The new Chinese GB standards and CCC conformity assessment systems are similar to their European counterparts. The GB standards are generally based on or borrowed from ISO and IEC standards. For most products, the CCC conformity assessment system is based on third party validation of a company quality control process. The CCC review criteria are patterned after ISO 9000.

There are differences between the EU and Chinese systems. There are no notified bodies in China. The China National Certification Agency is responsible for administering the CCC system. Instead of using notified bodies, quality control reviews will be conducted by another agency, the Chinese Certification Center.

The parallels between the EU and Chinese systems should make it easier for European manufacturers to enter Chinese markets. This will be particularly true for electrotechnical and telecommunications products where the differences between European and international standards are relatively small.

In contrast, the Chinese system could create problems for American manufacturers. The differences between the American and Chinese systems in standards and conformity assessment requirements are substantially larger than between the Chinese and European requirements. In addition, the US consular section has apparently encountered delays in processing the entry visas for the Chinese teams that are scheduled to conduct the US factory inspections. European manufacturers already have a significant advantage over their American competitors because of the similarities between the requirements of the CE marking and CCC systems. They could gain an added advantage if the EU immigration officials are able to process entry requests from the Chinese inspection teams in a reasonable period of time.

In Latin America, the European Union has entered into free trade agreements with Mexico and Mercosur (Mercado Comun del Sur: Argentina, Brazil, Paraguay and Uruguay, with Chile as an associate member). The EU has also entered into technical assistance programs for the national standards organizations for both regions. The goal of the programs is to promote the local adoption of CE marking and the use of harmonized standards. These programs include the cost–free donation of the rights to all harmonized standards to the national standards development organizations (European Council, 1995).

American standards development organizations have been working with their European counterparts to minimize the problems encountered in exporting products built in accordance with American standards to Latin America. However, these efforts have not been backed with the advocacy or resources of the US government.

7. AMERICAN ACCESS TO INTERNATIONAL MARKETS

We have discussed above what the Europeans have been doing to clean up the CE marking system and to expand the range of the markets in which CE marking is the accepted standard for regulating product safety. To the extent to which the Europeans are successful, European manufacturers will enjoy competitive advantages in market access.

What have the Americans been doing? In the early 1990s, NIST proposed the creation of SCUSA, the Standards Council of the United States of America. SCUSA would have been an agency of the United States government that would be charged with coordinating and helping to fund private sector standards development in the US. Supporters argued that SCUSA would have carried the status of official government backing in international discussions. SCUSA funding would have made it more likely that initiatives in US standards development would be based on business needs rather than on industry's willingness to pay. With government support and funding in hand, SCUSA would be able to coordinate the decentralized US standards community more effectively.

The US standards development community was almost unanimously opposed to the development of SCUSA. Opponents of SCUSA argued that it represented another government grab for regulatory authority over the private sector, that it was an organization in search of a mission and that government should stay out of the private sector standards development process. SCUSA was withdrawn after hearings at NIST before Congress had taken an interest in the proposal. Since the demise of SCUSA, there have been virtually no new initiatives for government coordination of private standards development in the US.

Since the defeat of SCUSA, ANSI has been one of the most active organizations in advocating new strategies for managing the US standards development process. The major vehicle for this initiative has been *A National Standards Strategy for the United States* (American National Standards Institute, 2000). The primary goal of the document is to improve the ability of American interests to influence the development of standards in Europe, with a focus on CEN and CENELEC.

> By taking an active role whenever and wherever possible, the US can work to influence the development of European product and service standards so that US interests are not disenfranchised from these markets. (American National Standards Institute, 1966)

The national strategy is intended to improve the standing of ANSI in the US standards development community by committing the organization to the perpetuation of the status quo. US standards development organizations, including ANSI, are to remain in the private sector and free from government involvement. These organizations are called upon to support ANSI's efforts to represent the US SDOs in the international arena. The enthusiastic implementation of the national strategy would result in more support for ANSI from the member organizations. However the critical issues, funding for standards development and competition over the control of standards, are not addressed. Neither would the implementation of the ANSI national strategy change the factors limiting international acceptance of US standards that were discussed in Capters 6 and 7.

ASTM International is also offering a new strategy that emphasizes the development of closer working relations with the IEC. This would lead to the coordination of new standards development between the two bodies and then a mutual willingness to withdraw conflicting standards if there is a better one already on the market (ASTM International, 2003).

The US government has also been pushing for improved international market access for American companies through a series of bilateral free trade agreements. Chile has been brought into NAFTA and stand-alone free trade agreements have been signed with Israel, Jordan and Singapore. The big prize would be the FTAA, the Free Trade Agreement of the Americas. The FTAA was proposed during the 1994 Summit of the Americas in Miami. Since then, negotiations for the FTAA have proceeded in fits and starts (Free Trade Agreement of the Americas, 2003a). The major issues are whether both Brazil, the most important skeptic in Latin America, and the US Congress really want to have an agreement.

The draft FTAA, like the concluded text of NAFTA, goes far beyond a mutual agreement on the reciprocal abolition of tariffs. The draft has a strong emphasis on the harmonization of trade procedures and regulations around a common set of international norms. A chapter of the draft FTAA concerns standards and technical barriers to trade (Free Trade Agreement of the Americas, 2003).

Virtually every provision in the text is under discussion so it is difficult to draft any conclusions about the final form of the treaty. If implemented as drafted, the member states would be required to strengthen their standards development and conformity assessment programs and to reduce non–tariff trade barriers arising from national differences in these areas. The TBT would be the governing document. National standards would be based, as much as possible, on international standards. The participation of national standards development organizations in ISO and the IEC would be encouraged. Regional standards organizations, such as the Pan American Standards Commission could help to coordinate national efforts.

Members of the FTAA could also be committed to accepting the equivalencies of technical regulations issued by other member states when the issuing state has demonstrated that they fulfill the importing state's legitimate objectives. Conformity assessment bodies from all member states would be eligible to be certified by any member states on terms that are no more restrictive than the conditions for national certification. To promote this process, FTAA members are pledged to participate in mutual recognition agreements under the Inter–American Accreditation Cooperation agreement.

Negotiations over the FTAA have involved the collection of data on national standards bodies, accreditation programs and international agreements. To summarize this data: most of the national standards development organizations in the major countries of the hemisphere are agents of their national governments. In general, ISO and IEC standards are used as the basis for developing national standards. Virtually all of the major FTAA countries are members of ISO. They all belong to regional standards organizations, such as the Pan American Commission on Technical

Standards), the Mercosur Standardization Committee or the Andean Committee on Standardization, Certification and Metrology (Free Trade Agreement of the Americas, 2003b).

The striking aspect of the draft FTAA is the extent to which it implicitly endorses the European interpretation of the TBT. Although ISO and the IEC are never mentioned by name, the draft treaty is based on an implicit assumption that the nature of the standards development organization, and not the level of international acceptance for the standard, defines an international standard. The mandate to participate in international standards development is more easily understood as referring to COPANT and ISO rather than to ASTM and ASME. The call for regional coordination on the basis of international organizations would further weaken the role of American standards development organizations.

8. AND SO. . . ?

The picture seems clear. he Europeans are working to improve the administration of the CE marking system. The scope of the CE marking system is being extended through the accession of new countries to the EU and by a fairly aggressive program of international promotion in the world outside the EU.

The American response is, at best, muted. Standards development in the US is considered to be a private sector function. The failure of SCUSA demonstrated the extent to which US standards development organizations can cooperate to resist government involvement in the world of US SDOs.

Regional trade and investment by US multinational corporations has already led to a high degree of acceptance of US standards in Latin America. However, US political initiatives in the region may have the effect of pushing Latin American governments towards the use of ISO and IEC standards instead. Given the close working relations between ISO and IEC on one hand and CEN, CENELEC and ETSI on the other, this should make it easier for European companies to enter Latin American markets.

REFERENCES

American National Standards Institute (1996), *American Access to the European Standardization Process*, Washington: ANSI.

American National Standards Institute (2000), *A National Standards Strategy for the United States*, Washington: ANSI.

ASTM International (2003), 'National standards strategy for the United States', at www.astm.org.

Country Monitor (2003), 'New approach to electronic waste', 27 January, pp. 3, 5.

Directorate General Enterprise (2003a), 'Better regulation' at http://europe.eu.int/comm/enterprise/regulation/better_regulation.

Directorate General Enterprise (2003b), 'Enlargement PECAs', at http://europe.eu.int/comm/enterprise/regulation/pecas/peca_hu.html

Directorate General Enterprise (2003c), 'Enlargement', at http://europa.eu.int/comm/enlargement/pas/Europe_agr.html.

Directorate General Environment (1998), *Integrated Product Policy.*

Directorate General Environment (2003a), 'How has the Commission developed IPP so far?', at http://europe.eu.int/comm/environment/ipp /2001developments.html.

Directorate General Environment (2003b), 'Climate change homepage; second ECCP progress report: can we meet our Kyoto targets?', at http://europe.eu.int/comm/environment/climat/eccp.html.

Directorate General Environment (2003c), 'Eco-management and audit scheme', at: http://europa.eu.int/comm/environment/emas/about/ summary.html.

Directorate General Environment (2004), 'Eco-label homepage', at http:// europa eu.int/comm/environment/ecolabel.html.

Directorate General Governance (2003), 'Impact assessment in the Commission: internal guidelines on the new impact assessment procedure developed for the Commission services', at http://europa..eu. int/comm/governance/suivi_ib_en.html.

Directorate General Health and Consumer Protection (2000), 'Commission adopts communication on precautionary principle', at http://Europa. eu.int/comm./dgs/health_consumer/library/press38_en.html.

Directorate General Internal Market (2003), 'Update on the single market: SLIM', at http://europa.eu.int/comm/internal_market/en/update/slim/ 5phase.html.

Directorate General Press and Communication (2003, 1999, 1995, 1991), 'Eurobarometer 60, 59, 53, 44, 34', at http://europa.eu.int/comm/public _opinion/archives.html.

EBN (2001), 'EU lead-ban weights on Industry–US Oems, suppliers see alternative technologies as too expensive', issue 1261, p. 1.

The Economist (2003a), 'That F–word' (2003A), 7 February, p. 1.

The Economist (2003b), 'Waste not, want not', 15 March, p. 12.

EE Times (2002a), 'Green laws fuel dumping', 4 March, p. 1.

EE Times (2002b), 'WEE message has failed in the UK', 21 October, p. 18.

Ernst & Young (2000), *Developing the Foundation for Integrated Product Policy in the EU*, Brussels: Directorate General Environment.

European Commission (1998), *Report from the Commission to the Council and the European Parliament: Efficiency and Accountability in European Standardization under the New Approach,* COM (1998) 291 final.

European Commission (2000), *White Paper on Environmental Liability,* COM(2000) 66 final.

European Commission (2001a), *White Paper: Strategy for a Future Chemicals Policy,* COM (2001) 88 final.

European Commission (2001b), *Report from the Commission to the Council and the European Parliament on Actions Taken Following the Resolutions on European Standardization Adopted by the Council and the European Parliament in 1999,* COM (2001) 527 final.

European Commission (2001c), *European Governance: A White Paper,* COM (2001) 428 final.

European Commission (2001d), *Staff Working Paper, Simpler Legislation for the Internal Market: Report on the Outcome of the 5th Phase of SLIM.*

European Commission (2001e), *Green Paper on Integrated Product Policy,* COM (2001) 68 final.

European Commission (2001f), *Summary of Discussions at the 6th Integrated Product Policy Expert Workshop: Standardization and the New Approach.* Brussels.

European Commission (2002a), *Communication from the Commission, Consultation Document; Towards a Reinforced Culture of Consultation and Dialog – Proposal for General Principles and Minimum Standards for Consultation of Interested Parties by the Commission,* COM (2002) 277 final. .

European Commission (2002b). 'The reality of precaution: comparing transatlantic approaches to risks and regulation', Group of Policy Advisors; Project 1 at http://europa.eu.int/commdgs/policy–advisers /activities/science_technology/ijndex_en.html.

European Commission (2003a), *Proposal for a Directive of the European Parliament and the of the Council; on Establishing a Framework for the Setting of Eco–Design Requirements for Energy–Using Products and amending Council Directive 92/42/EEU,* COM (2003) 453 final.

European Commission (2003b), *Continuing Enlargement: Strategy Paper and Report of the European Commission on the Progress Towards Accession by Bulgaria, Romania and Turk*ey.

European Commission, (2003c), *Communication from the Commission to the Council and the European Parliament: Enhancing the Implementation of the New Approach Directives* Brussels.,7.5.2003, COM (2003) 240 final.

European Convention (2003a), *Report from the Presidency of the Convention to the President of the European Council* CONV 851/03.

European Convention (2003b), *Rome Declaration.*

European Council (1983), *The Mutual Information Directive 83/189 of April 26; 1983.*

European Council (1994), *European Parliament and Council Directive 94/68/EC of 20 December 1994 on Packaging and Packaging Waste.*

European Council (1995), *Intergovernmental, Framework Agreement between the European Union and Mercosur* Madrid Summit, 16 December.

European Council (2002), *Directive 2002/96/EC of the European Parliament and of the Council of 27 January 2003 on Waste Electrical and Electronic Equipment.*

European Council (2003), *Directive 2002/95/EC of the European Parliament and Council of 27 January 2003 on the Restriction of the Use of Certain Hazardous Substances in Electrical and Electronic Equipment.*

European Council (Environment), 'Press release for the 235th Council Meeting', at http://ue.eu.int/newsroom/LoadDoc.asp?MAX=1& BID=89 &DID=66742&LANG=1.

European Parliament and Council (2003), *Directive 2002/95/EC of the European Parliament and of the Council of 27 January 2003 on the restrictions of the use of certain hazardous substances in electrical and electronic equipment.*

European Parliament, Committee on Economic and Monetary Affairs (2000), *Draft Opinion on the Results of the Third Phase of SLIM and Follow-up to the Implementation of the Recommendations of the First and Second Phases.* COM(2000) 104-C5-0209/2000-2000/2115(COS).

European Union Eco–labeling Board (2004), 'The European Eco–label award', at http://europe.eu.intcomm/environment/ecolabel/what_eco/ mission-statement_en.html.

Free Trade Agreement of the Americas (2002), *FTAA – Free Trade Area of the Americas: Draft Agreement,* Derestricted FTAA.TNC/w/133/Rev.2.

Free Trade Area of the Americas (2003a), 'Overview of the FTAA process', at http://www.ftaa.alca.org/View_e.asp.

Free Trade Area of the Americas (2003b), 'Inventory of national practices on standards, technical regulations and conformity assessment in the Western Hemisphere', at http://www.ftaa-alca.org/cp_tbt/english/ tbt_1b.asp.

Knight Ridder Tribune Business News (2003), 'Thai agency to check used electrical imports, monitor industrial waste', 12 August, p. 1.

Risk and Policy Analysts Ltd, Statistics Sweden (2002), *Assessment of the Impact of New Regulations in the Chemical Sector: Final Report.*

Science and Environmental Health Network (1998), 'Wingspread statement on the precautionary principle', *The Precautionary Principle in Action: A Handbook (1st ed.),* appendix XII.

Scolino, Elaine (2003), 'Europe drafting its constitution', *New York Times*, 15 June, p. 11.

10. What Can We Learn from CE Marking?

1. INTRODUCTION

In the first chapter of this work, we set out the basic issues. How is the CE marking system being implemented in the EU? That led us to a consideration of the elements of CE marking and some issues in their implementation. How does the CE marking system differ from the American system? This question led us to first examine the nature of the American standards system and the political context in which is it embedded. If the two systems are different, what is the impact of these differences on US–EU trade? If CE marking does have an impact, what is the effect likely to be on world trade in the long term? That question leads us to the issues at hand: how well are the American and European systems working? If a policy choice has to be made between the two systems, which one should be selected? If the choices are not favorable for American manufacturers, what could be done about it?

These issues, as we have argued in previous chapters, are important for world trade. CE marking is both an important issue in isolation and as an exemplar of an emerging class of international issues, the impact of inconsistent national regulations on international trade. What then, have we learned about the specific problems and general issues from this review of CE marking? We will use summaries of the arguments made in previous chapters to support our conclusions.

2. HOW WELL IS THE SYSTEM WORKING?

The New Approach to setting product safety standards was an integral part of the larger effort to promote the internal free market. The authors of the Cecchini Report (European Commission, 1998) argued that the elimination of internal trade restrictions would promote more trade, greater internal cohesion and higher levels of prosperity. We can't easily separate out the impact of the New Approach from the effects of enacting the other elements of the Cecchini plan. It is fair though to ask whether the enactment of the 1992 agenda has, overall, led to more trade and greater prosperity.

According to the European Union, it is working well. In *The Single Market Scorecard* (European Commission, 2000) the Commission reported that:

> Results from the business survey show increasing level of satisfaction among businesses with the operation of the Internal Market. . . .Three quarters of all business persons interviewed consider that the consolidation of the Internal Market will be either favorable or very favorable for their businesses. . . . A majority of businesses interviewed perceive a reduction in barriers over the last two years. (p. 2)

CE marking was an integral part of the 1992 program to complete the internal free market. If the CE mark has succeeded in lowering significant non–tariff trade barriers within the EU, then we would expect to see a significant growth in the economic importance of trade after 1985. The overall data are set forth in Table 10.1.

Table 10.1. Trade as a percentage of GNP

	1980	1985	1990	1995	2000
France	37	39	37	37	43
Germany	48	55	51	45	51
Italy	39	40	32	40	41
U.K.	48	53	48	47	48

Source: US Census Bureau, 2002

As Table 10.1 makes clear, the economic importance of international trade has increased for all four countries since 1995. However, there was no consistent pattern of change between 1980 and 1995.

According to the authors of the Cecchini Report, the development of a true internal free market would lead to rising rates of economic growth (European Commission, 1998). However, the record here is, at best spotty. The rebound in industrial production since 1985 has been relatively slow, see Table 10.2.

Analyzing the causes for trade diversion and slow growth in the EU since the mid-1980s is far beyond the task set out for this book. However, we can conclude that the 1992 reforms were not completely effective in addressing these issues. CE marking is certainly not the villain here. However, these data do not suggest that it is a hero either.

The author is not convinced that the CE marking system fully serves the interests of European industry. The EU had firmly adopted the preference for 'one standard, one test, world-wide'.

Table 10.2. Growth rates in European manufacturing

Indices of manufacturing production

	1953	1963	1973	1983	1993	2001
France	48	100	171	195	219	262.1
Germany	40	100	163	176	212	209.6
Italy	36	100	172	214	241	239.5
Netherlands	48	100	196	196	217	225.7

Percentage increases

	53-63	63-73	73-83	83-93	93-01
France	108	71	14	12	19
Germany	150	63	08	20	19
Italy	178	72	24	13	00
Netherlands	108	96	00	23	15

Source: US Census Bureau, 2002.

This position is a logical reflection of the coherence of the CE marking system and the working partnership between the European and international standards development organizations. After helping a substantial number of smaller businesses with CE marking, it seems that different compliance strategies would be more likely to help different companies. It would be useful to smaller companies to have a choice between design and performance standards or between a full design review and the use of certified components, if all approaches could provide equivalent levels of safety. Unlike the American system, CE marking is not likely to provide this level of choice.

3. CE MARKING AND THE EU

We argued in the first chapter that the process for developing the CE marking system would have an impact on the nature of the system that was developed. It should be clear from our analyses thus far that the development and enforcement of product standards is everywhere based on a partnership between government and business. Both parties are essential. Business can bring both technical expertise and a sensitivity to commercial interests to the table. Government provides the framework for defining and enforcing safety interests. However, the relations between the parties are configured differently in different regions. In the EU, government is the dominant partner. In the US, the balance favors the private sector.

We argued that the Europeans would benefit from stronger political leadership through the development of a more coherent regulatory system. The contrast between the US and EU systems for regulatory administration illustrates this process. In Europe, the CE marking system covers a very wide range of products and issues. DG Enterprise is responsible for the full range of CE mark directives. In the US, this regulatory jurisdiction is divided among at least nine Federal agencies and a large number of state and local agencies. In general, each agency has developed a separate set of policies and procedures.

On the other hand, we argued that the primacy of political leadership in Europe could lead to more intrusive regulation. In the US, politicians are unlikely to develop new regulatory programs until there is a clear constituency to support the move. These differences emerge in comparisons between the two systems. CE marking covers a lot of products that are essentially unregulated in the US. On the other hand, the US model also reflects the importance of tort litigation and the insurance industry in forcing product safety.

The differences in the positions of political leadership in the US and EU also emerge in the relatively wider acceptance of regulation in Europe. Broad programs such as the IPP, RoHS, EUP and the new chemicals policy are not likely to be accepted in the US. We are also not likely to find a broad acceptance of the precautionary principle in the US. Businesses are likely to resist regulation in the US; this resistance is likely to be overcome only where there is a showing of a concrete need to regulate.

This analysis also provides qualified support for the assertion that the policy leadership provided by the Commission and, in particular, Directorate General Enterprise, is relatively weak and that the member states are surprisingly strong. The complexities in developing and delays in implementing, for example, the Toy and Construction Products directives demonstrate how hard it can be for the Community leadership to develop a

Community consensus on specific New Approach issues. The relative inability of DG Enterprise to regulate the notified bodies and the speedy near collapse of EOTC are also suggestive of the political limitations facing the Commission and DG Enterprise. The Commission is also concerned about the wide range of competencies and strategies adopted by the surveillance authorities. This is another area in which they would find it difficult to act effectively.

On the other hand, the Commission seems to be in a stronger position in dealing with the accession countries. The PECA process constitutes a level of control over the soon to be notified bodies in Eastern Europe that could only be dreamed about in the West. If a 'super safeguards clause' is developed for the following (and possibly the last) wave of accession countries, the control of the EU over the new member states would be strengthened even more.

Market realities are strengthening the rigor and coherence of the notified body system. The earlier problems arising from excess exuberance in exercising the safeguards and failures to recognize decisions made by weak notified bodies have been largely overcome through political and commercial pressures among the member states.

It is also expected that larger notified bodies, with multi–directive, multinational authority, will increasingly dominate the system. This will also improve the coherence and expertise of the notified body system. The policy announced by Malta of offering a 'flag of convenience' for European notified bodies is one recognition of this reality. Instead of only promoting Maltese notified bodies, Malta will welcome applications from any qualified body in the EU.

In the long term, the political position of the Commission is likely to be strengthened. The commitments made under the PECA process are not likely to evaporate with accession. It is also unlikely that the Community will long tolerate two sets of rules governing notified bodies. One set of requirements would be based on existing law and apply to notified bodies in the original 15 countries, the other set would be based on the PECA process and would apply to the ten new members. It is more probable that something like the PECA requirements will eventually apply throughout. The proposals in the new draft constitution for strengthening the Commission would support that view.

4. CE MARKING AND THE POLITICS OF TRADE

The next question is whether, and to what extent, CE marking has reduced barriers to EU trade with the outside world. The gross evidence here is inconclusive. On one hand, the information in Table 10.1 suggests that CE marking may have benefited EU external trade more than internal trade. On the other hand, CE marking has also become the cause of a different set of US – EU trade barriers.

If CE marking were especially effective, we would expect to see an acceleration in the rate of economic integration within the EU. However, the fraction of total European international trade that is conducted with other members of the EU has actually been dropping since 1985 at a modest, but reasonably consistent rate, see Table 10.3. The EU argues that this pattern refutes the charge that the CE marking system is protectionist. The data suggest that the non–European manufacturers are major beneficiaries of the reforms in the internal free markets.

Table 10.3. Intra-EU trade as a percentage of total international trade

		1991	1995	1999	2001	Percentage change
France	Exports	62.1	63.5	64.2	61.1	-02
	Imports	61.1	63.5	61.6	58.4	-05
Germany	Exports	63.2	56.5	52.9	42.8	-32
	Imports	59.5	56.6	56.2	49.7	-16
Italy	Exports	62.2	56.9	57.8	53.3	-14
	Imports	61.8	60.5	61.1	56.0	-09
Netherlands	Exports	75.0	71.3	72.3	74.2	-01
	Imports	76.6	61.5	53.5	50.0	-34

Source: United Nations (2003).

A more detailed assessment of the impact of CE marking on international trade can begin with the question of intent. It is clear that the New Approach to product regulation was developed in order to mitigate problems that were clogging up the internal free market. If the EU has intended to use the CE marking system to build bridges to the larger world community, then we would expect the EU to use its political control over the CE marking system to reach out to international business interests. Instead, the CE marking system has developed in several important ways that exclude international commercial interests from consideration in the development of the system.

The evolution of the recommendations from the TABD illustrates this process. The earlier reports call for the mutual inclusion of the commercial interests of each party in the regulatory decision–making processes of the other. This was to be achieved through the vigorous exercise of political will by all parties. Through the permutations of the process though, this recommendation was diluted to a call for a special sensitivity by both parties to the trading interests of the other. In terms of active implementation, this recommendation has virtually disappeared.

These exclusions of international commercial interests also pop up strongly in the development of the harmonized standards. They start with the process of recruiting the TC members from the national standards development organizations. The TC members could be chosen on the basis of their technical skills and commercial interests, which would be global. Instead, they are chosen as 'national representatives', which are more clearly political. Under the 'national representative' criterion, representatives from many American multinationals are excluded from the process. They could have brought both additional technical expertise and a greater sensitivity to the impact of proposed standards on international trade. The ANSI case studies illustrate several instances in which European harmonized standards were being developed in ways that would prejudice US commercial interests.

The 'Japanese letter' was another example where the Commission blocked movement towards international convergence despite industry interests. The European members of ISO TC 11 had supported the development of an ISO standard that would simply have listed national standards governing boilers and pressure equipment. This was generally seen as a first step towards the recognition of equivalencies among different sets of boiler and pressure vessel codes. Directorate General Enterprise then persuaded the European mirror committees to oppose releasing the draft standard for fear that its passage could compromise the integrity of the Pressure Vessel Directive. The fact that the EU was apparently able to accomplish this task highlights the political nature of standards development in the EU. The fact that this step was taken points up the extent to which this power could be used to protect European interests from American competition at the international level.

The broad delegation of authority to the member states in the implementation of the CE marking system has also created problems. In the case of Dormont Manufacturing, an American company was largely kept out of the European market by an interpretation of a directive by the French government.

The impact of economic nationalism on CE marking and international trade also appears in the interpretations of the TBT. The Europeans have argued vigorously that there should be only one set of standards development organizations at each level of the polity. Furthermore, these SDOs should represent a wide range of civil interests. Finally, 'international' SDOs should not have any jurisdictional involvement in narrower industry or local interests. This is a clear definition of standards development in political terms. If accepted, this position would also bar any consideration of US standards in an international context.

The EU has also stated that notified bodies must be designated by the member states, listed by the EU and carry out critical aspects of their functions within the Community. These policies effectively eliminate the CB scheme as a model for international cooperation. Otherwise, product and quality reviews carried out by certified conformity assessment bodies in the United States might have been accepted by notified bodies in the EU for CE marking purposes. This could occur, for example, if the US subsidiary of a European notified body were given authority to conduct the notified body review for American clients in the United States, under the supervision of the European parent corporation. EU supervision of the process would take place through the European parent company. Given the Commission's policies, this is not now possible.

Because of this policy, the issue of international access to conformity assessments has to be handled through the MRA process. The prospects for success are more limited because the MRA is based on a policy of reciprocity. No one can participate unless both sides are equally involved. The fragmentation of the US regulatory landscape effectively limits the range of directives that can be covered under an MRA. Differences in national regulatory traditions make it difficult for either side to get past the confidence building period. We concluded that the US – EU MRA was not a useful tool for facilitating trade. This is not a unique experience; both the Canadians and Australians have come to similar conclusions.

Internationally, the EU has benefited from the political coherence of the CE marking system. CEN, CENELEC and ETSI have all been able to develop close working relations at the international level with ISO and IEC. The fact that the EU has 25 votes in the ISO and IEC since the 2004 accessions has added to the voice of European interests in international standards development.

The functional relationship between the ISO and the IEC with the Europeans is also based on the Vienna and Dresden agreements. The key question is why the US standards community has been neither a participant in these agreements nor a partner in similar arrangements. The answer points to the lack of strong administrative leadership in the US standards market.

The EU has been very successful in promoting the CE marking system internationally. The Technical Barriers to Trade convention pledges signatory countries to the use of international standards. The close ties between CEN, CENELEC and ETSI and the international standards development agencies in the development of international standards facilitates the international adoption of similar standards. The EU has developed clear arguments in favor of the European standards system and against considering American standards under the TBT. These arguments have been adopted into EU commercial and foreign assistance policies. In contrast, the USTR is not an effective advocate for the US standards market.

The political sponsorship of the CE marking system by the EU, coupled with an extensive system for international technical assistance, has also promoted the international acceptance of the CE marking system. The size of the market covered by the CE marking system is growing with the expansion of the European Union. There is also evidence that the system is being adopted outside the EEA. Australia and New Zealand are formally adopting the CE marking system for medical products. The Turkish customs authorities are insisting that all relevant imports from the US be CE marked. The Japanese customs authorities seem to be recognizing the CE mark from time to time as a substitute for Japanese marks. The Chinese CCC system is modeled in large part on CE marking. There is evidence that Mexico and Saudi Arabia may have, from time to time, adopted the EU interpretation of the TBT. All of these developments will help European exporters gain a competitive advantage over their American counterparts.

5. . . . AND THE AMERICAN SYSTEM?

Another perspective on the successes and failures of the New Approach can be gained by comparing the CE marking system with the American system for developing product standards.

Many American standards experts argue that the technical quality of US standards is generally higher than for their CE counterparts. Several reasons are advanced for this conclusion. US standards development organizations have to compete for a place in the market. Their patrons are often insurance companies and state regulatory authorities that have a very direct interest in product safety. Conformity assessment for American standards is not subject to the formal restraints of the EU system of modules and notified bodies. Many American SDOs have been active for a longer period than most of their European counterparts. They have been able to draw on a broader range of industrial experiences in standards development. Since the national SDOs are the members of CEN, CENELEC and ETSI, European standards tend to reflect compromises among the different national patterns. American SDOs are not subject to this restraint.

The American system also avoids a nagging problem encountered with the CE mark system, the span of time between the date a directive becomes effective and the time taken to develop the standards needed to implement the directive. Under the National Technology Transfer Act and OMB Circular A–119, US regulators are to use existing standards developed in the private sector for the purposes of public regulation as much as possible. US regulatory agencies are free to develop their own product requirements if private sector standards are not available or not appropriate for their intended purposes.

On the other hand, there is ample evidence that the American system for standards development leads to major problems with standards coordination and international integration. If the goal for the international community should be 'one standard, one test, world–wide', then the American system would create more obstacles than the European system. On the other hand, a diversified standards market in the US would be more likely to give manufacturers a choice among a broader range of approaches to the development of safe products.

The USTR has been an effective advocate for US standards interests, whenever standards issues have come within its jurisdiction. The two major initiatives were the negotiation of the US–EU MRA and the discussions over the definition of an 'international standard' in the triannual review of the TBT.

In the US though, the administrative involvement of the Federal government over standards development is limited. The product liability system administered by an independent court system provides the major incentive for manufacturing safe products. Regulatory oversight is also divided between state and Federal agencies. It is politically difficult for the Federal government to enact legislation that overrides well –established state government authority. At both levels, it is common for American regulatory agencies to use standards that have already been developed by private sector SDOs for other purposes or to allow manufacturers to choose among several sets of private standards and conformity assessment systems.

On the other hand, the US Department of Commerce has been funding efforts by American standards development organizations to participate in foreign standards activities in China and at the international level. Overall though, the role of the US government in promoting the international convergence of standards is relatively limited. As a result, the involvement of the USTR in promoting standards convergence is also limited. The USTR is concerned with the negotiation and enforcement of government–to–government agreements. Because of the international diversity in standards and conformity assessment systems and the limited role of the US government, there are only a few such agreements. One effort to develop a coordinating role, the SCUSA proposal, was roundly opposed by the private sector.

This limits the effectiveness of government–to–government negotiations to promote international coordination of national standards and conformity assessment requirements. Unlike the EU, there is no coherent official US standards policy that covers everything from US support for domestic standards development to technical assistance in international standards development through the foreign aid program.

There are American examples of governmental leadership for international standards convergence in the area of conformity assessment. NIST, for example, has promoted international recognition of US test laboratory results through the development of NVLAP, the National Voluntary Laboratory Accreditation Program and NVCASE, the National Volunteer Conformity Assessment Enterprise. However, the efforts of NIST and the USTR do not seem to be especially well–coordinated. This is consistent with an American political culture that emphasizes decentralization and compartmentalization.

Several US SDOs have organized an 'Alternative Path Coalition' to promote the view that US standards should be considered as 'international standards' under the Technical Barriers to Trade Convention. However, competition among US standards organization for revenues from the sale of standards has limited the willingness of American SDOs to submit their standards for international adoption.

On balance then, any technical advantages that the US standards development system may have are strongly counterbalanced by the difficulties experienced in the US with standards coordination and international integration.

6. MARKET DEMAND AND CONVERGENCE

We can start by recognizing that the development and enforcement of safety standards in a decentralized capitalist system will be based on functional partnerships among government, business and the standards development organizations. The evidence suggests that the private business partners in the process can be surprisingly effective in advancing their international goals and market interests through their involvement in the product safety regulation process.

The Transatlantic Business Dialog was organized by the governments of the USA and EU with a mandate to review a wide range of international trade issues from a business perspective. This was, for a while, a popular model, leading to the organization of a Transatlantic Small Business initiative and the Transatlantic Consumer Initiative.

The TABD recruited companies, organized committees and carried out studies. The resulting reports placed obvious issues in a sharper focus. For example, international differences in standards hurt international trade. However, the leaders of participating companies did not take the next logical step, to effectively lobby their governments to resolve these issues. This was probably due, at least in part, to the scope of the issues they were considering. Participating companies were reluctant to commit time, effort and political capital to a set of issues that were not all central to company interests.

Some industries are likely to have an interest in promoting international regulatory convergence. This is the situation for medical device manufacturers. This is an industry characterized by rapid innovation, short product life spans and global purchasing. Product innovation is generally led by smaller firms located in technology rich countries. In the US, for example, 40 per cent of US medical device production is exported. Governments, which generally are responsible for most medical purchasing, are usually interested in purchasing the latest equipment at the lowest price. Thus, both buyers and sellers have an interest in free trade.

Corporations are more likely to become involved in trade issues that directly affect their corporate interests. The Global Harmonization Task Force is a group of corporations manufacturing medical devices that have been organized by the relevant US and EU trade associations to promote for international convergence of medical product regulation. Unlike the TABD, the GHTF has actively lobbied five governments to adopt pro–convergence policies. They have had several significant successes.

The US Federal government passed legislation requiring the FDA to be more cooperative internationally. As a result, the FDA managers have developed close working relations with their British and French counterparts. Consequently, there are significant parallels between the New Approach Medical Device directives and the FDA regulatory system for medical equipment. The GHTF is now lobbying for the international adoption of a common application form for the regulatory review and approval of new medical devices.

Companies in industries such as international shipping and telecommunications are also likely to promote regulatory convergence. The similarities between the requirements of the Recreational Craft Directive and the corresponding regulations developed by the American Bureau of Shipping are not accidental. Both sets of regulatory requirements have been strongly influenced by the policies of the International Maritime Organization. The IMO, in turn, has been the heir to the international convergence in ship standards promoted by Lloyd's of London, an international marine insurance combine. The major elevator companies have also promoted global convergence in elevator standards. There are only a few leading companies in this industry and they all sell to global markets. The convergence of global standards makes it far easier to draw on global production facilities to meet local market needs.

The major players in the standards testing and conformity assessment industry also have an interest in a global perspective. Laboratories and conformity assessment bodies that are able to meet a wide range of international requirements are likely to take business from bodies that can only test and certify for local requirements. At the international level, the IEC has led the development of the GB program, a successful effort to promote the reciprocal recognition of conformity assessment results.

However, industries that are characterized by local sales and little international trade are more likely to resist any efforts to lower trade barriers. For example, the project managers in Directorate General Enterprise have encountered major difficulties in gaining intra–EU support for community acceptance for standards covering metals and construction products. The notified bodies were given responsibility for implementing the 'European approval of materials' clause in the Construction Products Directive because of the anticipated difficulties in having CEN develop European standards defining steel characteristics. If the task had gone to CEN, the steel company representatives on the relevant technical committees would have been charged with developing community–wide standards that could have eroded the security of their national markets.

The rate of technology change and the range of products in current use that are covered by older regulations will also have an effect on the ease of regulatory convergence. It is far easier to promote convergence for new standards than to try to reconcile widely used, well–established standards. The areas in which convergence efforts have been more successful, telecommunications and medical devices are areas of rapid technology development and on–going standards development. The major difficulties in promoting standards convergence have occurred in the metals and construction products industries, which are characterized by slow rates of technical innovation and widespread reliance on well established sets of standards and conformity assessment procedures.

Unfortunately, we cannot simply dismiss the impact of international standards as trade barriers by simply concluding that 'industries that want free trade are likely to get free trade'. Companies manufacturing materials and components and the companies that use their products do not always have the same interests in free trade. However, only the materials and component manufacturers are effectively represented in the development of the standards applicable to their products.

The fact that a manufacturer may not be interested in free trade does not mean that it would not be very important for the manufacturer's customers. For example, US–EU trade in a wide range of products incorporating hydraulic and pneumatic components has been impeded by difficulties encountered in developing European materials standards. The ability of European (and American) steel producers to impede free trade by supporting internationally inconsistent standards has a major negative impact on the companies that use the steel. All too often, pressure bearing components of American products covered by the Pressure Equipment Directive must be made from European materials. This can be expensive and inconvenient for smaller companies.

This suggests that our ideal system would offer ways to support the interests of buyers and the international community in the promotion of international convergence in standards and conformity assessment.

If product safety systems evolve on the basis of government business partnerships, then government cooperation is also likely to be required. This process of standards convergence through international regulatory cooperation is not likely to be successful without strong political leadership. The efforts of the GHTF led to the acceptance of a mutual recognition agreement on medical devices between the governments of the US and EU. With the successful implementation of the MRA, conformity assessments carried out by American organizations would be accepted by the Europeans and the FDA would accept product certifications from European agencies. However, this has not worked out in practice. The FDA has been unwilling to trust the judgment of the European conformity assessment review. This reflects the cautious, conservative organizational culture of the FDA. It would take sustained political pressure to overcome it.

This is not an example of the strength of government in the US system. Rather, the failures thus far of the MRA program reflects the lack of political leadership over regulatory policies in the US. If there were some similar entity in the US that could provide the sort of integrative functions that are provided by Directorate General Enterprise, then the MRA initiative would probably have worked.

7. A MODEST PROPOSAL

If neither the European nor the American systems fully meet the need for developing effective, compatible international standards systems, then what type of a system should we develop?

A few basics: the US government should develop a broad coherent policy of promoting US standards interests that could be consistently applied over a wide range of contexts. Such a policy could be used both to expand the range of government support of US standards interests and to promote more vigorous coordination of the programs that are already in place. Such a policy should cover government–to–government agreements, foreign technical assistance, government participation in standards development and government sponsored conformity assessment certification programs.

The diversity of the US standards development market should be protected. Because of the diversity and depth of industry involvement, the US is more likely to produce technically strong standards that can meet a diverse range of manufacturing interests.

Given the costs of standards development, diversity is an expensive option. It would therefore be helpful if Federal funding were available to support the administrative overhead and industry costs associated with standards development. Such a program could be used to promote small business involvement in standards development, at least in the comment stages.

The analysis developed in this book also suggests that the ISO goal for international convergence of 'one standard, one test, accepted everywhere' is probably unachievable. It has been relatively easy to promote standards convergence in industries characterized by global trade and rapid technological development. However, the problems are more formidable in efforts to promote convergence in industries characterized by domestic markets and stable technologies. There are major advantages to the involvement of manufacturers in the development of safety standards, but that is also likely to result in the representation of interests that may resist free trade in the standards development process. There are major advantages to giving industry a free reign to develop safety standards, but that also cuts into the probability of achieving international standards coordination via government –to–government negotiations.

An alternative approach would be to focus on the reciprocal recognition of different safety standards systems. Instead of looking to promote the convergence between the European and American safety standards for boilers and pressure vessels, the goal would be to have the US and EU regulatory authorities accept products built and certified in accordance with either the ASME Boiler Code or the Pressure Vessel Directive requirements. The discussions over the implementation of the mutual recognition agreement involve the issue of equivalency at the conformity assessment level.

Notified bodies and surveillance authorities would only be obligated to consider evidence concerning the relative effectiveness of different standards and to recognize equivalencies where it has been established on the record. The proponents of equivalency would have the burden of proof. Debates over the equivalencies of different standards would only emerge when proponents emerge that have a sufficiently strong interest to invest the time, effort and money needed to build a case. Either industry or the standards development organizations could take the lead in these discussions. This process would provide the American standards development organizations with a practical way to address their complaint that they are at a disadvantage in international discussions of standards convergence.

This principle could be implemented with relatively few amendments to the Technical Barriers to Trade Convention. Instead of requiring the signatories to 'adopt' international standards, an amended Convention could call on them to 'recognize' the equivalencies of these standards for the purposes of domestic regulation. Instead of defining international standards in terms of who drafted them, the language in the triannual review would be modified to refer to the sufficiency of the standards. This change would focus public discussions on the core issue, does a proposed standard effectively protect the public interest?

There are aspects of both the European and American regulatory programs that would support a mutual recognition approach. The decentralized American system can generate alternative standards whenever an SDO sees a commercial demand for them. The common state pattern of accepting all certifications that provide the necessary levels of protection is an example of a functioning equivalency system. As we have also pointed out, manufacturers selling in the EU are not required to use the harmonized standards, they only carry the presumption of conformity. American standards can be used if the manufacturer can show that they also meet the essential requirements. This feature of the New Approach is an implicit invitation to establish equivalencies. There are, however, no systems in the EU for developing alternative standards.

Several changes would have to be made in American regulatory policies in order to implement an equivalency policy. Statutory language that currently requires Federal regulatory agencies to consider adopting US private sector standards for public purposes would have to be amended to allow for the consideration of international equivalency. State and local regulators generally provide for the use of all products that are covered by an approved safety certification system. Federal legislation would probably be required to coordinate the review and approval processes for foreign certification systems as well. This could be done on an agency–by–agency basis, using the present FDA legislation as a model. This change would also help address a longstanding complaint of the Europeans, that many state programs do not comply with the international obligations of the Federal government.

A reciprocal recognition approach would have several advantages. By focusing on enforcement rather than the development of standards, it would promote resolutions through negotiations and the direct involvement of business would be limited. These negotiations would tend to emphasize outcome issues (Do the standards provide equivalent levels of safety?) instead of process issues (Which approach to standards development is better?). Like the GATT rounds over tariffs, the negotiations over standards equivalencies would probably be on–going. Like the GATT rounds, the long–term result would probably be international convergence in the underlying regulatory policies, which would have to be the ultimate outcome in any convergence process.

An emphasis on equivalency would not directly limit national strategies for standards development and would provide manufacturers with a range of options in deciding on which standards to use. If this approach were adopted, regulatory agencies would probably become involved in competitive negotiations over the relative adequacy of national requirements, and SDOs would compete on the international market for industry adoptions of their standards. These rivalries would probably improve both public regulation and private standards development efforts. Senior program managers in both the UK Medical Device Authority and the US FDA have commented on the extent to which the pressures for regulatory convergence have contributed to the effectiveness of the programs on both sides.

A reciprocal recognition approach to international conversion would not pre–empt other strategies where they are working well. There would be little need for reciprocal recognition in areas such as recreational craft, lifts, medical devices and telecommunications standards where there are strong market pressures for convergence. However, it could be a useful mechanism in more difficult areas, such as boiler and pressure vessel codes.

An equivalencies approach to international standards coordination would, however, entail a different set of problems. One major problem would be simply to define what constitutes an adequate level of public protection. There are significant international differences in attitudes towards product and environmental safety. Differences emerge in attitudes towards the inevitable gaps in the data. The Europeans rely more heavily on the "precautionary principle" while the Americans do not. Americans are more likely to argue that governments should mandate product requirements until a particular aspect has been shown to be harmful to individuals or to the environment. European regulatory agencies are more likely to assume that these aspects should be regulated until they have been proven not to be harmful.

This focus on international differences in regulatory expectations would not be unique to a reciprocal recognition strategy. These issues would be highly relevant to any efforts towards standards coordination. However, they are more likely to become buried in the discussion of less relevant issues in other strategies for promoting standards convergence. Neither is this issue unique to the standards harmonization efforts. The concept of the 'precautionary principle' entered international negotiations over global environmental treaties. It is likely to be a major issue in the anticipated conflicts between the US and EU before the WTO over genetically modified organisms.

A reciprocal recognition strategy would have to be applied cautiously in the area of environmental standards. A centerpiece of the proposed EUP directive is expected to be some form of product life cycle pollution assessment. A key principle of GATT/WTO is that products should be evaluated according to their properties, and not by their origins. Since the priorities given to pollution abatement alternatives are to depend as much on the physical environment as regulatory values, governments should be particularly careful in insisting on extraterritorial application of national manufacturing pollution requirements. Following this principle, governments should willingly grant reciprocal recognition for the national regulation of manufacturing pollution loads.

According to this logic though, governments would have the right to regulate the pollution loads generated by the use and disposition of imported products, since these take place on national territories. Thus, the careful application of the equivalency principle for standards convergence should not affect legitimate pollution control interests.

The strongest disagreements over national equivalencies might well concern conformity assessment procedures rather than standards. Insurance companies world–wide have a shared interest in making sure that national safety standards are up to international norms. International convergence in standards can be facilitated by simply exchanging information from national records on the frequency and nature of safety incidents. However, organizations may tend to have stronger vested interests in conformity assessment procedures. These are likely to involve professional jobs and company incomes. It has been easier for the FDA, for example, to accept the harmonization of regulatory standards than to accept the adequacy of conformity assessment decisions that would be made by European Conformity Assessment Bodies.

If so, the reader may ask, then why would anyone promote an equivalency recognition strategy? The EU–US mutual recognition agreement, which only focused on the conformity assessment portion of the problem, has been generally regarded as a failure. There are several responses to this argument.

First: a need for the reciprocal recognition of conformity assessment processes will emerge in any comprehensive discussion of international standards convergence. The change proposed here is simply to extend this approach to cover standards as well.

Second: the major disagreements have emerged in the medical device area, which, along with civilian aircraft, is generally subject to the most rigorous level of regulatory review.

Third: other problems have emerged in discussions over the MRA. In many cases, it would make little commercial sense for companies to use the reciprocal recognition route, if it were ever fully implemented.

Fourth: private efforts for the reciprocal recognition of conformity assessment, such as the IECs GB scheme, have been working well.

The international acceptance of the equivalency principle would have a dramatic impact on international negotiations, government data collections and the activities of the international standards organizations. The question of whether two standards provide equivalent levels of safety and environmental care can only be answered through comparisons of the safety records for products built under the two standards. In general, governments do not have this type of data. The EU has tried to develop this data for consumer products with the RAPEX system. However, the apparent national differences in the product safety levels seem to be due far more to national differences in enforcement and record keeping. The adequacy of national efforts to develop data on medical device use incidents seems to depend on whether the data are collected by manufacturers or by medical service providers. Developing an international commitment to accurate record-keeping and a consensus on connection strategies and data reporting formats would not be an easy task.

If this approach were to be developed, then the roles of ISO, IEC and the WTO would change significantly. ISO and IEC are government–industry partnerships. In order to implement a policy for international recognition of equivalent standards, the administrative processes of ISO and IEC would tend to tilt more towards the government side.

Under a policy promoting reciprocal recognition for equivalent standards, ISO and IEC would probably become involved in discussions of safety equivalencies. The advocates for the national alternatives would be as likely to represent government regulatory agencies as the national SDOs. There would be less of a need for the product experience and manufacturing expertise brought by private sector engineers and more of a need for the services of professional statisticians. In short, this process would resemble the discussions that have been going on between the US and the EU on the implementation of the MRAs, which pose very similar issues.

In order to support these activities, ISO and IEC would have to become quasi–public agencies providing specialized expertise rather than service organizations providing an administrative framework for private sector initiatives. The funding sources and levels would be expected to change. Since the protagonists would probably be the national regulatory agencies, the role of ISO and the IEC would more closely resemble the WTO than most standards development organizations.

8. . . . AND IF WE DON'T?

Implementing this strategy could be difficult. National differences in the importance attributed to international agreements could derail the efforts towards reciprocal recognition of equivalent standards.

Under international law, governments must accept or reject international agreements in their entirety. Within this limit, governments can withdraw from specific agreements at any time. The only ultimate enforcement comes from retaliation from other countries.

Different aspects of these basic principles are stressed in different ways in different countries. The historic experiment of the European Union is implicitly based on the assumption that international obligations are enduring and have the weight of law. The leaders of the European Union have significant latitude in pressing the smaller countries because the prospects of an effective political rebellion are slight. Europe would like to develop a world in which other countries would take their international obligations as seriously.

If so, then we would have the tools needed to shape domestic policies and processes through international agreements. This would significantly change the dynamics of international negotiations. Instead of focusing only on the costs and benefits of specific international agreements, the member states would have to focus on the advantages and disadvantages of the larger system of international regulation. Losses incurred in some areas of international negotiations could be offset by gains in other areas.

The American view seems to be that strong countries are immune to reprisals so they are free to selectively interpret or withdraw from international agreements at will. (This is being written a few weeks after the Second Gulf War.) International arrangements are not binding and do not represent permanent obligations. The policies of governments can be driven more by national power than any sense of obligation to the international community. International agreements would therefore have to be viewed according to their agreement–specific, short–term costs and benefits. This will make it more difficult to convince governments that international negotiations are worthwhile. If so, then we should not count on the prospects for developing an international commitment to a policy of international recognition of equivalent national standards.

Therefore, we should expect a continuation of the present piecemeal process. Standards for products developed for new technologies and for international markets will become increasingly harmonized through industry pressures. However, products will continue to incorporate commonplace materials and components, which are exactly the areas in which the international convergence of national standards has been the most difficult to achieve. This problem will not go away with continued technical change.

Our world is not likely to crumble if the international community does not effectively harmonize international differences in inconsistent national product standards. However, a failure to address this issue would be far from costless. If the world community does not effectively address the issue of non–tariff trade barriers in general and standards convergence in particular, then we will have missed an opportunity to effectively promote the economic and political integration of the developed countries.

It is more likely that the New Approach will gradually become the dominant international model for product standards and conformity assessment. The level of safety provided by the harmonized standards is at least acceptable. The European system has the advantages of administrative simplicity, political decentralization and strong EU sponsorship. The New Approach also meets TBT obligations through the close working relationships between the European standards associations and the leading international standards organizations. In contrast, it would be more difficult for a government to adopt the American system since government involvement is limited. It is also a very decentralized system that could only develop in a large, highly competitive economy.

The evolution of the Chinese standards and conformity assessment system is an example of this process. The GB standards are generally based on ISO/CEN equivalents. The CCC system of conformity assessment for high risk products is also based on a combination of product testing and third party reviews of factory quality systems on the model of ISO 9000. Unlike the New Approach though, the factory inspections and product tests are carried out by state agencies rather than notified bodies.

This movement towards the recognition of the New Approach as the dominant international model for product standards and conformity assessments could be promoted by international efforts to promote national convergences. The governments of Australia and New Zealand, both párticipants in the GHTF, have adopted the New Approach for the national regulation of medical devices.

If the world harmonizes around the European model, then US manufacturing exports will increasingly be alone in facing the problems of inconsistent national product standards. The prospects for the unilateral harmonization of US standards to European and international norms are dim, at best. The US system is too decentralized and the prospects for vigorous leadership by either the government or ANSI are limited by vigorous competition among US SDOs.

We would expect instead to see a continuing weakness in the development of US export markets. This would accentuate present patterns; investment capital is increasingly more mobile than merchandise trade. Within the trade area, imports would continue to grow far more rapidly than exports. The development of US export markets is, in fact, even lagging behind the growth of the US economy as a whole.

We can put human faces to these dry economic abstractions. The rising tide of international investments is a consequence of the growing internationalization of the major corporations in the US and elsewhere. The world economy is increasingly dominated by effectively stateless corporations. The problems of global standards convergence are less pressing for the multinational corporations; they have the ability to shift production to facilities that are dedicated to foreign markets.

Smaller US corporations do not have this advantage. For smaller companies, international orders have to be filled by modifying products that have been primarily designed and built to meet the requirements of national markets. This contributes to the continuing erosion of US manufacturing employment and cuts into the viability of smaller manufacturers in a global marketplace.

This pattern has promoted the simultaneous prosperity of American multinational corporations and the loss of manufacturing jobs. At some point, we should be as concerned about the welfare of our workers and the US technology base as the balance sheets of our largest corporations.

REFERENCES

Directorate General Enterprise (2001), *Consultation Document Prepared by the Directorate General Enterprise on the Review of the New Approach* 13 December, p. 12.

European Commission (1998), *Technical Barriers to Trade in the EU: An Illustration by Six Industries, Volume 6, The Cost of Non–Europe: BasicFindings.* Luxembourg: European Commission.

European Commission (2000), *The Single Market Scorecard* Brussels, European Commission, November, No. 7.

Mitchell, B.R. (1998), *International Historical Statistics: Europe 1750-1993 (4th ed)*, New York: Stockton Press.

Transatlantic Consumer Dialog (1999), 'Commission's consultation on certain elements of the New Approach; reply from the UK', in *TACD Recommendations on Food, Electronic Commerce and Trade and European Commission Services' Responses.*

United Nations (2003), *2001 International Trade Statistics Yearbook, Volume 1; Trade by Country,* New York: United Nations.

Glossary

A2LA. American Association for Laboratory Accreditation. A private sector agency that accredits US laboratories to the same standards used by the Europeans for notified bodies and test houses.

AAMI. American Association for Medical Instrumentation. A US trade association for medical device manufacturers.

Accession states. The ten countries that joined the European Union on 1 May 2004. They are: Cyprus, Czech Republic, Estonia, Latvia, Lithuania, Hungary, Malta, Poland, Slovakia and Slovenia.

AdCo's. Committees of notified bodies sponsored by EOTC in order to promote the harmonization of standards interpretation in the EU.

AFNOR. Asociacion Francaise de Normalizaction. The lead French standards development organization.

Alternative Path Coalition. A coalition of American standards development organizations that was organized to promote the acceptance of American standards as international standards.

ANSI. The American National Standards Institute. ANSI is the lead US standards organization. It represents US interests in ISO and the IEC. The major US standards development organizations are members of ANSI. ANSI does not develop new standards.

ASME. American Society for Mechanical Engineering. AMSE also develops standards. The ASME boiler ands pressure vessel code is particularly important.

ASTM International. A major US standards development organization. ASTM is one of the leaders in the Alternative Path Coalition.

ATEX. The Explosive Atmospheres Directive.

BEE. The European Environmental Bureau. Directorate General Enterprise has encouraged BEE to represent environmental issues in the development of the CE mark materials and standards.

BG system. A system of government mandated mutual insurance companies that provide workplace inspection and workman's compensation insurance for German companies.

BSI. British Standards Institute. The lead British SDO.

CAB. Conformity Assessment Body. Bodies that are certified outside of the EU to perform notified body services, either under a PECA Agreement or a MRA, are called CAB's.

CB Scheme. A system sponsored by the IEC and NEMA to encourage the reciprocal recognition of test results among CB scheme participants on an international basis.

CEN. Comite Europeen de Normalizacion. CEN is the EU SDO that is responsible for the development of harmonized standards for the CE mark system in areas that are not handled by CENELEC or ETSI.

CENELEC. Comite Europeen de Normalizacion Electrotecnique. CENELEC is the EU SDO that is responsible for developing "electrotechnical" standards.

Comitology. An evolving area of EU law and public policy that concerns the widespread use of private sector advisory committees in the development and implementation of EU policy.

COREPER. Committee of the Permanent Representatives, manages with work of the European Council.

Conformity assessment. The prices of confirming that a product or process has been developed in accordance with the relevant requirements.

CPSC. The US Consumer Product Safety Commission.

DG Enterprise. Roughly speaking, the Commission is responsible for planning and policy execution in the EU. The Commission is divided into nineteen directorates general. DG Enterprise is responsible for the CE marking program.

DIN. Deutsche Industrie Normal. The lead German SDO.

Directives. Orders from the EU to the member states on to how to conform their laws to meet EU policy requirements. The so-called New Approach directives establish the legal requirements of the CE marking system.

Dresden Agreement. Task sharing agreement between CENELEC and the IEC.

EC. Name given to the common market after 1992. It is one component of the EU.

ECU. European currency unit. This is the composite value of a basket of EU currencies under the EMS.

EEA. The EU plus the other countries that participate in the common market. These basically include the EFTA countries and the accession countries.

EEC. Name for the European common market from 1957 to xxxx when the European Coal and Steel Community and Euratom had separate management.

EFTA. European Free Trade Area. Originally set up as a competitor to the EU, EFTA is now an association of countries that participate in some, but not all, of the EU programs. ETFA includes Switzerland, Iceland, Norway and Liechtenstein. Iceland, Norway and Liechtenstein participate in the CE Marking system.

EMAS. Environmental management assessment system. One component of the developing system for regulating the environmental impact of products in the EU.

EMC. The Electromagnetic Compatibility Directive.

EMS. The European monetary system. The name given to the program for stabilizing exchange rates among the EU members before currency unification and the development of the euro. The ECU was the fictitious unit of exchange used under the EMS for accounting purposes.

EN. European Norm. The prefix given to standards developed by CEN, CENELEC and ETSI.

EOTA. The European Organization for Technical Approvals, an organization sponsored by DG Enterprise and organized through EOTC for the purposes of coordinating technical approvals at the national level under the Construction Product Directive.

EOTC. European Organization for Testing and Conformity. An organization set up by DG Enterprise to help coordinate notified bodies.

ETSI. European telecommunications Standards Institute. One of the three EU wide SDO's involved in developing standards for the CE Marking system.

EU. European Union. The name given to the totality of the common market after the Maastricht Agreement in 1992.

EUP. The proposed Energy Using Products directive. This is part of the developing program for the regulation of products from an environmental perspective.

European Council. The unit in the government of the EU in which the governments of the member states are represented directly.

FDA. US Food and Drug Administration.

FTAA. The proposed Free Trade Agreement of the Americas, a super NAFTA.

GHTF. Global Harmonization Task Force. An industry led effort to promote the international convergence on the regulation of medical devices.

Global Approach. A variation on the New Approach and CE marking.

Green paper. A document issued by the EU concerning proposed policies that have not yet been adopted.

Guidance documents. Non-binding but influential interpretations of CE mark issues that are developed by representatives of the major notified bodies and surveillance authorities in cooperation with DG Enterprise.

Harmonized standards. Standards developed by CEN, CENELEC or ETSI under a mandate from DG Enterprise that have been approved by the Commission for the implementation of the New Approach directives.

IEC. International Electrotechnical Commission. The international commission that develops or approves electrotechnical standards at the highest international level.

IEEE. Institute for Electronic and Electrical Engineering. A major US SDO.

ISO. The International Standards Organization. ISO develops and/or approves all other standards at the highest international level.

ISO 9000. The most commonly accepted standard for developing or certifying business quality control systems. It forms the basis for several of the CE mark conformity assessment modules.

ISO 14000. The most commonly accepted standard for developing or certifying business pollution control systems. It is used in the EU as a component of the EMAS program.

LVD. Low Voltage Directive.

MEDDEV's. Medical device guidance documents.

MD. The Machinery Directive.

MDD. The Medical Device directive.

Modules. Standardized procedures for conformity assessment for CE marking.

MRA. A mutual recognition agreement. These are signed between the EU and non-member states in an attempt to develop conformity assessment bodies outside of the EU that could be recognized as equivalent to notified bodies inside of the EU.

NIST. National Institute for Science and Technology. The agency in the US Department of Commerce that has primary concern for US standards and conformity assessment policies and programs.

Notified body. A private organization in the EU that has been authorized ("notified") by a member state to implement one or more of the CE marking conformity assessment modules for manufacturers.

NTTAA. National Technology Transfer Administration Act. The NTTAA directed US federal regulatory agencies to the use private standards for public purposes whenever feasible.

NVLAP. National Volunteer Laboratory Accreditation Program. A program sponsored by NIST to promote the accreditation of US testing laboratories to EU/world standards.

Old Approach. The EU approach to product safety regulation before the development of the New Approach. Under the old approach, the Commission was responsible for developing all of the technical requirements and there was no use of the modules or involvement of the notified bodies.

OTA. Office of Technology Assessment. A research arm of the US Congress in the Library of Congress.

PECA. Protocol for the Evaluation of Conformity Assessment. A program for qualifying the notified bodies in the accession countries. The PECA agreements are signed when the candidate notified bodies (called "conformity assessment bodies") are approved.

PPWD. The Packaging and Packaging Waste Directive.

RAPEX. The EU wide database in which all member countries are to post their reports of consumer safety incidents.

Regulations. Issued by the EU under the authority of a directive and are legally enforceable without having to be transposed into national law.

ROHS. The Removal of Hazardous Substances directive.

RTTE. Radio and Telecommunications Terminal Equipment Directive.

Safeguards clause. A provision in each of the New Approach directives that authorizes the surveillance authorities to take an unsafe product off the market or out of service, even if it is properly CE marked. The Commission must be informed and has the right to review the action.

SCUSA. The Standards Council of the USA, a NIST proposal for strengthening the US standards community that was never adopted.

SDO. The generic acronym for a 'standards development organization'.

SLIM. Simplified Legislation for the Internal Market. A program sponsored by the Commission for the periodic review and updating of all directives.

Standstill process. A procedure under the Mutual Information Directive. The member states are obligated to notify the Commission about proposed measures that could impact the common market. The Commission can call for a standstill period in order to determine whether there is a need to invoke Community-wide legislation.

Subsidiarity. An EU policy and law that mandates the decentralization of activities to the maximum feasible level.

Surveillance authorities. Regulatory agencies of the member states that are charged with responsibility for enforcing the CE marking system.

TABD. Transatlantic Business Dialog. A private sector initiative involving US and EU business leaders who have been asked to review US-EU commercial relations and to make recommendations.

TACD. Transatlantic Consumer Dialog. An off-shoot of the TABD.

TASBI. Transatlantic Small Business Initiative. An off-shoot of the TABD.

TBT. The Agreement on Technical Barriers to Trade. The international Agreement governing the development and use of standards and technical requirements that is sponsored by the WTO.

TC. A "technical committee", a group of private sector representatives that is organized and sponsored by a SDO which is directly involved in the process of developing standards. A TC is generally assigned the task of developing standards in a specific technical area. Different "working groups" within a TC are responsible for individual projects.

Technical requirement. The equivalent of a standard except it is developed and enforced by a government agency.

Treaty of Rome. The 1957 Treaty that founded the European Economic Community.

TUV. A leading German notified body that also offers independent quality and safety marks.

UL. Underwriters Laboratory. A major US non-profit research, standards development and conformity assessment house. UL affiliates have become very active in the EU as notified bodies.

UNECE. The United Nations Economic Committee for Europe. UNECE has worked very closely with the EU in promoting the development of the infrastructure of the larger Europe, including highway safety and automobile standards.

User inspectorate. A program or self-regulation authorized under the Pressure Equipment Directive. Approved user inspectorates can mandate the use of their own pressure equipment requirements, as long as they provide a level of safety that is at least equivalent to that provided by the PED.

USTR. United States Trade Representative. The USTR works for the president and is responsible for negotiating and reviewing the international agreements of the United States.

Vienna Agreement. The agreement between CEN and ISO on the division of work.

WEEED. The Waste from Electrical and Electronic Equipment Directive.

White paper. A document from the Council or Commission discussing a polcy that has already been approved.

Working Group. A subcommittee of a TC that is involved in the development of one particular draft standard.

Index

Italy, Italians 15, 45, 75, 85, 95, 103, 132, 179, 200, 203

Japan, 2, 3, 15, 141, 158, 159, 204, 206

Kitemark 106
K-Mart 15
Kyoto targets 181

Lander 74, 100
Latvia 184, 185
Lifts Directive 50, 73, 80, 81, 112, 134
Lithuania 184, 185
Lloyds 84, 133, 209
Low Voltage Directive 44, 49, 51, 60, 69, 72, 80, 103, 104, 112, 127, 134, 155, 172, 173

Maastricht Treaty 25, 26, 37, 81, 82
Machinery Directive 51, 58, 69, 71, 72, 80, 112, 134, 171, 185
Malta 184, 187, 202
Medical Device Authority 157, 214
Medical Devices Directive 50, 59, 78–80, 83, 91, 105, 112, 114
MERCOSUR 190, 193
Metric system 134
Mexico 190, 206
Microsoft 6, 15
Mirror committees 138, 141, 142
Montgomery Ward 15
Mutual Information Directive 21, 61, 182
Mutual Recognition Agreement (MRA) 95, 151, 153–60, 163, 167, 205, 207, 211, 216

National Center for Standards and Certification Information 109
National Concrete Masonry Association 117
National Cooperation for Laboratory Accreditation (NVCASE) 164, 208
National Electrical Manufacturers Association 117
National Fire Prevention Association 114, 122, 123
National Institute for Science and Technology (NIST) 109, 119, 120, 125, 190, 191, 208
National Technology Transfer Act 120
National Voluntary Laboratory Accreditation Program (NVLAP) 125, 163, 164, 208
NATO 29
Netherlands 92, 158, 199, 202
New Approach 2, 3, 33, 37, 38, 44–51, 53–8, 60–62, 65, 69–71, 74, 79, 80, 82, 85, 86, 89, 94, 96, 98, 102, 112, 129, 133, 136, 158, 170, 172–74, 176 180, 186
New Transatlantic Agenda 152
New Transatlantic Marketplace 152
New Zealand 206, 218
Noise Directive 86, 111
Non-automatic Weighing Instruments Directive 50, 80, 112
North American Free Trade Agreement (NAFTA) 192
Notification Process 56, 57